TOUSSAINT LOUVERTURE

| | | | |

D1069743

THE C. L. R. JAMES ARCHIVES
recovers and reproduces for a contemporary
audience the works of one of the great intellectual figures of the twentieth century, in all
their rich texture, and will also present, over
and above historical works, new and current
scholarly explorations of James's oeuvre.

Robert A. Hill, Series Editor

TOUSSAINT
LOUVERTURE

| | | | |

The Story of the Only Successful
Slave Revolt in History

A PLAY IN THREE ACTS

C. L. R. JAMES

Edited and Introduced by Christian Høgsbjerg
With a Foreword by Laurent Dubois

DUKE UNIVERSITY PRESS   DURHAM AND LONDON   2013

© 2013 Duke University Press
All rights reserved
Designed by Heather Hensley
Typeset in Arno Pro by Tseng Information Systems, Inc.
Library of Congress Cataloging-in-Publication Data appear on
the last printed page of this book.

CONTENTS

Mr. C. L. R. James, law student and writer, is a member of The League of Coloured Peoples

C. L. R. James, 1933 (*Tit-Bits*, 5 August 1933, p. 16). © The British Library Board. All Rights Reserved, 26 March 2012.

"I would have far preferred to write on Toussaint L'Ouverture," C. L. R. James wrote wearily in 1931. He had, instead, been forced to respond at length to a racist article published by the eminent Dr. Sidney Harland, an English scientist teaching at the Imperial College of Tropical Agriculture in Trinidad. The "scientist" had, among other things, ranked Toussaint Louverture in his classificatory scheme as a member of "Class F," the "lowest of the superior classes." In other words, James seethed, Harland thought the world was quite full of men like Louverture: "He will pick a Toussaint from every tree." But, as James insisted in his response—and as he would show in the coming decade within brilliant works of theatre and history—there was really only one Louverture. And there was no way to twist reality around so thoroughly as to make him proof of racial inferiority. Louverture's story, and those of the events and people who made it, must serve as inspiration—and as a weapon.

It was in this 1931 article ("The Intelligence of the Negro," reprinted in the appendix), that James first took on a task that in a way became one of his great life missions: wresting the story of Louverture, and of Haiti, away from those in Europe and North America who for too long had distorted it—turning it into a cautionary or ironic tale, using it to create an intriguing whiff of exoticism, or (all too often, as in Harland's case) employing it as a justification for racism. The achievements of the Haitian Revolution, James insisted instead, were among the most remarkable and important in the history of mankind. He did research in Paris, reading both books and archives from the revolutionary period itself. James largely depended on accounts— often hostile ones—written by white contemporaries and white historians in crafting his own vision of the Haitian Revolution. "All my quotations are from white historians," James noted in his riposte to Harland. Though he found some accounts that in fact shared his admiration for the successes of the revolution, in other cases he culled details from accounts with very different intentions and turned them to new ends. Using such tools, he produced what remains the greatest account of the epic of the Haitian Revolution, *The Black Jacobins*.

He wrote this story first, however, not as history but as theatre in his 1934 play *Toussaint Louverture*. That fact has been known for some time among those familiar with James's trajectory. But too many readers of James—including, I must admit apologetically, me—have seen his work of theatre as a kind of unsuccessful prequel to his legendary work of history. That has been a mistake. For as this edition of James's play *Toussaint Louverture* allows us to see, this literary work is as crucial a contribution as *The Black Jacobins* has been. Written in a different register, and to different ends, it nevertheless captures the density and drama of the Haitian Revolution. It bridges time and space, remarkably condensing an incredibly complex period into a series of memorable scenes and characters. It brings together the sense of an epic event with the apt portrayal of historical characters. By offering us, in full, the original play—published here for the first time—Christian Høgsbjerg allows us to fully enjoy James's work of political theatre.

"Oh, Dessalines! Dessalines! You were right after all!" Toussaint Louverture shouts as he dies, alone in prison, in James's play. The words—absorbed by silent walls, lost to history—are imagined into being in *Toussaint Louverture*. Shouted out by Paul Robeson on the London stage in 1936, they must have been impressive. James might have, like many writers before and since, ended his story with the death of Louverture in the cold prison of the Jura. But James returns his audience to Haiti for a final, rousing scene, putting on stage the creation of the Haitian flag out of the French tricolour, the white ripped out and trod underfoot. Though the play is called *Toussaint Louverture*, and many commentators focused in particular on the portrayal of that character by Robeson, it is in fact much more than that: this is a drama that, remarkably, seeks to tell the whole history of the Haitian Revolution, of international imperial rivalry, of the emergence of a revolutionary consciousness, and of the creation of both a nation and a people.

James effectively creates some composite characters in the play. Roume, the French commissioner, for instance, was a historical figure, and his role in negotiating with the insurgents is drawn directly from contemporary accounts. However, in the play, Roume also takes on the role of later French commissioners and officers, including Léger-Félicité Sonthonax, who abolished slavery in the colony, and Etienne Laveaux, who negotiated with Louverture to join the Republic. The various insurgents — the early leaders Jean-François, Jeannot, and Biassou, along with Louverture's longtime companions Jean-Jacques Dessalines and Henry Christophe — are made to represent different trajectories but also different perspectives on the strategy of revolution, the usefulness of vengeance, and the meaning of freedom and independence. At the same time, James manages to capture the transatlantic dimensions of the revolution, with a curtain opening up behind Louverture to show the dramatic events that led to the abolition of slavery by the French National Convention in February 1794. Later, discussions about the Leclerc expedition in Paris provide the crucial background to understanding the layers of secrecy and treachery at work in Saint-Domingue in 1802 and 1803.[1]

One particularly fascinating figure in the play is General Macoya, inspired by the figure of Macaya, an African-born insurgent leader who clearly caught James's attention. Macaya is described in one of the most important early accounts of the Haitian Revolution, the memoirs of the French General Pamphile de Lacroix, which James drew on in several places in writing his play (and later *The Black Jacobins*).[2] In particular, Lacroix published a remarkable explanation given by Macaya for his loyalty to "three kings" — those of France, Spain, and the Congo — which James both quotes and then dwells on at length in the play. It is a striking reminder of the fact that, already in the 1930s, James had identified what remains perhaps the key issue in understanding the Haitian Revolution: the role that the African-born majority played in creating and theorizing politics during this period. Macaya's quote, for instance, is at the center of one of the most important recent articles by the Africanist historian John Thornton about Africans and the Haitian Revolution.[3] Interestingly, this particular theme is actually more foregrounded in the play *Toussaint Louverture* than in *The Black Jacobins*. Perhaps simply because James found so little historical work through which to deepen this question, he ultimately didn't really take it on fully as an analytical problem in his historical writing. But he was able to foreground it, quite powerfully, in his work of theatre.

As Høgsbjerg notes, during one performance of the play, C. L. R. James was forced to stand in for an absent actor: the one playing the role of General Macoya. So it was that, in London in 1936, the elusive and revolutionary words of a Congo-born insurgent, captured and written down by a French general, were spoken aloud by a man thoroughly inhabited by the story of that revolution. More than anyone else, James made sure that the story of Haiti would be remembered and retold outside of the country, through the twentieth century, and into the twenty-first. As one of the many who owe a massive debt to James for his impassioned and brilliant channeling of this revolutionary history, I am comforted to know that, on that one night, James was able to be among the insurgents in 1793, letting them speak through him. On stage that night, I imagine that in the rousing conclusion of the play, James joined the rest of the chorus in singing "Grenadiers à l'assaut!" ("To the attack, grenadiers!") — his singular voice at last at home, surrounded by the sound of a revolution without end.

Notes

1. On Sonthonax's role in the abolition of slavery, see Robert Louis Stein, *Léger Félicité Sonthonax: The Lost Sentinel of the Republic* (Rutherford, N.J.: Fairleigh Dickinson University Press, 1985), and Jeremy D. Popkin, *You Are All Free: The Haitian Revolution and the Abolition of Slavery* (New York: Cambridge University Press, 2010). For a general history of the revolution, see Laurent Dubois, *Avengers of the New World: The Story of the Haitian Revolution* (Cambridge, Mass.: Belknap Press of Harvard University Press, 2004).

2. Pamphile Lacroix, *La Révolution de Haïti* (Paris: Karthala, 1995).

3. John K. Thornton, "I Am the Subject of the King of Congo: African Political Ideology and the Haitian Revolution," *Journal of World History*, 4 (Fall 1993), 181–214.

ACKNOWLEDGMENTS

The compilation of this volume would have been impossible without the kind cooperation of the staff of many archives and libraries. I wish to take this opportunity to express my gratitude first to the staff of the archives of the Brynmor Jones Library, University of Hull, for their kind assistance over several years. I am also indebted to Judy Burg, the University of Hull's archivist, for generously permitting me to reproduce a photograph of the conferment of an honorary Doctorate of Letters on C. L. R. James at Thwaites Hall, University of Hull, on 28 July 1983. (For more background on this ceremony, see David Richardson's collection *Abolition and Its Aftermath: The Historical Context, 1790–1916* [London: Frank Cass, 1985], viii.) I also owe debts of gratitude to the staff of the Theatre Museum collection at the Victoria and Albert Museum, London; the British Library; particularly the Newspaper Library at Colindale; the Moorland-Spingarn Research Center at Howard University; the British Film Institute; Nelson Library; and the libraries of the University of Leeds and the University of York; and the Salford Working Class Movement Library.

I would also like to thank the following for permission to reprint copyrighted material: the Estate of C. L. R. James; the British Library Board; the Victoria and Albert Museum, London; the Illustrated London News Picture Library; the *Daily Telegraph*; *Daily Mail*; *Evening Standard*; Associated Newspapers Ltd.; Mirrorpix; News International Trading Ltd.; and the *Nelson Leader*. Every effort has been made to trace all copyright holders.

There are very many other people who deserve acknowledgment, particularly at Leeds Metropolitan University and the University of York, but here I would just like to express particular thanks to Talat Ahmed, Henrice Altink, Ian Birchall, Paul Blackledge, Stephen Bourne, Colin Chambers, Raj Chetty, Rachel Douglas, Allison Drew, Joellen El-Bashir, Alan Forrest, Charles Forsdick, Peter Fraser, David Goodway, Gráinne Goodwin, the late Stephen P. Hill, Christian Holder, Selma James, Minkah Makalani, Aldon Lynn Nielsen, David Renton, Helen E. Roberts, the late Eric E. Robinson, Bill Schwarz, David Scott, Marika Sherwood, Liz Stainforth, and Fionnghuala Sweeney. I have benefited greatly from the opportunity to present some of my research and developing thoughts on *Toussaint Louverture* at conferences at the University of Liverpool and the University of Warwick. I am indebted to my parents for their unconditional support.

Finally, I owe particular debts of gratitude to David Howell for extensive comments on my introduction, to Margaret Busby for her expertise in helping skillfully edit it for publication, and to Laurent Dubois for his illuminating foreword. I would also like to thank the two anonymous readers for their thoughtful and helpful reports on my introduction and the manuscript as a whole, and to the team at Duke University Press, in particular Gisela Fosado, for their support and advice. Robert A. Hill not only granted me a great honour by inviting me to write this introduction, but he also provided expert editorial assistance and kind support and encouragement at every point. Any remaining errors in transcription or in the introduction are, of course, mine alone.

INTRODUCTION | CHRISTIAN HØGSBJERG

In 2005, early in my research for a doctoral thesis on C. L. R. James's life and work in 1930s Britain, I went to inspect the Jock Haston Papers at the Brynmor Jones Library at the University of Hull, in the north of England. Like James, Haston had been a Trotskyist in Britain during the 1930s, and listed among the Haston Papers was a file entitled simply "Toussaint Louverture."[1] Daring to hope to discover perhaps a programme from the original 1936 production of James's play about the Haitian Revolution, a rare enough and valuable find in itself, I decided to save examining this file until the end. After several hours spent wondering at some of the forgotten struggles and squabbles revealed among the minutiae of internal documents relating to the tiny early British Trotskyist movement, I finally rewarded myself by turning to the intriguing folder. Opening it up, I found to my amazement a yellowing mass of thin oilskin paper headed "Toussaint Louverture: The story of the only successful slave revolt in history." All that was missing from what I recognised immediately as the long-lost original playscript was its author's name on the front—C. L. R. James.

At that moment, the extraordinary providence of the find dawned on me in a way that must have eluded those historians of British Trotskyism who over the years had gone through the Haston Papers. It is not clear how James's play about the Haitian Revolution ended up with Jock Haston (1912–86). Haston had broken from the Communist Party in 1934, and he had set up a discussion group sympathetic to Trotskyism. Around 1935–36, Haston's group met for discussions with the three British Trotskyist groups then in existence, including James's Marxist Group, then part of the Independent Labour Party (ILP). It is possible that, during these discussions, James gave a copy of *Toussaint Louverture* to Haston, who may well have seen the play performed.[2]

It is hard to overstate the significance of the discovery of James's original playscript—the last major missing piece of his writing yet to be published. The play should not be seen as an early preliminary work superseded by the publication of James's classic history of the Haitian Revolution, *The Black Jacobins*, in 1938. Rather, as Robert Hill first suggested to me, *Toussaint Louverture* must be seen as the indispensable companion work to *The Black Jacobins*. The play is a literary supplement to the magisterial history and had allowed James to give his imagination full rein. In the play's portrayal of Toussaint, "the first and greatest of West Indians,"[3] it might be argued that James demonstrates the full tragedy and heroism of this world-historical individual in a more powerful way than in both his history and in his later co-written play about the Haitian Revolution, *The Black Jacobins* (1967), which evolved out of *Toussaint Louverture*.

The production of *Toussaint Louverture* in 1936 at the Westminster Theatre in London is also of considerable importance for the light it sheds on imperial metropolitan culture in 1930s Britain, or rather the radical counterculture that has always existed in the "dark heart" of the British Empire. The presence of that gentle giant of stage and screen, the black American star Paul Robeson, alongside other black actors from the Caribbean and Africa, meant that the two performances of *Toussaint Louverture* on 15 and 16 March 1936 were the first time that black professionals had ever performed on the British stage in a play written by a black playwright.[4] Back in 1926, Robeson had told an interviewer that he dreamed "of a great play about Haiti, a play about Negroes, written by a Negro, and acted by Negroes . . . of a moving drama that will have none of the themes that offer targets for race supremacy advocates."[5] Ten years later, Robeson clearly gave his all in his portrayal of Toussaint. *Toussaint Louverture* was to be "the only play in which Robeson appeared that was written by a writer of African heritage."[6]

Although James's play has been celebrated as a pioneering production in the history of black British theatre, and an important moment in the history of African and Caribbean theatre, *Toussaint Louverture* also stands as an outstanding contribution to what the late Trinidadian dramatist and scholar Errol Hill once described as "the revolutionary tradition in black drama," a "tradition of writing and producing plays that deal directly with black liberation."[7] This revolutionary tradition dates at least as far back as the Haitian Revolution itself, for after Toussaint seized the power to rule as black Consul in Saint-Domingue, James noted in *The Black Jacobins* that "the theatres began to play again, and some of the Negro players showed a remarkable talent."[8] In the 1820s, William Henry Brown, a West Indian seaman domiciled in New York who seems to have experienced the wider wave of slave revolt and national liberation that swept across the Caribbean during the 1790s, formed the African Company and founded a small theatre for black Americans. In 1822 Brown wrote and produced what was billed as "an entirely new play . . . called *Shotaway*; or the Insurrection of the Caribs," about the Second Carib War of 1795–96 on St. Vincent, led by the Carib chief Chatoyer. As Shane White notes, "This was the first African American dramatic production," and *Shotaway* drew from the *New York Spectator* the comment that "it seems that these descendants of Africa are determined to carry into full practice the doctrine of liberty and equality, physically by acting plays, and mentally by writing them."[9] Though no text of the play has been found, as Errol Hill notes, "in the 1820s, there were over two million black slaves in America," so "the staging of the struggle of Chatoyer and his tribe could be interpreted as a vivid antislavery statement," making King Shotaway, the title role, "the first revolutionary hero in black drama."[10] As James would later insist, West Indians have "straight plays bursting out of our history."[11]

The wider historic importance of James's own play *Toussaint Louverture* and its production in Britain in 1936 emerges then not simply from the remarkable talent of its own cast, drawn from across the African diaspora and with Paul Robeson in the title role, nor from its immediate audience, which would have included such Pan-African figures as George Padmore, Jomo Kenyatta, and Eric Williams. For at the heart of James's play was a pioneering recovery of the collective memory of the historic experience uniting people of the African diaspora: the experience of enslavement and the resistance to it. This introduction will begin by exploring the conceptual and ideological formation that led James to write such a play about the Haitian Revolution, "the most epic struggle to end slavery in the Americas."[12]

Conceiving *Toussaint Louverture*

"The play was conceived four years ago and was completely finished by the autumn of 1934," James writes in his author's note in the original 1936 programme of *Toussaint Louverture*. In the crucial year of 1932 the thirty-one-year-old aspiring novelist decided to leave his native colonial Trinidad for the Mother Country of imperial Britain. Unlike the manuscripts James brought with him from Trinidad—a soon-to-be-published biography, *The Life of Captain Cipriani: An Account of British Government in the West Indies* (1932), and the novel *Minty Alley* (1936)—*Toussaint Louverture* was actually composed in Britain. Yet if a play about the leader of the Haitian Revolution therefore stands as the defining literary work born out of James's experience of the "voyage in," such a project was fundamentally inspired and shaped by James's earlier environment, the colonial Caribbean society in which he was born and grew to intellectual maturity.[13]

C. L. R. James was, in the eloquent words of George Lamming, "a spirit that came to life in the rich and humble soil of a British colony in the Caribbean."[14] Certainly the fact that James wrote a play so soon after leaving would not have surprised those closest to him back home. The young James had involved himself in amateur dramatics soon after leaving the elite school to which he had won a scholarship, Queen's Royal College (QRC), a place where he recalled "we learned Shakespeare, Goldsmith, Shaw" and other famous dramatists "of high morality."[15] In 1919, he landed a job at a private school in Port of Spain as an English teacher, and he took his passion for drama into the classroom. A friend from QRC, William Besson, recalled:

> Nello told me he was going to stage "The Merchant of Venice" in a cinema in Port of Spain; and he actually got his pupils to learn Shakespeare and put on the show. But unfortunately the people of Port of Spain had not reached the stage to appreciate that. . . . I took a young lady . . . to see the play and there was just a sprinkling of people in this huge cinema. But Nello pressed on. The play was staged in front of the curtain and his pupils performed the whole of "The Merchant of Venice." So there you see, when Nello read Shakespeare it wasn't just a book he was reading but he saw life behind it, and he had to present that life.[16]

In the 1920s, James became secretary of the Maverick Club, a social club independent of the white colonial elite; he later recalled how "for the most part we were Black people and one brown . . . we would give concerts."[17] Kent Worcester notes that "at the age of 21, he directed an operetta, *Gypsy Rover* (and played a jester); at the age of 28, he directed Molière's *Le Bourgeois Gentilhomme* for the Maverick Club."[18] Paul Buhle has described how after James returned to QRC to teach English and History, "he staged with his class a

The Maverick Club, 1919. Top row: V. L. Burton, Meta Davis, G. A. Busby, Beryl Davis, Inez Grosvenor, Milly Busby; middle row: Evelyn James, C. L. R. James, Kathleen Davis, M. A. J. Forrester, Mabel James, H. O'Neil, R. Cumberbatch, A. S. Berridge, E. Isaacs; bottom row: Ruby James, J. T. C. Prescott, Ellen James, Millie Davis, Milly Grosvenor, E. S. Berridge, C. T. W. E. Worrell, Wilhelmina Grosvenor, May Chandler, J. Arthur Procope, Vivien Pollard. Courtesy of Christian Holder.

full public version of *Othello*. It drew an enthusiastic response, and James went on to write a now-vanished drama about local life and to produce it with his students, for the public."[19] James's cultural activism throughout the 1920s was increasingly accompanied by a growth of political conscious-ness, expressed in support for the growing nationalist movement around the social-democratic Trinidad Workingmen's Association (TWA), led by the charismatic self-declared "champion of the barefoot man," Captain Arthur

Andrew Cipriani. In the late 1920s and early 1930s, James was at the forefront of "the Trinidad Awakening" by contributing implicitly anticolonialist short stories to *Trinidad* and *The Beacon*, both literary journals with nationalist leanings. "My hitherto vague ideas of freedom crystallised around a political commitment: we should be free to govern ourselves," James later recalled.[20]

While teaching at QRC, James began to research the rich, hidden history of the Caribbean. "I was tired of hearing that the West Indians were oppressed, that we were black and miserable, that we had been brought from Africa, and that we were living there and that we were being exploited."[21] James remembers he was "one of the pioneers" in introducing "West Indian history" in school, something not then on the official curriculum.[22] One friend from the *Beacon* group, Ralph de Boissière, later recalled James's early "opposition to colonialism had a solidly grounded historical base, something that none of us possessed" and that "C. L. R. delivered telling blows with history."[23] No doubt mindful of the plight of Haiti itself—since 1915 under American military occupation—James was soon "reading everything" he could on the Haitian Revolution, including a couple of books written by British writers during the 1850s, including Reverend J. R. Beard's short 1855 biography of Toussaint. However, he was grievously disappointed not to find any books of "serious historical value" while in colonial Trinidad. James remembered his reaction on reading one "very bad" biography of Toussaint, Percy Waxman's *The Black Napoleon: The Story of Toussaint Louverture* (1931): "What the goddam hell is this?"[24]

Insult was added when Dr. Sidney Harland, a "distinguished scientist" from England who was at the Imperial College of Tropical Agriculture in Trinidad, "foolishly took it upon himself to write an article proving that Negroes were as a race inferior in intelligence to whites." James wrote, "I wasn't going to stand for that and in our little local magazine I tore him apart."[25] Harland's 1931 article "Race Admixture" utilized Francis Galton's *Hereditary Genius: An Inquiry into Its Laws and Consequences* (1869) to assert different classes of intelligence linked to such features as race. Harland had also brought Toussaint Louverture into his discussion, ascribing his intelligence as best befitting Class F, "the lowest of the superior classes." James sprang to Toussaint's defence to expose this "absurdity," and his glorious counterblast to Harland's racism, "The Intelligence of the Negro," published in *The Beacon* in August 1931 (and reproduced here in the appendix), stands as his first written appreciation of Toussaint's astonishing achievements.[26] Robert Hill has rightly emphasised "the over-riding vindicatory nature" of James's discussion of Toussaint in 1931, noting that "in the context of the domination of European colonialism, vindication was . . . a cultural and ideological necessity."[27]

Vindication of black accomplishments in the face of racism then provides the first underlying motivation for James's *Toussaint Louverture*, and David Scott in his important and insightful work *Conscripts of Modernity* has noted that "Haiti has very often played a prominent role" in "black vindicationist discourse." Scott cites as an example an extraordinary lecture given in the 1850s by the black American Reverend James Theodore Holly, "A Vindication of the Capacity of the Negro Race for Self-Government, and Civilized Progress," which hailed the Haitian Revolution as one of the "noblest, grandest, and most justifiable outbursts against tyrannical oppression that is recorded on the pages of the world's history."[28] James's second motivation in conceiving *Toussaint Louverture* was also a vindicatory one, and he was concerned with what he later called (in the title of a pamphlet) "The Case for West Indian Self-Government." He had begun work researching and writing a "political biography" of the TWA leader Captain Cipriani, and in this work James would tear into the British government's line of "self-government when fit for it," demonstrating that the recent growth of the TWA was proof, if proof was needed, that the black majority societies of the Caribbean had always been manifestly "fit" to govern themselves.[29] James's championing of Toussaint in "The Intelligence of the Negro" was critically part of this wider struggle for West Indian sovereignty and self-determination.[30]

Amidst the rising movement for West Indian self-government in 1920s Trinidad, James could not have also failed to register the power and inspiration of either the Harlem Renaissance or Garveyism. Marcus Garvey, the Jamaican founder of the Universal Negro Improvement Association, had played a pathbreaking role in the attempt to develop an indigenous Caribbean theatre. Garvey wrote three plays that were performed on consecutive nights in Kingston, Jamaica, in August 1930: *The Coronation of an African King, Roaming Jamaicans,* and *Slavery—from Hut to Mansion,* which "described the horrors of slavery and the slave traffic, the agitation for freedom, emancipation, and progress thereafter."[31]

James was also aware that others had written plays about Toussaint. As

Percy Waxman had noted in *The Black Napoleon*, the great radical French Romantic historian Alphonse de Lamartine had "composed a poetical drama with Toussaint as its hero," a play that was staged in Paris in 1850. Indeed, despite its weaknesses as a work of historical scholarship, Waxman's *The Black Napoleon* itself evoked some sense of the dramatic clash of personalities involved and even the Haitian Revolution's world-historic significance: "For the first time in the world's history an enslaved people had succeeded in gaining their own freedom."[32]

After arriving in London in March 1932, James moved in May to the Lancashire cotton town of Nelson to stay with the family of his fellow Trinidadian, the professional cricketer Learie Constantine. Though in Nelson officially to help Constantine write his autobiography, it would be Constantine who first helped James publish *The Life of Captain Cipriani: An Account of British Government in the West Indies*, with a local printing firm in Nelson, Coulton & Co.[33] James recalls how after sending it "back to the West Indies," he felt "free to get down to my own business. I had a completed novel with me. But that was only my 'prentice hand . . . the real *magnum opus* was to be my second novel."[34]

However, it was James's play *Toussaint Louverture* that materialised instead of a second novel; he tells us, "Fiction-writing drained out of me and was replaced by politics." As a result of his tireless campaigning for West Indian self-government in Britain, West Indian history remained of central importance: as he recalled, "in the back of my head for years was the project of writing a biography of Toussaint Louverture. . . . I had not been long in Nelson before I began to import from France the books I would need to prepare."[35] By the time James left the Constantines in late March 1933 in order to return to London and work as a cricket reporter for the *Manchester Guardian*, he had begun turning his historical research on the Haitian Revolution into a play.

FROM IMPERIAL BRITISHNESS TO MILITANT PAN-AFRICANISM

On 29 May 1933, as part of the commemoration of the centenary of the official abolition of slavery throughout the British Empire, James was invited to give a talk on BBC Radio as part of a series on "Slavery, 1833–1933," and the broadcast was published in *The Listener* as "A Century of Freedom" (see the appendix).[36] As James remembered, "I visualized my audience as people who had to be made to understand that West Indians were a Westernized people. I must have stressed the point too hard, in fact I know I did. Colonial officials in England, and others, began their protests to the BBC almost before I had finished speaking."[37] Despite his active campaigning for West Indian self-government, James's broadcast gives some insight into his continuing identification with imperial Britain, and abandoning this would clearly not happen quickly, even for someone of James's intellect. "For a non-white colonial to adjust his sights to England and not to lose focus is the devil's own job and the devil pays great attention to it," he later reflected.[38]

In London, James joined the League of Coloured Peoples, a multiracial pressure group formed in 1931. Amidst the rise of fascism in Europe, including the seizure of power by Hitler's Nazis in Germany, James now increasingly adopted a defiant and more radical transnational identification with black people and their culture. In the summer of 1933, James attended a meeting in London to hear George Padmore, the leading black figure in the international Communist movement, speak. Besides his relentless anticolonialist agitation, Padmore was also a prolific pamphleteer, and his *The Life and Struggles of Negro Toilers* (1931) was already something of a classic. James would not regret going to that meeting, as "George Padmore" turned out to be his boyhood friend from Trinidad, Malcolm Nurse. The two had not seen each other for about eight years, since Nurse had left for America.[39] Hearing the inspirational and authoritative Padmore speak about the "coming African revolution" helped to open James's eyes to new possibilities and potentialities.

Critical to James's movement toward Pan-Africanism, however, was to be the six months he spent during the winter of 1933 in France, researching the Haitian Revolution in the archives in Paris.[40] Paris at that time has been described as the "capital of the Black Atlantic" for its apparently enlightened attitude toward race and the fact that black journals such as *La Revue du Monde Noir* and anticolonial organizations such as the Ligue Nationale de Défence des Intérêts de la Race Nègre flourished.[41] It was in Paris that Nancy Cunard finished compiling her monumental eight-hundred-page *Negro Anthology* (1934).[42] James's six months in France were also critical for his decision to become a revolutionary socialist. In early February 1934, he witnessed a spontaneous general strike erupt in Paris against the threat of a fascist coup. James later paid tribute to "the sure instinct of the Paris workers," noting how "the stock of 1789 and the 10th August, 1792, of 1830, of 1848 and 1871, came out in their thousands," effectively destroying the hopes of those trying to emulate Hitler's success the year before.[43]

"I had not been in Europe two years before I came to the conclusion that European civilisation as it then existed was doomed," James later recalled of his early experience of a continent still scarred irrevocably by the horrors of the Great War and then engulfed by the Great Depression and the rise of fascism.[44] After making an independent study of Marxism, on his return to Britain in early 1934, James decided to become an organised revolutionary and to join the Trotskyist movement.[45] As he put it in 1944, "Ten years ago something came into my life and altered its whole course."[46] James's embrace of revolutionary Marxism complemented his newfound militant Pan-Africanism, as demonstrated in a lecture on "The Negro" he gave in Nelson in March 1934: he damned the British Empire for the racism it fostered not only abroad but also "at home," in the metropolis itself. James also stressed the achievements of African civilization, and he was quoted as declaring that "there was going to be a tremendous revolt in Africa someday."[47]

The Playscript: Plot and Politics

James's *Toussaint Louverture* is panoramic in its dramatisation of the Haitian Revolution, eleven scenes spread over three acts, ranging from vodou rituals in the forests of colonial Saint-Domingue to a skilful reenactment of the French Convention that passed a decree abolishing colonial slavery in Paris in 1794, and to Napoleon Bonaparte in his apartment declaring his desire to restore slavery. There is music throughout, opening with Mozart's minuet from the opera *Don Giovanni*, and going on to include African drumming, Toussaint singing a spiritual hymn in captivity, and the armies of former slaves singing "To the Attack, Grenadiers," to the tune of the Marseillaise, the anthem of revolutionary France. The play is not without humour; some characters seem almost to have been written in to provide an element of comic relief. However, once the Haitian revolt begins, the action becomes faster paced, reflecting the frenzied ecstasy of revolution, and things build to an exhilarating finale as Dessalines declares Haiti independent.

The action begins in 1791, in colonial Saint-Domingue. The play opens in the villa of a wealthy white planter, Monsieur Bullet, the president of the Colonial Assembly, who is entertaining Colonel Vincent, a visiting representative of the moderate liberal government in France. The French Revolution is in its second year, and the new legislative assemblies in Paris are caught in a contradiction between their professed ideals of liberty, equality, and fraternity, and the continuing obscenity of colonial slavery. Such contradictions play havoc in Saint-Domingue among the twenty thousand or so whites, as royalists fight republicans, and with the thirty thousand free mulattoes demanding full political rights. M. Bullet's response to a petition demanding equality for mulattoes is uncompromising—he openly demonstrates that he will defend white supremacy on the island with violence and terror.

James's play shows how the five hundred thousand enslaved blacks on the island were drawn into this conflict. One stormy night in August 1791, at a huge open meeting in the forests of a northern mountain, they decide to strike out for freedom under the leadership of Boukman. Drawing strength and courage from vodou, they pledge to rise in revolt under the slogan "Liberty or Death!" James then moves to 1793, with the rebel army of former slaves at war with both the whites and some of the mulattoes. Unknown to them, however, the revolutionary process in France has risen to a new level of radicalisation under the threat of foreign invasion: the Paris masses have begun to take matters into their own hands. The power of the Bourbon monarchy has been completely smashed and the Girondins now lead the new Republic. The rebel slave army leaders receive Commissioner Roume from France but are not impressed, because the French Republican Convention does not stand for the abolition of slavery and has executed King Louis XVI. They decide instead to accept the offer of an alliance with the Spanish Empire in order to gain arms. By 1794, the rebel slave army, with Spanish help and under Toussaint's leadership, succeeded in taking control of the north of Saint-Domingue. The desperate colonial planters look for support from the British Empire, but Toussaint sees through the British and planters' intrigues.

Meanwhile in France the Jacobins under Robespierre have come to power after leading the defence of the revolution. In February 1794, the Convention in Paris officially abolishes slavery in all French colonies.[48] Though the British fleet prevented material assistance from France reaching the rebel slave army, Toussaint decides to side with the French Jacobins, taking the name "Louverture," "the opening."[49] "I feel that the only European Government which will do its duty by the Negroes is the Government of the Revolution," Toussaint is quoted as saying, making a personal commitment by sending his two sons to be educated in Paris.

Act II opens five years later, in 1799, by which time Toussaint's revolutionary armies have fought off the British army of intervention. However, while Toussaint is still loyal to the French Republic, in France the Jacobins have long been swept from power by a tide of reaction. A new French Commissioner, Hédouville, enters the scene as a representative of the government of the conservative Directory. The French plot with their official enemies, the British, to end "black domination" in the colony, to break the power of Toussaint, a man described by the British General Maitland as "this audacious and all-conquering Negro." Yet Toussaint, after defeating those mulattoes who rebel against him with the backing of the French and British, stands firm with France. By 1801, however, and the rise of Napoleon Bonaparte to power as First Consul in France, there are growing fears that the French will move to restore slavery. Colonel Vincent in vain presents Toussaint's Constitution, which would leave Saint-Domingue an autonomous part of the French Empire, to Bonaparte. Bonaparte, however, refuses to "abandon the fairest and richest prize of all the colonies to this upstart," and he orders his brother-in-law, General Leclerc, to mount an expedition to reclaim Saint-Domingue for the old slaveowners.

Act III tells of Leclerc's attempt to restore slavery on Saint-Domingue in 1802. His promises of coming in the name of "liberty and the happiness of all" appeal to many of Toussaint's tired generals, and Toussaint is himself eventually forced to the negotiating table, only to be betrayed and captured by the French. His last warning to those who arrest him will be vindicated by the play's end: "Do with me what you will. In destroying me you destroy only the trunk. But the tree of Negro liberty will flourish again, for its roots are many and deep." The penultimate scene shows the destruction of Toussaint, defiant to the end, in his prison cell in the Alps. But by the time news of his death reaches Saint-Domingue, Dessalines has already led the black former slaves to victory over Leclerc, before uniting with the mulattoes to proclaim independence for the colony, now renamed Haiti. As Dessalines triumphantly declares, "Haiti, the first free and independent Negro state in the new world. Toussaint died for it. We shall live and fight for it!"

As James notes in his stage directions for Act I, Scene 2, the moment the enslaved of Saint-Domingue gather to plot their uprising in the depths of the forest, "they, the Negro slaves, are the most important character in the play. Toussaint did not make the revolt. It was the revolt that made Toussaint." But James's play was also concerned with the vital question of revolutionary leadership. In the Haitian Revolution, the ideals of the Enlightenment, of liberty, equality, and fraternity, became embodied in the rebel slave army. During their mighty collective struggle for freedom, cherished African beliefs in kingship, rooted in ancient tradition, began to be transcended.

It was above all Toussaint himself who ensured that the new ideas triumphed over the old, enabling the enslaved themselves to make "the only successful slave revolt in history."[50] As James stressed in *The Black Jacobins*, Toussaint's revolutionary leadership was critical, for "it is the tragedy of mass movements that they need and can only too rarely find adequate leadership."[51] The play ends with a reenactment of the performance of "one of the most revolutionary symbolic and enlightened gestures in the history of the struggle for independence in the Americas. Eager to differentiate the revolutionary army from the French enemy, Dessalines designs a new flag by removing the white from the French tricouleur."[52]

Toussaint: A Tragic Hero of Colonial Enlightenment

Yet if James's Toussaint was a hero, his ultimate destruction underlines the fact that he was a tragic hero. Robert Hill has drawn attention to "the cultural dilemma of the West Indian intellectual," rooted in the struggle for national liberation amid material and cultural backwardness, and he notes that "James was the first commentator to recognize the significance of this dilemma for the fate of the Haitian revolution."[53] Perhaps because James was wrestling with a similar identity crisis in respect of his own "Britishness," he could so vividly explore Toussaint's "Frenchness" and his ultimately doomed attempt to overcome the backwardness of Saint-Domingue through a relationship with French culture and capital. This dilemma is made explicit in James's play through a discussion of Placide and Isaac, Toussaint's two sons who were sent to study in France, and their different views when they return to Saint-Domingue. In exploring Placide's and Isaac's conflicting loyalties, James was following other dramatists of the Haitian Revolution, including Alphonse de Lamartine.[54]

Tragedy was the dramatic form James used to portray the way Toussaint was caught between the barbaric realities of New World slavery and the modern ideals of the Enlightenment embodied in the French Revolution. "All great tragedies," as he would later point out with respect to Shakespeare's *Hamlet*, deal with "the confrontation of two ideas of society and they deal with it according to the innermost essence of the drama—the two societies confront one another within the mind of a single person."[55] James focused on the human personality of Toussaint. As Stuart Hall notes, "James imagined Toussaint as a Shakespearean figure with the tragic form built in" and "had classical Greek tragedy and Shakespeare at the very forefront of his mind at every turn."[56]

Toussaint is shown from the first to be someone who is torn between the enslaved Africans' old faith in vodou and kingship and the new revolutionary ideals of the Enlightenment: he is pulled first one way, then the other. Toussaint's Christianity, thoughtfulness, literacy, hesitancy to participate in the vodou ritual drinking of the blood of a stuck pig, and ability to write clearly mark him out from most of the other rebel slaves in Act I, Scene 2. In Act I, Scene 3, we see him drawing strength from re-reading the Abbé Raynal, the French priest and Enlightenment *philosophe*, and his famous history of French colonialism, *Philosophical and Political History of the Establishments and Commerce of the Europeans in the Two Indies* (1770). As Raynal had warned, for the enslaved to end slavery, "a courageous chief only is wanted. Where is he? That great man whom Nature owes to her vexed, oppressed and tormented children?" James's Toussaint delivers a soliloquy after re-reading Raynal: "White men see Negroes as slaves. If the Negro is to be free, he must free himself. We have courage, we have endurance, we have numbers. . . . Thou hast shown me the light, oh God! I shall be that leader."

Yet the barbaric oppressions of colonial slavery mean that for James's enlightened Toussaint, the mass of black rebel slaves were fit only to be led like "children" into the "light" and were not intellectually mature enough for liberty. Even as late as 1799, after leading the ex-slaves to victory after victory under the slogan "Liberty or Death," Toussaint still has the comparative backwardness of Saint-Domingue at the forefront of his mind. It is not that James's Toussaint cannot conceive of the possibilities of independence. "God knows that in my dreams sometimes I see not only an independent black San Domingo. I see all these West Indian islands free and independent communities of black men reaping the reward of the long years of cruelty and suffering which our parents bore." Yet when Dessalines urges him to strike there and then for complete independence, Toussaint urges caution:

Freedom—yes—but freedom is not everything. Dessalines, look at the state of the people. We who live here shall never see Africa again—some of us born here have never seen it. Language we have none—French is now our language. We have no education—the little that some of us know we have learnt from France. Those few of us who are Christians follow the French religion. We must stay with France as long as she does not seek to restore slavery. (Act II, Scene 1)

Only after he is betrayed and captured by the French, in his last lines of the play, "Oh, Dessalines! Dessalines! You were right after all!" do we see Toussaint acknowledging his tragic failing not to have placed more trust in the black masses and chosen Haitian independence over French civilization at the critical moment (Act III, Scene 4). As James recalled it in 1938,

Toussaint's error sprang from the very qualities that made him what he was. It is easy to see today, as his generals saw after he was dead, where he had erred. It did not mean that they or any of us would have done better in his place. If Dessalines could see so clearly and simply, it was because the ties that bound this uneducated soldier to French civilization were of the slenderest. He saw what was under his nose so well because he saw no further. Toussaint's failure was the failure of enlightenment, not of darkness.[57]

Yet because his error "sprang from the very qualities that made him what he was," Toussaint remains a representative figure, the precursor of the tradition of West Indian intellectual and cultural thought.

The impact of Athenian tragedy on James's *Toussaint Louverture* can be seen in the way that the black masses of Saint-Domingue function as a kind of Greek chorus. From the very opening of the play, when "there is a faint but insistent beating of drums. In moments of tenseness the drums beat louder and with accelerated rhythm," the rebellious slaves steadily make their presence felt more and more throughout the play. Act I, Scene II, sees "a great rattle of the drums" as the enslaved Africans take centre stage, meeting in the forest to plan their uprising, drawing strength from vodou. Once fighting for liberation in Act I, Scene III, the chorus of ex-slaves seems almost to be using the drums to comment on the ideas put forward by their leaders, in particular Boukman's hopes in the King of Congo and then Toussaint's view that liberation for all would mean "the whole country will be ruined." The chorus cheers Toussaint's victory over the mulattoes at Jacmel (Act II, Scene 1) and fights bravely against Leclerc's forces (Act III, Scene 2). Finally, singing "To the Attack, Grenadiers," "Toussaint and his soldiers march in, the band off-stage coming to a great climax" in its playing of the Marseillaise, an anthem appropriated by the black revolution, to meet Leclerc to negotiate peace (Act III, Scene 3).

The final scene of revolutionary history sees what James would in 1963 describe as "the entry of the chorus, of the ex-slaves themselves, as the arbiters of their own fate," making for an ending to a drama that no Greek tragedian or even someone with the far-reaching imagination of Shakespeare could have envisaged.[58] The play's thrilling climax serves to place Toussaint's defeat within the context of the wider collective victory of the Haitian Revolution, so the tragedy of *Toussaint Louverture* paradoxically ends with an act representative of a certain vindication of Enlightenment values, one achieved by the slaves themselves. That it falls to Dessalines to lead this final struggle suggests that, as Paul B. Miller notes, "his resolve to declare Haiti independent qualifies him to a certain extent as *more enlightened than Toussaint*, more eager to throw off the yoke of arbitrary and tyrannical authority. Dessalines merely embodies the same paradox as Toussaint, though now inverted: emancipation achieved through barbarous autonomy rather than civilized tutelage."[59]

Black and Radical Theatre in Imperial Britain

Such an ambitious project as attempting to put the Haitian Revolution on the British stage was something new. For over a century, portrayals of black people on the British stage were, in general, racial mockery — "nigger" minstrelsy, or melodramatic "slave plays" where black people were simply shown as suffering until liberation comes with the arrival of some great white man, usually an English imperial hero such as a naval officer.[60] There seems to have been only one direct attempt to stage the Haitian Revolution in Britain before James. This was by the radical-leaning Victorian writer George Dibdin Pitt, most famous for a drama about Sweeney Todd the Barber, "The Fiend of Fleet Street." Pitt's blackface minstrel play *Toussaint L'Ouverture, or The Black Spartacus*, was performed at the Britannia Theatre in London's East End in 1846. Though only Act I survives, Pitt's play has been described by Hazel Waters as "an uneasy mix of comedy and melodrama" that depicted Toussaint's main concern as "saving his owner's family from the black revolution."[61]

By the 1930s, the representation of black people on the British stage was beginning to be challenged. While James was in France, in November 1933, *At What a Price*, a pioneering production written and directed by the Jamaican feminist Una Marson, the secretary of the League of Coloured Peoples, had been staged in London. With an amateur cast composed of League members, this play about family life in Jamaica then went on to enjoy a brief run at the Scala Theatre in January 1934.[62] Until Marson's play, as Deirdre Osborne has noted, "the presence of black people on the British stage into the early twentieth century remained by and large that of touring African-American individuals and groups," most notably the Shakespearean actor Ira Aldridge, the singer and dancer Florence Mills, and, of course, since the mid-1920s, Paul Robeson.[63]

James recalled that, after his return from France in March 1934, he had had the fortune to meet Robeson, the icon of the American and British stage, "at various places" in London, including "at the houses of English people who were happy to invite Blacks as well as whites to their parties."[64] Born in Princeton, New Jersey, in 1898, Paul Robeson from an early age displayed outstanding talents as a singer, athlete, and actor, though it was as a law student that he moved in 1919 to Harlem, New York, "the Negro capital of the world." There he joined the Amateur Players, a group of black students, and from that moment his phenomenal career on the stage (and screen) took off.[65] As James recalled, Robeson "was not only a very famous man in England but he was very much loved by everybody. . . . To have spent half an hour in his company or to have ten minutes alone with him, was something that you remembered for days, and if I had to sum up his personality in one word, or rather two, I would say it was the combination of immense power and great gentleness."[66] As Robert Hill notes, "At a very profound and fundamental level, Robeson as a man *shattered* James's colonial conception of the Black Physique. In its place the magnificent stature of Robeson gave to him a new appreciation of the powerful and extraordinary capacities which the African possessed, in both head and body."[67]

Robeson had starred in several important productions on the British stage, including Eugene O'Neill's *Emperor Jones* (1925), *The Hairy Ape* (1931), and *All God's Chillun Got Wings* (1933); Oscar Hammerstein's *Show Boat* (1928); and Shakespeare's *Othello* (1930).[68] In May 1935, Robeson starred in *Stevedore*, by the Americans Paul Peters and George Sklar. This play was a dynamic social realist portrayal of a multiracial dock strike in America begun after a black docker was falsely accused of rape. As Marie Seton, an English actress who had become a theatre and art critic, recalled, "*Stevedore* was an important play: for the first time in the theatre Negroes were shown fighting for their rights and their lives, with white workers joining them in their resistance to a racist mob."[69] What made it truly remarkable was the cast of West Indian and African amateurs supporting Robeson on the London stage, including Kathleen Davis, James's friend from the Maverick Club in Trinidad, as Ruby.[70]

Central to assembling such a cast was Amy Ashwood Garvey, the former wife of Marcus Garvey. Amy Ashwood Garvey, also Jamaican and a playwright and theatre producer in her own right, had taken her shows across America and the Caribbean in the 1920s. After moving to London in 1934 she investigated the possibility of taking a company of artists of African descent to West Africa. However, when this plan fell through, she and her partner, the Trinidadian musician and actor Sam Manning, opened the Florence Mills Social Parlour in London's Carnaby Street, which became "a haunt of black intellectuals."[71] In London, Manning put on black musical and comic revues with "singers and actors from Liverpool, Cardiff and the West Indies."[72] The production of *Stevedore* in May 1935 seems to have been a critical and inspiring breakthrough for all concerned. Its talented director, André van Gyseghem, who had also directed Robeson in *All God's Chillun Got Wings*, was soon to leave for South Africa to help establish the Bantu People's Theatre.[73] Paul Robeson declared that it was his aim to establish a "Negro theatre" in London, possibly on the model of the Negro People's Theatre being formed in Harlem after the riots of March 1935.[74]

James may well have been aware of a separate shift toward the medium of radical theatre among leading young English intellectuals at this time, who, like him, had radicalized politically amid the economic crisis and a rising threat of fascism. Most notable were the "Left Poets" around W. H. Auden, Stephen Spender, Cecil Day-Lewis, and Christopher Isherwood, who, while studying at Oxford and Cambridge, embraced a "Marxism of the heart," which Stuart Samuels has described as "a philosophy of personal action, a moral force for good." Inspired in part by the Anglo-American poet T. S. Eliot, whose poem *The Wasteland* (1922) captured the imagination of many growing up after the devastation of the Great War, and who had himself turned to writing religious plays in the 1930s, the Auden Group was attracted to the Group Theatre, founded in 1932. The Group Theatre was closely associated with London's Westminster Theatre, and in February 1934, the Group produced its first big production, Auden's *The Dance of Death*, a satirical attack on bourgeois civilization.[75]

While James was perhaps encouraged by such movements as the Group Theatre and the unapologetically amateur Workers' Theatre Movement around the Communist Party, one suspects his vision of political theatre was on a far grander scale. It was closer to that of a less well-known third artistic current among British socialist playwrights, the Left Theatre group. Formed in 1934, it tried to bring some of the more sophisticated European developments in theatre — pioneered by the likes of Bertolt Brecht and Ernst Toller — to England. The Left Theatre group was searching for creative new forms of political theatre, and it aspired to "Total Theatre," combining dance, music, and drama — and James's *Toussaint Louverture* might be best seen as in this mould.[76]

Countercultures of Modernity

C. L. R. James, having written *Toussaint Louverture*, decided to show his playscript to Marie Seton, "a good friend."[77] In 1935, when James must have passed his script to her, Seton had recently returned from a trip to the Soviet Union with Paul and Eslanda Robeson. The visit had been organised at the behest of the Soviet filmmaker Sergei Eisenstein, an artistic genius of the twentieth century, whom she had first met in 1932 on a visit to the Soviet Union.[78] Eisenstein was interested in having Robeson star in a proposed film about the Haitian Revolution. The director of such classic films about the Russian Revolution as *Strike* (1924), *Battleship Potemkin* (1925), and *October* (1927), Eisenstein had become fascinated by Haitian history and had purchased a copy of John W. Vandercook's dramatic novel *Black Majesty: The Life of Christophe, King of Haiti* (1928) for a dollar in 1930, while in Hollywood working for Paramount. Eisenstein corresponded with the British socialist filmmaker Ivor Montagu and Paul Robeson about the prospect of filming *Black Majesty* but had no illusions about Paramount's support. As Montagu recalled, the idea of making the film "did not come into the running . . . we knew too much about the Hollywood set-up to imagine for a moment that such a subject could be acceptable to a big Hollywood corporation."[79] The fact that Haiti itself was under American military occupation at the time hardly helped matters.

Yet Eisenstein did not abandon his dream. He was able to learn more about Robeson from Marie Seton when they met in 1932, after his return to Moscow. Seton had seen Robeson play the character of Joe in a London production of *Show Boat* in April 1928, though she had not met him until 1930, when he played Othello opposite the twenty-two-year-old Peggy Ashcroft at London's Savoy Theatre.[80] Eisenstein asked Seton "to act as intermediary and persuade Robeson to come to Moscow so that he could discuss the proposed film."[81] It is doubtful that Robeson took much persuading. The son of a former slave, he had brought his father to tears when, at seventeen, he had given an impassioned oration of Wendell Phillips's tribute to Toussaint Louverture in a high school contest. One of his earliest film roles was in O'Neill's *The Emperor Jones* (1933), about a black American who, more by accident than design, ends up ruling an unnamed Caribbean island, not unlike Haiti.[82]

The stage was then set for a tremendous meeting of minds when Robeson (with Marie Seton and his wife, Eslanda) made the voyage to meet Eisenstein, arriving in Moscow in late December 1934. Seton described their intense discussions: "After knowing Robeson for twenty-four hours, Eisenstein, who was a sceptical critic of great men, attributed human genius to Robeson because he was without falseness. Six days later Robeson, who had met many of the greatest artists and thinkers of the twentieth century, said that meeting Eisenstein was one of the greatest experiences of his life."[83] There now seemed at least a chance that Eisenstein's film on the Haitian Revolution would finally go ahead with Robeson in the lead. On 6 January 1935, the Robesons and Seton left Russia to return to Britain.[84] Two days later, Eisenstein addressed the All-Union Creative Conference of Soviet Filmworkers, called to celebrate fifteen years of Soviet film. No doubt fully conscious of the hostile bureaucratic forces ranged against him among the Soviet film authorities, Eisenstein himself was now distinctly circumspect in his comments. As he explained in a reflective and retrospective manner, he *had* planned to produce as a film "the *best* episodes from the Haitian Revolution," starring "the remarkable black actor Paul Robeson, whom we welcomed here as our guest not so long ago."[85]

On her return to London from Moscow, and after being presented with a copy of *Toussaint Louverture* by James, Marie Seton took the playscript to the

Stage Society. Once described as a "quasi-Fabian dramatic club," the Stage Society had been set up in 1899 to circumvent the Lord Chamberlain's draconian censorship of the British stage by presenting private performances. It successfully established its reputation as a force in the British theatre world after putting on the first performances of plays by George Bernard Shaw and Arnold Bennett. Moreover, it was also committed to "introduce to the English public the best plays of contemporary foreign dramatists," staging the first productions in Britain of work by world-famous playwrights, including Anton Chekhov, Henrik Ibsen, Somerset Maugham, Eugene O'Neill, Ernst Toller, and Leo Tolstoy.[86] In 1935, the officials of the Stage Society found themselves considering James's *Toussaint Louverture*, and in keeping with their progressive internationalist tradition they made him an offer. As James recalled, "A very courteous old gentleman at the Stage Society said if I could get Paul Robeson to play the part, they would put it on."[87]

This was easier said than done. Tracking Robeson down proved difficult. By early 1935, after a tour of concerts across England, Scotland, Ireland, and Wales, Robeson was not merely the toast of London's theatre world but a popular singing idol in Britain. Offers for work were pouring in. Jacob ("Jack") Isaacs of the Stage Society "spent several months trying to reach Robeson by telephone and letter." Seton explained:

> This seeming elusiveness was not because Robeson ranked himself and his talent so high, but that his experience with producers had been discouraging and often exceedingly painful. It was not pleasant to be offered all sorts of inferior material because the outlook of the white world towards black people was reflected in plays with Negro roles that corresponded in no way to reality and were often extremely offensive.[88]

Indeed, in April 1935, Robeson had an "exceedingly painful" experience when Alexander Korda's film of Edgar Wallace's *Sanders of the River* was released. Like James, Robeson had "discovered Africa" in London, studying at what is now the School of Oriental and African Studies, and he clearly hoped *Sanders of the River*, in which he played the character of the African chief Bosambo, would for once portray something of the majesty of the African continent for a mass audience.[89] Instead, the film ended up glorifying the British Empire.[90]

Enter Mussolini, Stage Right . . .

An even more titanic clash of fiction and reality with respect to Africa was by now well under way. In early 1935, the murderous intentions of Mussolini, the dictator of fascist Italy, to conquer the African state of Ethiopia (then called Abyssinia) became apparent. To justify such nineteenth-century-style empire building, in time-honoured fashion, the criminal invasion and occupation of a sovereign nation was declared to be "a war of civilization and liberation."[91]

Robert Hill has drawn attention to how Italy's invasion of Ethiopia "marked the turning-point of nineteenth-century and post-war Black nationalism and paved the way for the emergence of an explicitly political Pan-Africanism," noting that "the contribution of C. L .R. James would prove to be one of the essential factors in clearly establishing the changed outlook."[92] As Italian war drums beat ever louder, James remembered that Amy Ashwood Garvey and he both "felt that there ought to be an opposition" in Britain to Mussolini's looming war and that she had "a unique capacity to concentrate all the forces available and needed for the matter in hand."[93] Together they revived an ad hoc committee formed in 1934 to aid the Gold Coast Aborigines' Rights Protection Society's deputation to England.[94] James became the chairman of the resulting International African Friends of Abyssinia (IAFA).[95] The first public meeting of the IAFA held to protest against the looming war was in London on 23 July 1935. *West Africa* described it as "crowded" with "men and women of African descent." The meeting sent "resolutions of sympathy with Abyssinians in their resolve to maintain independence" and began a fund to either "send an ambulance" or "found a permanent hospital if there is no war."[96]

On Sunday, 28 July 1935, the IAFA held its second public meeting. As *West Africa* reported, "a crowded meeting of sympathisers with Abyssinia, was held, presided over by Mrs A. A. Garvey, of the West Indies. The speakers represented several African territories."

> The first speaker was Mr C. L. R. James, a West Indian writer and journalist, one of whose short stories was adjudged among the best of a recent year. He surveyed the history of Abyssinia's intercourse with foreign Powers. His plea may be summarised as follows: Africans and persons of African descent all over the world have always looked with zealous pride

at Abyssinia, which, alone of ancient African kingdoms, still maintains independence. They therefore viewed with alarm and indignation the desire expressed on behalf of Italy, of conquering Abyssinia and the concentration of Italian troops and armaments on the Abyssinian frontiers. . . . Mr James expressed the belief that many Africans would be willing to offer themselves for the frontline, or for any auxiliary form of service in the event of war.[97]

The IAFA did consider organizing an "International Brigade" to go from Britain and fight fascism in Ethiopia.[98] At an IAFA rally in London's Trafalgar Square on 25 August 1935, James declared "the question of Ethiopia has brought about a union of sentiment between black men in Africa, America, the West Indies and all over the world. . . . Ethiopia's cause is our cause and we will defend it by every means in our power."[99] James's speeches in August 1935 give a sense of how Ethiopia and his study of the Haitian Revolution fired his imagination. Toussaint had defeated the European armies through a ruthless guerrilla war waged from the mountains of Haiti, and the Ethiopians' victory at Adowa in 1896 had been achieved in a similar manner, through adopting a "scorched earth" strategy and retreating into the mountains, before falling on the cut-off Italian army.[100] James put it to an IAFA public meeting on 16 August 1935 that the Ethiopians should "destroy their country rather than hand it over to the invader. Let them burn down Addis Ababa, let them poison their wells and water holes, let them destroy every blade of vegetation."[101]

In late August or September 1935, James was at last able to propose the idea of his play to Paul Robeson. "[Jack] Isaacs and I ran him down at some party, told him about it and he agreed to read the script." Robeson was at the height of his powers and reputation at this time. Martin Duberman notes that "James's play was one of four on various aspects of the Haitian revolution that Robeson had been considering." But Robeson, according to James, "read it and with great simplicity and directness said, yes, he would be ready to play the role."[102] Robeson had just been offered the chance of recreating his character Joe in a film version of *Show Boat*, but he felt that James's play would "satisfy his political needs." In September 1935, the Robesons left for Hollywood. "The [*Show Boat*] shoot was condensed into a two-month period so Robeson could get back to London in time for rehearsals of C. L. R. James's play about Toussaint."[103] From October 1935, as Mussolini waged war on the people of Ethiopia, notices about the play began appearing in the British press.

The Performance of *Toussaint Louverture*

In order to help prepare *Toussaint Louverture* for the stage, in February 1936 James took a break from an intensive speaking tour across Britain and Ireland. From an examination of the actual 1936 programme and comparison of the scenes described there with the longer 1934 script, it is clear the original script was too long at eleven scenes for a play that would only have two performances by the Stage Society, so cuts were necessary. James removed three scenes (Scenes 1 and 4 from Act I and Scene 1 from Act III) and he made abridgements so that the story still flowed relatively smoothly.[104] One consequence of the revisions however was that some characters (including Toussaint's wife and sons) were completely removed. Any regrets James may have had about cuts were doubtless outweighed by the excitement of knowing his play was going into production with Paul Robeson in the lead.

The director was Peter Godfrey, "a young man . . . who later came to Hollywood and made films," although at times when Godfrey was occupied James himself had to rehearse the cast.[105] As James recalls:

[Paul Robeson] was here, as elsewhere, always the centre of attention, a not easy role to fill. Besides playing the lead, he was his own extraordinary self and not only players but all who were connected with the stages where we rehearsed had their eyes fastened on him and were all ears when he spoke. Yet he continued to be that extraordinary combination of immense power enclosed in a pervading gentleness. Paul listened all the time to what Peter Godfrey or I had to say. I was somewhat naïve then and was always ready to say exactly how I thought the words of the character should be said and what the character ought to do. Paul was always ready to listen and to oblige, far more so than one or two others in the cast.[106]

The weeks in rehearsal with Robeson, whom James regarded as "the most remarkable human being [he had] ever met," must have been one of the most incredible experiences of James's life up to that point.[107] As James, interviewed in November 1983, recalled, "The moment he came onto the stage, the whole damn thing changed. It's not a question of acting . . . the physique and the voice, the *spirit* behind him — you could see it when he was on stage."[108]

The cast assembled around Robeson was remarkable, featuring as it did other black professional actors from throughout the African diaspora, including Robert Adams, who played Dessalines. Adams, born in British Guiana, had, like James, been a distinguished schoolteacher who produced and acted in amateur productions before coming to Britain. He had worked with Paul Robeson in *Sanders of the River* and *Midshipman Easy,* and in 1935 he made his London stage debut in *Stevedore.*[109] Also recruited from *Stevedore* was the Nigerian Orlando Martins, who played the role of Boukman.[110] Black amateur actors — including other veterans of *Stevedore,* such as John Ahuma, Rufus E. Fennell, and Charles Johnson — were included, while the remaining cast was recruited through the Stage Society itself, many of whom were experienced professional actors or rising stars such as Harry Andrews.[111]

The play was staged at the 730-seat Westminster Theatre, on the fringes of London's West End in Palace Street. The owner of the Westminster Theatre during this period was A. B. Horne, and it was managed by Anmer Hall. Michael Sidnell notes that Hall learnt that "Sunday performances were a way of getting a hearing for new or neglected plays without going to great expense." With its quite liberal management, it is not surprising that the Westminster Theatre was a home for the radical Group Theatre, and James's *Toussaint Louverture* had followed a series of plays by "the Auden Group," most notably Auden and Isherwood's *The Dog beneath the Skin.*[112] The famous theatre critic Herbert Farjeon noted at the end of the 1930s that "the Westminster Theatre has probably housed during the present decade a higher percentage of interesting plays than any other theatre north of the Thames." In 1955, the Westminster Theatre produced an all-African play, *Freedom,* which toured Europe and was filmed in Nigeria in 1956 with a cast of thousands.[113]

Those wishing to see the performance had to pay at least one guinea, the basic annual membership subscription to the Stage Society.[114] As well as the Sunday evening performance on 15 March, there was a matinee the next day, and for this final performance James himself was called upon to step in for Rufus E. Fennell, the actor playing the "small part" of Macoya. "I was in it by accident. . . . I wanted to sit in the back and watch the play . . . not to be mixed up in it. But I dressed myself up and played it."[115] Overall, though the production went well, James would always remember it was Paul Robeson who stole the show.[116]

While James's *Toussaint Louverture* was being performed, the British film *Rhodes of Africa* was just out in cinemas. In the film, Cecil Rhodes is quoted as saying, "I think of the natives as little children who must be educated— and sometimes punished."[117] James's play not only represented a much-needed antidote to such imperial propaganda, but also symbolised in an important sense the Ethiopian resistance to Mussolini.[118] The first review of the play appeared in the *New York Times*, which noted that "although unevenly written and produced, the episodic drama of the rebellion of San Domingo slaves at the end of the eighteenth century nevertheless held an appreciative audience's attention throughout, receiving an ovation at the final curtain."[119] Astute critics such as Ivor Brown grasped some of the real depth of the play, noting that James's "Toussaint was a real tragedy hero, and Mr Robeson bestowed tremendous power on the picture of this tribal hero in victory and frustration."[120] *Toussaint Louverture* was widely regarded as a success, and it must surely stand as the most outstanding anti-imperialist play ever to make it onto London's West End during the interwar period. As the *New Leader* noted:

> The whole play cogently puts the problem of empire with its exploitation and slavery of the coloured people. The "civilising" missions of the Capitalist Governments, their promises solemnly made and lightly scrapped, their trickery, makes a pretty picture for an audience whose rulers have the largest empire in the world under their domination. The production, with its minimum of scenery, is excellently done by Peter Godfrey, and the large cast, many of them Negroes, succeeds in convincing the audience that an Empire is nothing of which any white civilisation can be proud.[121]

After the shows in March 1936, Robeson himself was "pleased" with how *Toussaint Louverture* had gone; as James remembers, "We agreed that we should seek ways and means to do it commercially."[122] Indeed, at the time this must have seemed a real possibility, and James had even "received a cable from a Broadway producer asking him to arrange a production in New York."[123]

Toussaint Louverture's Place in History

In 1963, a revised edition of *The Black Jacobins* was published. As well as adding footnotes and an appendix, "From Toussaint Louverture to Fidel Castro," James added six new paragraphs at the start of his last chapter on "The War of Independence," which contain his most concentrated meditations on the nature of Toussaint's tragedy. In David Scott's judgment, "These are magnificent passages . . . among James's most poignant sentences ever. And yet they bear rereading several times over not only for their somber quality of beauty, but for their attempt to refigure our understanding of Toussaint Louverture and the predicament he engaged."[124]

Perhaps as part of this project of refiguring Toussaint, James now helped his fellow Trinidadian, Dexter Lyndersay, adapt *The Black Jacobins* into a new play of that title. James felt the victory of many national liberation movements internationally in the postwar world meant that, as he later recalled, "the idea I was expressing should be differently expressed . . . writing about the struggle for independence in 1956 or 1960 was very different from what it was in 1936."[125] As James told Reinhard Sander, "After twenty-five years the colonial revolution had made great strides so about that time I began to rewrite it [the play] in view of the new historical happenings."[126] The play version of *The Black Jacobins* was first performed at the University of Ibadan in Nigeria in 1967, directed by Lyndersay amid the tumult of civil war to an enthusiastic reception.[127] It has since been staged numerous times, and this later script has necessarily formed the basis of scholarly discussion of "James's play."[128]

The later play essentially followed the same chronological structure as *Toussaint Louverture*. There is the same humour, the lively music, drumming ebbing and flowing into the action, and there are still moments of rare dramatic power. Yet by the 1960s James had experienced for himself, in Trinidad with Eric Williams and in Ghana with Kwame Nkrumah, both the excitement and the disappointment generated by movements for colonial liberation in the Caribbean and in Africa. If *Toussaint Louverture* was about the vindication of national liberation struggles written in the age of colonialism, in *The Black Jacobins* James and Lyndersay explored what lessons the Haitian Revolution might hold for national liberation struggles in the age of decolonisation. While Toussaint and Dessalines were still portrayed as heroic revolutionary leaders, other more radical leaders were developed as characters. The condemned Moïse castigates Toussaint as a dreamer: "Pitiful old Toussaint . . . you will remain just an old man with a dream of an impossible fraternity."[129] The play version of *The Black Jacobins* ends with Dessalines portrayed not defiantly leading the Haitian masses to victory but as a corrupt tyrant, toasting his new position as "Emperor," having personally betrayed Toussaint to the French.

James seems to have had two other concerns in the play of *The Black Jacobins*. First, the role of the ordinary slaves is given even greater emphasis: stage directions specify that "crowds say little but their presence is felt powerfully at all critical moments . . . this is the key point of the play." Second, James seems more conscious of the experience of women during the Haitian Revolution, whether being sexually abused by cruel slaveowners or engaging in relationships with the likes of Toussaint and Dessalines. Yet the richness of character that defines *Toussaint Louverture* is absent from *The Black Jacobins*. The judgment of the British playwright Arnold Wesker on the play *The Black Jacobins*, expressed in a letter to James in 1968, seems fair. According to Wesker,

> Your canvas is enormous and I was fascinated to read the way you handled it. . . . But there is a spark which is missing from the whole work. Forgive me, but there does seem to be something wooden about the play. The construction is dramatic; the dialogue carries the story and the dialectic of what you want to say, but when all the component parts are put together, it doesn't work.[130]

The publication of *Toussaint Louverture*, more than seventy-five years after it was first performed, will now make it possible to compare it to the play version of *The Black Jacobins* as well as to the many other classic plays written about the Haitian Revolution, such as those by Lamartine, Jean Brierre, Langston Hughes, Aimé Césaire, Derek Walcott, and Édouard Glissant.[131] In a short preface written in January 1986 to introduce the London production of *The Black Jacobins*, James himself remained hopeful that an audience still existed for the subject of his play:

> The play has been successful with audiences in Europe, Africa, America and in the Caribbean. But nowhere has it swept the audience off its feet. However, it was written fifty years ago. Fifty years is a long time and what did not happen then can happen now. Lift the curtain, gentlemen.[132]

Notes

1. The fragile playscript was catalogued "Toussaint Louverture [DJH/21]" and located among material dated 1943-45 in the Haston Papers, donated to the University of Hull in 1967. For more on how the historian John Saville secured Haston's papers for the university archives at Hull, see John Saville, *Memoirs from the Left* (London: Merlin, 2003), 138-39. The Haston Papers, like the university archives themselves, are now located in the Hull History Centre.

2. See Sam Bornstein and Al Richardson, *Against the Stream: A History of the Trotskyist Movement in Britain, 1924-1938* (London: Socialist Platform, 1986), 251-52. In the 1940s, Haston became a leading British Trotskyist, the first and only general secretary of the Revolutionary Communist Party, before leaving the movement in 1950. See John McIlroy, "James Ritchie (Jock) Haston," *Dictionary of Labour Biography*, XII (2005): 124-36.

3. C. L. R. James, *The Black Jacobins: Toussaint L'Ouverture and the San Domingo Revolution* (London: Penguin, 2001), 326.

4. Deirdre Osborne, "Writing Black Back: An Overview of Black Theatre and Performance in Britain," *Studies in Theatre and Performance*, 26, no. 1 (2006), 21.

5. Martin B. Duberman, *Paul Robeson* (London: New Press, 1989), 105.

6. Colin Chambers, *Black and Asian Theatre in Britain: A History* (London: Routledge, 2011), 98.

7. Errol Hill, "The Revolutionary Tradition in Black Drama," *Theatre Journal*, 38, no. 4 (1986), 408. See also Chambers, *Black and Asian Theatre in Britain*; Martin Banham, Errol Hill, and George Woodyard, eds., *The Cambridge Guide to African and Caribbean Theatre* (Cambridge: Cambridge University Press, 1994), 148, 226-27; and Judy Stone, *Theatre* (London: Macmillan Caribbean, 1994).

8. James, *Black Jacobins*, 201. In *Toussaint Louverture* and *Black Jacobins*, James used the anglicised term for Saint-Domingue, "San Domingo," or "St. Domingo," almost certainly to make it easier for a British audience to comprehend. The first recorded political play about the Haitian Revolution itself, *La Liberté Général, ou Les Colons à Paris*—"General Liberty, or The Planters in Paris" by an unidentified author, a certain citizen B, "a comedy glorifying abolitionist sentiments expressed by mulatto freedmen," was written and performed in Saint-Domingue in 1796. See VèVè A. Clark, "Haiti's Tragic Overture: (Mis)Representations of the Haitian Revolution in World Drama (1796-1975)," in James A. W. Heffernan, ed., *Representing the French Revolution: Literature, Historiography, and Art* (Hanover, N.H.: Dartmouth College, 1992), 242, 255. See also the discussion in Sibylle Fischer, *Modernity Disavowed: Haiti and the Cultures of Slavery in the Age of Revolution* (Durham: Duke University Press, 2005), 214-26.

9. Shane White, *Stories of Freedom in Black New York* (Cambridge, Mass.: Harvard University Press, 2002), 72-73, 86-88.

10. Hill, "Revolutionary Tradition in Black Drama," 408-9.

11. C. L. R. James, "Introduction," in Errol Hill, ed., *Caribbean Plays*, Vol. 2 (St. Augustine: University of the West Indies, 1965), viii.

12. Hill, "Revolutionary Tradition in Black Drama," 414.

13. For more on James's "voyage in," see Nicholas Laughlin, ed., *Letters from London: Seven Essays by C. L. R. James* (Oxford: Signal Books, 2003), which contains articles James published in the *Port of Spain Gazette* in 1932, collected together with a useful introduction by Kenneth Ramchand.

14. George Lamming, *The Pleasures of Exile* (London: Michael Joseph, 1960), 150.

15. Chris Searle, "Language and the Seizure of Power: An Interview with C. L. R. James," *Race and Class*, 50, no. 1 (2008), 82. While formal theatre never had popular roots in Trinidad, Selwyn Cudjoe has noted that "open-air, communal theatre in the form of Carnival, ramleelas, and hosay were always an integral part of the society, the product of the non-European people of the culture." See Selwyn R. Cudjoe, *Beyond Boundaries: The Intellectual Tradition of Trinidad and Tobago in the Nineteenth Century* (Wellesley, Mass.: Calaloux, 2003), 336.

16. Jean Besson, ed., *Caribbean Reflections: The Life and Times of a Trinidad Scholar (1901–1986): An Oral History Narrated by William W. Besson* (London: Karia Press, 1989), 55. James was known to friends and family as "Nello," a nickname for Lionel.

17. Richard Small, "The Training of an Intellectual, the Making of a Marxist," in Paul Buhle, ed., *C. L. R. James: His Life and Work* (London: Allison & Busby, 1986), 56.

18. Kent Worcester, *C. L. R. James: A Political Biography* (Albany: State University of New York Press, 1996), 248.

19. Paul Buhle, *C. L. R. James: The Artist as Revolutionary* (London: Verso, 1993), 22.

20. See Reinhard W. Sander, *The Trinidad Awakening: West Indian Literature of the Nineteen-Thirties* (London: Greenwood, 1988), and C. L. R. James, *Beyond a Boundary* (London: Hutchinson, 1969), 119.

21. Stuart Hall, "A Conversation with C. L. R. James," in Grant Farred, ed., *Rethinking C. L. R. James* (Oxford: Blackwell, 1996), 21.

22. Paul Buhle, "The Making of a Literary Life: C. L. R. James Interviewed," in Paget Henry and Paul Buhle, eds., *C. L. R. James's Caribbean* (Durham: Duke University Press, 1992), 58. It was not until 1939 that West Indian history was recognized formally as a subject for a certificate and as part of school curriculum.

23. Kenneth Ramchand, ed., *Life on the Edge: The Autobiography of Ralph de Boissière* (Caroni: Lexicon Trinidad Limited, 2010), 59.

24. See the interview with C. L. R. James in MARHO: The Radical Historians Organization, eds., *Visions of History* (Manchester: Manchester University Press, 1984), 267, and James, *Black Jacobins*, xv, 336. James would later describe Waxman's biography as "superficial."

25. James, *Beyond a Boundary*, 117. The offending article, "Race Admixture" by Dr. Sidney Harland, appeared in *The Beacon*, 1, no. 4 (July 1931) and asserted that "while it is not apparent to what extent the negro is inferior in intelligence to the white man, there is little doubt that on the average he is inferior."

26. James's intellectual demolition of Harland is discussed further in David Scott, *Conscripts of Modernity: The Tragedy of Colonial Enlightenment* (Durham: Duke University Press, 2004), 80–81.

27. Robert A. Hill, "C. L. R. James: The Myth of Western Civilisation," in George Lamming, ed., *Enterprise of the Indies* (Port of Spain: Trinidad and Tobago Institute of the West Indies, 1999), 256–57.

28. Scott, *Conscripts of Modernity*, 83, 85.

29. In this James was following in the footsteps of other Trinidadian nationalists. See Selwyn Cudjoe, "CLR James and the Trinidad and Tobago Intellectual Tradition," *New Left Review*, 223 (1997).

30. James perhaps drew inspiration while taking on Harland from an earlier intervention made by John Jacob Thomas, another black Trinidadian schoolmaster, in response to James Anthony Froude, the famous English "man of letters" and a biographer and friend of Thomas Carlyle. In 1887, Froude had visited the British West Indies, and on his return to Britain he published *The English in the West Indies, or the bow of Ulysses* (1888). Froude's book deployed the most blatant and vicious racism, particularly against the people of Haiti, in order to challenge the increasingly popular argument that the West Indian colonies should now be given Home Rule, or self-government. Thomas, despite his ill health, now travelled to England and published a justly famous riposte to Froude, *Froudacity: West Indian Fables Explained* (1889). Yet despite the brilliance of *Froudacity*, Thomas remained strikingly silent about the Haitian Revolution itself, possibly on the grounds that he felt it more important to put a clear case for West Indian self-government by avoiding plunging into complicated historical controversies. It is possible that James felt a certain frustration while in colonial Trinidad because of this. After all, Froude, who would eventually become Regius Professor of Modern History at Oxford University, had included a brief "history" of the Haitian Revolution in *The English in the West Indies*, yet as James later demonstrated, "every sentence that Froude writes is absolutely and completely wrong. *Every single sentence.*" See C. L. R. James, "The West Indian Intellectual," in J. J. Thomas, *Froudacity: West Indian Fables Explained* (London: New Beacon, 1969), 39 (emphasis in original).

31. Errol Hill, "Emergence of a National Drama in the West Indies," *Caribbean Quarterly*, 18, no. 4 (1972), 39–40. See also Kole Omotoso, *The Theatrical into Theatre: A Study of the Drama and Theatre of the English-Speaking Caribbean* (London: New Beacon, 1982), 47, 131.

32. Percy Waxman, *The Black Napoleon: The Story of Toussaint Louverture* (New York: Harcourt, Brace, 1931), 6, 293. James had read some Lamartine while in Trinidad and would read Lamartine's play in the course of his research. See Frank Rosengarten, *Urbane Revolutionary: C. L. R. James and the Struggle for a New Society* (Jackson: University Press of Mississippi, 2008), 17, and James, *Black Jacobins*, 348. On Waxman, see Scott, *Conscripts of Modernity*, 81, 243.

33. See C. L. R. James, *The Life of Captain Cipriani: An Account of British Government in the West Indies* (Nelson: Coulton & Co., 1932). The work sparked extensive discussion in colonial Trinidad, in particular in the pages of *The Beacon*. See Christian Høgsbjerg, "'A Thorn in the Side of Great Britain': C. L. R. James and the Caribbean Labour Rebellions of the 1930s," *Small Axe*, 35 (July 2011).

34. James, *Beyond a Boundary*, 119. The completed novel that James carried with him was *Minty Alley*, which he had written in the summer of 1928 and which would be published by Secker & Warburg in the summer of 1936.

35. James, *Beyond a Boundary*, 122, 149. See also James, *Black Jacobins*, xv. On 22 January 1933, James spoke at a local ILP meeting in Nelson on the topic "Coloured Peoples under British Rule." By this stage, the local ILP could already describe James as "a well-known, intelligent and capable speaker." See *Nelson Leader*, 22 and 27 January 1933.

36. Other contributors included Sir John Harris, Parliamentary Secretary to the Anti-Slavery and Aborigines Protection Society and author of *A Century of Emancipation* (1933); Charles Kingsley Webster, Professor of International History at the London School of Economics; and Reginald Coupland, Beit Professor of Colonial History at the University of Oxford and author of works such as *Wilberforce* (1923) and *The British Anti-Slavery Movement* (1933). What these representatives of the great and good had to say was epitomized in a quote from Coupland, who insisted that, after abolishing the slave trade in 1807, "Britain once more led the way in abolishing slavery itself." See *The Listener*, 26 April 1933, 3; 10 and 31 May 1933.

37. James, *Beyond a Boundary*, 121. James remembers Constantine was "very, very pleased" by the broadcast while Harold Moody of the League of Coloured Peoples also paid tribute to James's intervention. See *The Keys*, 1, no. 1 (July 1933), 17. James replied to the storm of protest from colonial officials by making sure "A Century of Freedom" was "circulated far and wide," including publishing it back home in the *Port of Spain Gazette* on 17 June 1933.

38. James, *Beyond a Boundary*, 115.

39. C. L. R. James, "Towards the Seventh: The Pan-African Congress [1976]," in C. L. R. James, *At the Rendezvous of Victory: Selected Writings*, Vol. 3 (London: Allison & Busby, 1984), 240.

40. James would always pay tribute to his good friend Harry Spencer (c. 1894–1965), who with his wife, Elizabeth, ran a bakery and tea room in Nelson, Lancashire, and who funded James's research visit to Paris. See *Nelson Leader*, 17 February 1933 and an obituary notice in *Nelson Leader*, 23 December 1965. In Paris, James was very proud that, as a black colonial subject from the West Indies, he was able to surprise librarians at La Bibliothèque Nationale with his knowledge of the French language. See Stuart Hall and Bill Schwarz, "Breaking Bread with History: C. L. R. James and *The Black Jacobins*," *History Workshop Journal*, 46 (1998), 19.

41. J. P. Eburne and J. Braddock, "Introduction: Paris, Capital of the Black Atlantic," *Modern Fiction Studies*, 51, no. 4 (2005), 733. The Martinican poet Aimé Césaire coined the term "Negritude" in the March 1935 issue of *L'Etudiant Noir*, a French journal. See Aimé Césaire, *Discourse on Colonialism* (New York: Monthly Review Press, 2000), 12.

42. For more on Cunard, see Barbara Bush, " 'Britain's Conscience on Africa': White Women, Race and Imperial Politics in Inter-war Britain," in Clare Midgley, ed., *Gender and Imperialism* (Manchester: Manchester University Press, 1998), and Maroula Joannou, "Nancy Cunard's English Journey," *Feminist Review*, 78 (2004).

43. C. L. R. James, *World Revolution 1917–1936: The Rise and Fall of the Communist International* (New Jersey: Humanities Press, 1994), 379–81. On the French events of 1934, see Chris Harman, *A People's History of the World* (London: Bookmarks, 1999), 494.

44. C. L. R. James, *Mariners, Renegades, and Castaways: The Story of Herman Melville and the World We Live In* (London: Allison & Busby, 1985), 162.

45. Al Richardson, Clarence Chrysostom, and Anna Grimshaw, *C. L. R. James and British Trotskyism: An Interview* (London: Socialist Platform, 1987), 2.

46. Anna Grimshaw, ed., *Special Delivery: The Letters of C. L. R. James to Constance Webb, 1939–1948* (Oxford: Blackwell, 1990), 136.

47. "Racial Prejudice in England," *Nelson Leader*, 16 March 1934.

48. On 29 August 1793, a new Jacobin Commissioner in Saint-Domingue, Sonthonax, "hemmed in on all sides" and, recognising the fact that "the slaves who had not yet revolted, kindled by the revolutionary ferment around them, refused to be slaves any longer," had proclaimed emancipation from slavery on the island. See James, *Black Jacobins*, 104.

49. "Polverel is said to have exclaimed at the news of another victory by Toussaint: 'This man makes an opening everywhere', whence the new name began. It is not improbable that the slaves called him Louverture from the gap in his teeth" (James, *Black Jacobins*, 344). Others have suggested the name relates to Toussaint's personal vodou practice.

50. *Toussaint Louverture's* subtitle was "the only successful slave revolt in history."

51. James, *Black Jacobins*, 20.

52. Paul B. Miller, *Elusive Origins: The Enlightenment in the Modern Caribbean Historical Imagination* (Charlottesville: University of Virginia Press, 2010), 78.

53. Hill, "C. L. R. James: The Myth of Western Civilization," 256.

54. See Clark, "Haiti's Tragic Overture," 244–45.

55. C. L. R. James, "Notes on Hamlet [1953]," in Anna Grimshaw, ed., *The C. L. R. James Reader* (Oxford: Blackwell, 1992), 243.

56. Hall and Schwarz, "Breaking Bread with History," 20–21, 27.

57. James, *Black Jacobins*, 234.

58. Ibid., 237.

59. See Miller, *Elusive Origins*, 78.

60. J. S. Bratton, Richard Allen Cave, Breandan Gregory, Heidi J. Holder, and Michael Pickering, *Acts of Supremacy: The British Empire and the Stage, 1790–1930* (Manchester: Manchester University Press, 1991).

61. Hazel Waters, *Racism on the Victorian Stage: Representation of Slavery and the Black Character* (Cambridge: Cambridge University Press, 2007), 118, 122, 190, 214.

62. Delia Jarrett-Macauley, *The Life of Una Marson, 1905–1965* (Manchester: Manchester University Press, 1998), 54, and Chambers, *Black and Asian Theatre in Britain*, 99.

63. Osborne, "Writing Black Back," 19, 21.

64. James, "Paul Robeson: Black Star [1970]," in C. L. R. James, *Spheres of Existence: Selected Writings*, Vol. 2 (London: Allison & Busby, 1980), 256. In this incredibly important memoir, first published in *Black World*, James tells us he had not known Robeson

before the publication of Robeson's article "The Culture of the Negro" in *The Spectator*, 15 June 1934.

65. Duberman, *Paul Robeson*, 32, 43.

66. James, "Paul Robeson," 256.

67. Robert A. Hill, "In England, 1932–1938," in Buhle, *C. L. R. James*, 73.

68. Duberman, *Paul Robeson*, 148–49, 165, and Marie Seton, *Paul Robeson* (London: Dennis Dobson, 1958), 63. For a discussion of O'Neill's *The Emperor Jones*, see Hazel V. Carby, *Race Men* (Cambridge, Mass.: Harvard University Press, 1998), 77–79.

69. Seton, *Paul Robeson*, 102, and Duberman, *Paul Robeson*, 192. *The Times* of London described *Stevedore* as "a swift and exciting drama of a race riot seasoned with class propaganda." For the impact of *Stevedore* in Harlem in 1934, see Mark Naison, *Communists in Harlem during the Depression* (Urbana: University of Illinois Press, 2005), 152.

70. Seton, *Paul Robeson*, 100. As Ronald Adam, the owner of the progressive Embassy Theatre which staged *Stevedore*, put it, "In assembling a cast of Negroes around Paul, I knew there would be unity of atmosphere in the performance."

71. Marika Sherwood, "Amy Ashwood Garvey," in Hakim Adi and Marika Sherwood, *Pan-African History: Political Figures from Africa and the Diaspora since 1787* (London: Routledge, 2003), 70; Tony Martin, *Amy Ashwood Garvey* (Dover: Majority Press, 2007); Barbara Bush, *Imperialism, Race and Resistance: Africa and Britain, 1919–1945* (London: Routledge, 1999), 211; and Duberman, *Paul Robeson*, 192. See also Errol G. Hill, "The Caribbean Connection," in Errol G. Hill and James V. Hatch, eds., *A History of African American Theatre* (Cambridge: Cambridge University Press, 2005), 278–79.

72. *News Chronicle*, 25 February 1935.

73. Seton, *Paul Robeson*, 103, and Colin Chambers, *The Story of Unity Theatre* (London: Lawrence & Wishart, 1989), 33. Van Gyseghem later returned to Britain to become the first President of Unity Theatre.

74. *News Chronicle*, 30 May 1935. On black theatre in Harlem, see Naison, *Communists in Harlem during the Depression*, 151, 204–9.

75. Stuart Samuels, "English Intellectuals and Politics in the 1930s," in Philip Rieff, ed., *On Intellectuals* (New York: Doubleday, 1969), 198, 207, 224.

76. Michael J. Sidnell, *Dances of Death: The Group Theatre of London in the Thirties* (London: Faber and Faber, 1984), 168, 260, and Chambers, *Story of Unity Theatre*, 33–34. The Left Theatre lasted from 1934 to 1937, and members included André van Gyseghem and the playwright and theatre critic Hubert Griffith. Their second production in 1934 was John Wexley's *They Shall Not Die*, a protest at the racism of the Scottsboro case in America.

77. James, "Paul Robeson," 257, and Alex Hamilton, "Profile: An Interview with C. L. R. James," *Guardian*, 25 June 1980.

78. Marie Seton, *Sergei M. Eisenstein* (London: J. Lane, 1952), 251.

79. Ivor Montagu, *With Eisenstein in Hollywood* (Berlin, Seven Seas, 1968), 345, and Richard Taylor, ed., *S. M. Eisenstein; Selected Works, Vol. IV: Beyond the Stars: The Memoirs of Sergei Eisenstein* (London: British Film Institute, 1995), 369. Black actors rarely appeared in any films made at this time, and those films in which they did appear the characters they played were in a deeply racist fashion, as they appeared only as servants or savages. See Peter Noble, *The Negro in Films* (London: Skelton, 1948), 48, 56.

80. Seton, *Paul Robeson*, 55, and Duberman, *Paul Robeson*, 134.

81. Seton, *Paul Robeson*, 79, and Seton, *Sergei M. Eisenstein*, 317. At Seton's suggestion, Eisenstein wrote a letter of invitation to Robeson in March 1934. See Paul Robeson Jr., *The Undiscovered Paul Robeson: The Early Years, 1898–1939* (New York: Wiley, 2001), 213–14.

82. Duberman, *Paul Robeson*, 17, 167. It might be noted that criticisms of a residual primitivism in the main character of Brutus Jones persist, making direct connections with the Haitian Revolution in *The Emperor Jones* problematic.

83. Seton, *Paul Robeson*, 86, and Yon Barna, *Eisenstein* (London: Secker & Warburg, 1973), 189–90. See also Sergei M. Eisenstein, *Immoral Memories: An Autobiography* (London: Owen, 1983), 213.

84. Seton, *Paul Robeson*, 96, and Seton, *Sergei M. Eisenstein*, 329. In Moscow, Robeson told a reporter that "the most important development in Soviet culture I have seen is in the moving picture field." See Philip S. Foner, ed., *Paul Robeson Speaks: Writings, Speeches, Interviews, 1918–1974* (London: Quartet, 1978), 102.

85. Richard Taylor, ed., *S. M. Eisenstein: Selected Works, Vol. III: Writings, 1934–1947* (London: British Film Institute, 1996), 23.

86. Ian Britain, *Fabianism and Culture: A Study in British Socialism and the Arts c. 1884–1918* (Cambridge: Cambridge University Press, 1982), 174–75, 264, 300.

87. Hamilton, "Profile: An Interview with C. L. R. James."

88. Seton, *Paul Robeson*, 76.

89. See Duberman, *Paul Robeson*, 171, and James, "Paul Robeson," 260.

90. Duberman, *Paul Robeson*, 178–80, 627. *The Times* of London noted on 3 April 1935 that *Sanders of the River* "will bring no discredit on Imperial authority," while the *Sunday Times* on 7 April 1935 added that the film provided "a grand insight into our special English difficulties in the governing of savage races." Korda, an Anglophile Hungarian, had links to the Conservative Party Film Association and was committed to making propaganda films for the British Empire. See John M. Mackenzie, *Propaganda and Empire: The Manipulation of British Public Opinion, 1880–1960* (Manchester: Manchester University Press, 1985), 80, 89, 91, and Jeffrey Richards, "Boy's Own Empire: Feature Films and Imperialism in the 1930s," in John M. MacKenzie, ed., *Imperialism and Popular Culture* (Manchester: Manchester University Press, 1986), 145.

91. This quote from Mussolini is from a speech he gave at Pontinia, 18 December 1935, quoted in *The Times* of London, 20 December 1935. See George Padmore, *Africa and World Peace* (London: F. Cass, 1972), 153.

92. Hill, "In England, 1932–38," 69.

93. Richardson et al., *C. L. R. James and British Trotskyism*, 5–6, and James, *Beyond a Boundary*, 250.

94. Bush, *Imperialism, Race and Resistance*, 240.

95. Peter Fryer, *Staying Power: The History of Black People in Britain* (London: Pluto Press, 1987), 340, 345. Amy Ashwood Garvey was the honourary treasurer, and T. A. Marryshow and Jomo Kenyatta were also leading members. For more on other IAFA members, see George Padmore, *Pan-Africanism or Communism? The Coming Struggle for Africa* (London: Dennis Dobson, 1956), 145. The IAFA disbanded after "major combat operations" had finished in Ethiopia and after others had formed the Abyssinian Association, active in April 1936.

96. *West Africa*, 27 July 1935. See also Hakim Adi, *West Africans in Britain, 1900–1960: Nationalism, Pan-Africanism and Communism* (London: Lawrence & Wishart, 1998), 67–70, and Marika Sherwood, "Ethiopia and Black Organizations in the UK 1935–36," *Black and Asian Studies Association Newsletter*, 43 (September 2005).

97. *West Africa*, 3 August 1935.

98. See C. L. R. James, "Black Intellectuals in Britain," in Bhikhu Parekh, ed., *Colour, Class and Consciousness: Immigrant Intellectuals in Britain* (London: Allen & Unwin, 1974), 158–59. As James recalled, "We wanted to form a military organisation which would go to fight with the Abyssinians against the Italians. I think I can say here with confidence that it would have been comparatively easy to organise a detachment of blacks in Britain to go to Ethiopia."

99. *Nottingham Evening Post*, 26 August 1935. In a letter to his friends in the ILP, James explained that he hoped to join the Ethiopian army to make contact with "the masses of the Abyssinians and other Africans" (*New Leader*, 3 June 1936). The letter is reprinted in James, "Black Intellectuals in Britain," 158–59.

100. As James described in *The Black Jacobins*, "Toussaint, with half his 18,000 troops in the ranks of the enemy, could only delay and harass the advance, devastate the country and deprive Leclerc of supplies, while retiring slowly to the mountains . . . he would raid Leclerc's outposts, make surprise attacks, lay ambushes, give the French no peace, while avoiding major engagements. With the coming of the rains, the French, worn out, would fall victims in thousands to the fever, and the blacks would descend and drive them into the sea" (248).

101. S. K. B. Asante, *Pan-African Protest: West Africa and the Italo-Ethiopian Crisis, 1934–1941* (London: Longman, 1977), 46.

102. James, "Paul Robeson," 257, and Duberman, *Paul Robeson*, 633. Philip Foner notes that Robeson had "hoped to appear in a play about Dessalines in London in 1935, but the plans for the play were never realized" (Foner, *Paul Robeson Speaks*, 510).

103. Duberman, *Paul Robeson*, 194–96.

104. Until a copy of the final 1936 script is found, we have only one scene from it (Act II, Scene 1, published in the journal *Life and Letters Today*, 14, no. 3 [Spring 1936]) to compare with the original. This scene is included in this book, following the complete original 1934 playscript.

105. James, "Paul Robeson," 257. Peter Godfrey with his wife, Molly Veness, had founded and run the pioneering Gate Theatre, where he had directed the first British production of *All God's Chillun Got Wings* in 1926 and his own version of *Uncle Tom's Cabin* in 1933

(Chambers, *Black and Asian Theatre in Britain*, 96). For more on Godfrey, see Norman Marshall, *The Other Theatre* (London: Lehmann, 1947), 42–52.

106. James, "Paul Robeson," 257–58.

107. C. L. R. James, "The Old World and the New [1971]," in James, *At the Rendezvous of Victory*, 207.

108. Duberman, *Paul Robeson*, 197. James even revised his play so that Robeson could sing. "One or two people thought that it would be a mistake for Paul to play and not to sing. I was not too anxious for singing to be injected into what I had written in reality for the sake of hearing a marvellous voice, but I looked at Paul and his attitude was: 'I am not particular but if you all want me to sing I will sing.'" Lawrence Brown, Robeson's pianist and assistant and who had previously acted alongside Robeson in *Stevedore*, was already a member of the cast, playing Toussaint's aide, Mars Plaisir, and so "an opening was made and he sang a song" (James, "Paul Robeson," 258). See the stage instructions of Act III, Scene 4: "Before the curtain rises Toussaint is heard singing hymns with Mars Plaisir."

109. After *Toussaint Louverture*, Adams's further stage and screen successes included the films *Song of Freedom* (1936) and *King Solomon's Mines* (1937) alongside Robeson, but the highpoint of his career was starring in the 1946 film *Men of Two Worlds*. In 1944, Adams, by then Britain's leading black actor, became the president of the Society for the Prevention of Racial Discrimination in Britain and planned to establish a black theatre company in Britain, the Negro Repertory Theatre; this sadly failed to find enough support to mount more than one production, *All God's Chillun Got Wings*, in 1944. In 1947, Adams became the first black actor to play a Shakespearean role on British television, the Prince of Morocco in *The Merchant of Venice*. See Stephen Bourne, "Adams, (Wilfred) Robert, (c. 1900–1965), Actor," in *Oxford Dictionary of National Biography* (Oxford: Oxford University Press, 2004).

110. Martins had left for London in 1917, serving intermittently in the British merchant marine until the end of the war. Aside from an early theatrical appearance in 1920 with the Diaghilev Ballet, Martins took various jobs, including working at Billingsgate fish market, wrestling (as "Black Butcher Johnson"), and snake charming for a circus. From 1926, he again found work on the stage and screen, notably appearing in the play *They Shall Not Die* (1934) and in the films *Tiger Bay* (1933), *Sanders of the River* (1935), and *Song of Freedom* (1936). His performance in the film *Men of Two Worlds* (1946) helped continue his on-screen career into the 1970s. He returned to Nigeria in 1959 and in 1983 was presented with the National Award of Theatre Arts by the Society of Nigerian Theatre Artistes. He later told his biographer, "I am very happy to say that I am one of the pioneers, if not *the* pioneer African film star." See Stephen Bourne, "Martins, Emmanuel Alhandu [Orlando] (1899–1985)," *Oxford Dictionary of National Biography*; Stephen Bourne, *Black in the British Frame: The Black Experience in British Film and Television* (London: Continuum, 2001), 76–79; and Noble, *The Negro in Films*, 127, 177–78.

111. Particularly experienced among the group of professional actors were Townsend Whitling (1875–1952), Fred O'Donovan (1889–1952), and Wilfred Walter (1882–1958), who all warranted entries in John Parker, ed., *Who's Who in the Theatre: A Biographical*

Record of the Contemporary Stage (London: Sir Isaac Pitman & Sons, 1936). Aside from Harry Andrews (1911–89), who after *Toussaint Louverture* went on to star in many television programmes and films, other rising stars in the cast were Charles Maunsell, Norman Shelley (1903–80), Kynaston Reeves (1893–1971), and Geoffrey Wincott.

112. See Sidnell, *Dances of Death*, 47, 76.

113. See K. D. Belden, *The Story of the Westminster Theatre* (London: Westminster Productions, 1965), 19–21.

114. *The Observer*, 8 March 1936. This worked out as about the going rate for a play admission in London's West End. For the price of a night out at the London theatre around this time, see the letter in the *Sunday Referee*, 22 March 1936.

115. *The Era*, 18 March 1936, and Hall, "A Conversation with C. L. R. James," 33. The *News Chronicle* on 17 March 1936 noted "an actor who had played the part of Macoya stepped forward and took the applause as author yesterday afternoon." Fennell (1887–1974) was a black American who had served in the British army during the Great War and bravely defended Cardiff's black community during the 1919 race riots. Fennell later acted in a number of plays and films, including the 1937 film *Jericho*, also starring Robeson. See Christian Høgsbjerg, "Rufus E. Fennell: A Literary Pan-Africanist in Britain," *Race and Class* 56, no. 1 (2014), and Jacqueline Jenkinson, *Black 1919: Riots, Racism and Resistance in Imperial Britain* (Liverpool: Liverpool University Press, 2009), 120–23.

116. James, "Paul Robeson," 258. Norman Marshall listed the Stage Society production of *Toussaint Louverture* as possibly the "best work" Peter Godfrey ever did—no mean tribute. See Marshall, *The Other Theatre*, 75–76.

117. See *Sunday Referee*, 22 March 1936.

118. I am indebted to Robert Hill for this last suggestion.

119. *New York Times*, 16 March 1936.

120. *The Sketch*, 25 March 1936.

121. *New Leader*, 20 March 1936.

122. James, "Paul Robeson," 259. Martin Duberman's belief that the film rights to James's *Toussaint Louverture* were bought by the *Show Boat* director James Whale is mistaken: this came about because he confused James's play with a proposed film starring Robeson based on Vandercook's novel *Black Majesty*. See Duberman, *Paul Robeson*, 196, 634; Foner, *Paul Robeson Speaks*, 105, 512; and Robeson Jr., *Undiscovered Paul Robeson*, 236.

123. *Port of Spain Gazette*, 19 April 1936. James sought to stage *Toussaint Louverture* in New York after his arrival in November 1938. See *New York Amsterdam News*, 5 November 1938, cited in Minkah Makalani, *In the Cause of Freedom: Radical Black Internationalism from Harlem to London, 1917–1939* (Chapel Hill: University of North Carolina Press, 2011), 223.

124. Scott, *Conscripts of Modernity*, 152.

125. Daryl Cumber Dance, "Conversation with C. L. R. James [1980]," in Daryl Cumber Dance, *New World Adams: Conversations with Contemporary West Indian Writers* (Leeds, U.K.: Peepal Tree, 1992), 115.

126. Reinhard W. Sander, "C. L. R. James and the Haitian Revolution," *World Literature in English*, 26, no. 2 (1986), 278. In 1953, after his forced return to Britain from McCarthyist America, James sent a manuscript of *Toussaint Louverture* to the Haitian Embassy in London to discuss the possibility of staging his play in Haiti itself. See the letter from Gerard Jean-Baptiste of the Haitian Embassy to James, dated 15 September 1953, in the University of the West Indies, St. Augustine, Trinidad and Tobago, the Alma Jordan Library, West Indiana and Special Collections, C. L. R. James collection, box 7, folder 190. I am indebted to Raj Chetty for this intriguing reference.

127. Hill, "Emergence of a National Drama in the West Indies," 21, and Colin Chambers, ed., *The Continuum Companion to Twentieth-Century Theatre* (London: Continuum, 2002), 399.

128. *The Black Jacobins* was produced by BBC Radio in 1971; for the stage by, among others, Rawle Gibbons and the Yard Theatre in Trinidad in 1979; by the Graduate Theatre Company of the Jamaica School of Drama in Kingston, Jamaica, in 1982; by Yvonne Brewster and the Talawa Theatre Company at the Riverside Studios in London in 1986; and by the Theatre Arts Faculty at the University of the West Indies, St. Augustine, in 1993. See C. L. R. James, "*The Black Jacobins*," in Grimshaw, *The C. L. R. James Reader*, 67–111, 418, 424; Selwyn R. Cudjoe, "C. L. R. James Misbound," *Transition*, 58 (1992), 127; Nicole King, "C. L. R. James, Genre and Cultural Politics," in Christopher Gair, ed., *Beyond Boundaries: C. L. R. James and Postnational Studies* (London: Pluto Press, 2006), 32; Stone, *Theatre*, 152; Rosengarten, *Urbane Revolutionary*; and Mary Lou Emery, *Modernism, the Visual, and Caribbean Literature* (Cambridge: Cambridge University Press, 2007), 259.

129. James, "*Black Jacobins*," 96.

130. Grimshaw, *C. L. R. James Reader*, 418.

131. Clark, "Haiti's Tragic Overture," 255–56. For a discussion of Glissant's *Monsieur Toussaint* (1961), Césaire's *La Tragédie du roi Christophe* (1963), and Vincent Placoly's *Dessalines* (1983), see Bridget Jones, "'We Were Going to Found a Nation . . .': Dramatic Representations of Haitian History by Three Martinican Writers," in Bridget Brereton and Kevin A. Yelvington, eds., *The Colonial Caribbean in Transition* (Kingston: University of the West Indies Press, 1999).

132. James's quote is from the programme of *The Black Jacobins*, the 1986 London production by the Talawa Theatre Company, and it suggests he was content for the audience to believe they were seeing essentially the same play that had been performed fifty years before.

C. L. R. James's *Toussaint Louverture*, published in this special edition for the first time, is reproduced from the 1934 playscript now held in the Hull History Centre (DJH/21), and before then in the archives of the Brynmor Jones Library at the University of Hull. It should be noted that I have made a small number of changes. The spelling of some words and the names of some of the characters and places have been brought in line with modern usage (as used in the 2001 Penguin edition of James's *The Black Jacobins*), so "Bouckman" becomes "Boukman," and so on. James had used "è" and "é" haphazardly and inconsistently in the original text, so again I have followed the spellings as found. I have retained James's original spelling of "Louverture," and I compiled a list of characters in order of appearance at the start of the play.

The original playscript contains several corrections made with pen over the typed manuscript. It is not known when these were made, or even by whom, but I have assumed these were made by James himself at the time and I have respected them accordingly. There is also an issue concerning the dating of the scenes in Act III. In the 1934 playscript, Act III, Scene 1, is described as being set in "early 1802"; Act III, Scene 2, is "March 24th 1802, about six o'clock in the evening"; Act III, Scene 3, "late in 1801"; Act III, Scene 4, "late in 1801" (though corrected by hand later to "late in 1802"); and Act III, Scene 5, in "May 1802." The 1936 production cut out Act III, Scene 1, completely, and the 1936 programme dated the four remaining scenes of Act III, respectively, as follows: "March 24th, 1801, about six o'clock in the evening," "late 1801," "late 1801," and then "May 1802." The fact that James could specify that a scene took place at "about six o'clock in the evening" but change the year from 1802 to 1801 suggests that his main concern was not that the dates he gave at the start of each scene precisely matched the events of the Haitian Revolution. I have resolved this rather tricky matter by again referring to the historical record as it appears in *The Black Jacobins* and by ensuring that the scenes are dated in chronological order. For Act III, the scenes are as follows: Scene 1 remains set in "early 1802"; Scene 2, "March 24th 1802, about six o'clock in the evening"; Scene 3, "late in 1802"; Scene 4, "late in 1802"; and finally Scene 5, "May 1803." This order seems to more accurately relate to the Haitian Revolution than either set of dates given in the original playscript or the 1936 programme, though readers should be aware of the change.

Finally, the manuscript of *Toussaint Louverture* published here stands as representative of the most complete original 1934 playscript we have. That said, in the interests of future scholarship it might be noted here briefly that it has become apparent to a select but growing number of scholars recently that a number of other original playscripts of *Toussaint Louverture* besides the version at the University of Hull exist. An essentially identical 1934 playscript, for reasons that may be related to a letter written by George Padmore to Alain Locke (see the appendix), for example, can be found among the Alain Locke Papers at the Moorland-Spingarn Research Center at Howard University, Washington, D.C.[1] A number of other very slightly different versions of both the playscripts *Toussaint Louverture* (1934) and *The Black Jacobins* (1967), the later play that evolved out of *Toussaint Louverture*, have also come to light. The C. L. R. James Collection, held in the West Indiana and Special Collections of the Alma Jordan Library, University of West Indies, St. Augustine, Trinidad and Tobago, has versions of both these 1934 and 1967 playscripts, alongside other relevant material regarding the writing of *The Black Jacobins* play.[2] Among the Richard Wright Papers of the Beinecke Rare Book and Manuscript Library at Yale University Library there is another version of the 1934 playscript.[3] C. L. R. James, when he was placed under house arrest in Trinidad in 1965, gave a copy of his 1934 playscript to Errol Hill, and this can be found among the Errol Hill Papers, Rauner Special Collections Library, Dartmouth College.[4]

Errol Hill would himself publish one version of the 1967 playscript of *The Black Jacobins* in his edited 1976 anthology, *A Time . . . and a Season: Eight Caribbean Plays*. This version informed Yvonne Brewster and the Talawa Theatre Company's production of *The Black Jacobins* in 1986, and there is extensive material about this production in the Records of the Talawa Theatre Company, Theatre Collections, Victoria and Albert Museum, London. In

1992, this version of the 1967 playscript was republished by Anna Grimshaw in *The C. L. R. James Reader*. However, Sibylle Fischer and Frank Rosengarten have more recently drawn attention to a slightly longer version of the 1967 playscript with an additional "epilogue" that is in the Playscript Collection, Schomberg Centre for Research in Black Culture, New York Public Library.[5] The Special Collections Library of Penn State University now also has two slightly differing versions of the 1967 playscript of *The Black Jacobins*.[6] There is also relevant material among the C. L. R. James Papers in the Rare Book and Manuscript Library, Columbia University Library.[7] Scholars, including Rachel Douglas of the University of Glasgow and Raj Chetty of St. John's University, are currently at work elucidating the exact nature of the differing revisions and rewriting of James's play on the Haitian Revolution over the course of his life, and this is not the place to preempt their work. Other versions of James's playscripts may exist unknown to this editor, and it is not impossible that perhaps one day the much shorter version of the 1934 playscript that was used in the actual 1936 production of *Toussaint Louverture* itself may also come to light.

Characters in Order of Appearance

Colonel Vincent, an officer of the French army
Monsieur Bullet, President of the Colonial Assembly of San Domingo
Jeannot, an enslaved African
Monsieur Ferrand de Baudière, a white resident of San Domingo
Antoine, an enslaved African
Boukman, a leading rebel slave
Jean-François, a leading rebel slave
Toussaint Louverture, a leading rebel slave
Jean-Jacques Dessalines, a leading rebel slave
General Macoya, an officer in the Spanish army
Henri Christophe, a leading rebel slave
Commissioner Roume, a member of the French Revolutionary
    Government
Madame Louverture, the wife of Toussaint
Mars Plaisir, a civilian aide of Toussaint
General Maitland, an officer of the British army
General Pétion, a leading mulatto

Commander Hédouville, an officer of the French army
Tobias Lear, the American Consul
General Leclerc, an officer of the French army and Bonaparte's brother-in-law
Pauline Leclerc, the wife of General Leclerc
Napoleon Bonaparte, the First Consul of France
Isaac, a son of Toussaint
Placide, a son of Toussaint
Father Coignon, a French priest
Captain Verny, a military aide to Toussaint
Suzanne, a mulatto
General Lemmonier-Delafosse, an officer in the French army
Governor Baille, the Commandant of the Fort-de-Joux prison
General Caffarelli, an officer in the French army

French officers
Soldiers
Enslaved Africans
Members of and delegates to the French Convention

Notes

1. See Fionnghuala Sweeney, "The Haitian Play: C. L. R. James' *Toussaint Louverture* (1936)," *International Journal of Francophone Studies*, 14, no. 1–2 (2011), 143–63. The playscript can be found in the Alain Locke Papers in box 164–86, "Writings by Others," folder 8.

2. Relevant sections of the collection are box 7, folder 190; box 9, folders 228 and 230; box 10, folders 240 and 241; and box 12, folder 280.

3. In the Richard Wright Papers, see JWJ MSS3 89 1102a. For some discussion of the 1934 playscripts at St. Augustine and Yale, see Mary Lou Emery, *Modernism, the Visual, and Caribbean Literature* (Cambridge: Cambridge University Press, 2007), 259–60.

4. In the Errol Hill Papers, see ML77, box 70.

5. The relevant manuscript information for the New York Public Library is SC MG 53. Also see Sibylle Fischer, *Modernity Disavowed: Haiti and the Cultures of Slavery in the Age of Revolution* (Durham: Duke University Press, 2005), 349, and Frank Rosengarten, *Urbane Revolutionary: C. L. R. James and the Struggle for a New Society* (Jackson: University Press of Mississippi, 2008), 220–24.

6. In the Penn State collection, see VF Lit 0581R.

7. See box 5, folders 14–19.

In 1789, the West Indian Island of San Domingo, a few miles from Jamaica, was owned partly by the Spaniards and partly by the French. French San Domingo was the richest colony in the world, with a population of thirty thousand whites, thirty thousand mulattoes, and half a million Negro slaves.

The native Carib population, nearly a million in number, had dropped to less than fifty thousand after twenty years of European occupation.

The French Revolution was the starting point of a cruel struggle between whites and mulattoes. The mulattoes could own land and slaves, but were denied political rights and social equality. It was only after seeing their masters torture and murder each other for two years that the slaves began their own revolution. The play is the story of that revolution, and is substantially true to history. The independence so hardly won has been maintained. The former French colony of San Domingo, today Haiti, is a member of the League of Nations, and Colonel Nemours, its representative, a man of colour, presided over the eighth assembly of the League. The closest and most cordial relationship exists today between white France and coloured San Domingo. The French take a deep interest in a people whose language, cultural traditions and aspirations are entirely French. The Haitians look on France as their spiritual home and many of them fought in the French army during the war of 1914–18. The play was conceived four years ago and was completely finished by the autumn of 1934.

TOUSSAINT LOUVERTURE

| | | | |

The Story of the Only Successful

Slave Revolt in History

A PLAY IN THREE ACTS

TOUSSAINT LOUVERTURE

THE STORY OF THE ONLY SUCCESSFUL SLAVE REVOLT IN HISTORY.

A Play in 3 Acts.

(Act 1. Scene 1. A moonlight evening.
The verandah of M. Bullet's villa on
the outskirts of Cap Francois, the
largest town in the West Indian island
of San Domingo.   In the villa the
Minuet to Don Giovanni is being played
and there are glimpses of women and
men dancing in the brightly lighted
drawing-room. All through the scene
there is a faint but insistent beating
of drums. In moments of tenseness the
drums beat louder and with accelerated
rhythm, though they remain always in
the distance.   M. Bullet and Colonel
Vincent are sitting at a small table.

VINCENT

San Domingo - the very name is beautiful. On the boat I was always regretting
Paris, and now after forty-eight hours
here I have forgotten Paris completely -
almost.

(He walks to the end of the verandah
and looks out into the night.)

BULLET

Colonel Vincent, ~~it is the most marvellous colony in the world, and it is a
pity that the King's Government never
fully appreciated what we in the West
Indies have been doing for France.~~
We produce more sugar here than in all
the British West Indian Islands put
together.   In fact, no part of the
civilised world produces as much wealth
in proportion to its size as the French
~~portion~~ *past* of the island of San Domingo.

Jamaica
Barbadoes

VINCENT

They tell me that the soil is as
fertile as the scenery is beautiful.

"Toussaint Louverture." Hull History Centre (DJH/21), p. 1.

Act I SCENE 1

A moonlight evening. The verandah of M. Bullet's villa on the outskirts of Cap François, the largest town in the West Indian island of San Domingo. In the villa the minuet to Don Giovanni *is being played and there are glimpses of women and men dancing in the brightly lighted drawing-room. All through the scene there is a faint but insistent beating of drums. In moments of tenseness the drums beat louder and with accelerated rhythm, though they remain always in the distance. M. Bullet and Colonel Vincent are sitting at a small table.*

VINCENT   San Domingo — the very name is beautiful. On the boat I was always regretting Paris, and now after forty-eight hours here I have forgotten Paris completely — almost.

(He walks to the end of the verandah and looks out into the night.)

BULLET   Colonel Vincent, we produce more sugar here than in Jamaica, Barbados, and all the British West Indian Islands put together. In fact, no part of the civilised world produces as much wealth in proportion to its size as the French part of the island of San Domingo.

VINCENT   They tell me that the soil is as fertile as the scenery is beautiful.

BULLET   There is more to it than that. The Spaniards own twice as much of the island as we do. Yet Spanish San Domingo is all decay and corruption.

VINCENT   The Revolutionary Government in France which has sent me here, M. Bullet, is fully aware of the importance of San Domingo to the trade and prosperity of the mother-country. The new government in Paris is anxious to redress your grievances.

BULLET   Most of our people have supported the Revolution and still do so. But why do you allow these abolitionists to abuse freedom by preaching against slavery and advocating equal rights for all men whatever their colour?

VINCENT   M. Bullet, if the Revolution stands for anything it stands for freedom of speech.

BULLET   *(Losing his temper)* Colonel Vincent, we have half a million slaves in this colony, and we could not exist without them. God made the Negro black to distinguish him from the rest of us and strong to work for the white man in tropical climates. Thirty thousand of us whites keep them in subjection. What further proof do you want of their inferiority? If slavery were interfered with we would declare ourselves independent.

VINCENT   The Revolutionary Government does not intend to abolish slavery, despite the extremists. But the Government is sympathetic to the claims of the mulattoes to have equal rights.

BULLET   Never! *(Enter Jeannot, a slave.)* What do you want?

JEANNOT   There is a M. Ferrand de Baudière to see you, master. He has travelled far.

BULLET   Let him come in. No, stay, Colonel Vincent.

(Enter M. Ferrand de Baudière, old, white-bearded. He comes up the steps onto the verandah. His black servant stays below.)

BAUDIÈRE   You are M. Bullet, the President of the Colonial Assembly of San Domingo?

BULLET   I am. You are welcome, M. Baudière. You come from the South Province? I have heard of you. You will have a glass of wine? *(Baudière refuses.)* What can I do for you?

BAUDIÈRE   I must apologise for coming so late. But I was delayed on the way. I bring a petition signed by citizens of the South Province, and I hope to get your goodwill before I present it to the Assembly tomorrow.

BULLET   What does it deal with?

BAUDIÈRE   The claims of a large number of citizens in our island, some rich, God-fearing, all obedient to the law, and yet deprived of their just rights.

BULLET State their grievances. In these days of liberty, equality, and fraternity no section of the community will seek its rights in vain.

BAUDIÈRE I refer to the mulattoes of this colony —

BULLET What!

BAUDIÈRE Yes, the mulattoes. The Revolutionary Government in France has decreed —

BULLET (*Beside himself with rage*) Jeannot! Antoine! Louis! (*Slaves appear.*) Seize him!

(*Other slaves rush in. The music stops suddenly and the dancers appear on the verandah. The slaves seize de Baudière.*)

A WOMAN What is it?

BULLET He demands equal rights for mulattoes. (*There is a chorus of horror and execration.*) You, a white man, so far forget your colour as to ask equality for mulattoes, men whose mothers were slaves–

BAUDIÈRE And whose fathers were white men. (*Murmurs among the listeners.*) I know them well, and you know them too. They are men of industry, thrift, education, and character. The great Revolution in France has decreed liberty, equality, and fraternity for all men. That does not refer to slaves, but mulattoes are free men. My petition here states their grievances and the legitimate remedies. I had hoped to have some sympathy from you. I had heard that you were liberal in your ideas, and devoted to the principles of the Revolution. I see that I am wrong. Tell your slaves to free me. I am no criminal. Tomorrow at the bar of the Assembly I shall seek justice for my fellow-citizens.

BULLET You expect that I shall allow you, a white man, to raise this question in open Council and further disturb the unsettled state of the country? Give me that petition.

(*The slaves take it from de Baudière, and Bullet glances at the first few lines.*)

BULLET	*(Reading)* In the name of the Father, the Son, and the Holy Ghost–
BAUDIÈRE	Yes. The rights I demand are not only conferred by the Revolutionary Government in France, but are founded on the eternal principles of justice laid down by our Lord and Master.
BULLET	This is no way to begin a petition. This is blasphemy. You women, go inside. *(They hesitate.)* Inside at once, I say! *(They go in.)* Ferrand de Baudière, you come to the President of the Colonial Assembly, and the President of the Colonial Assembly will deal with you. On my own responsibility I condemn you immediately to death by hanging for propounding ideas dangerous to religion, to the State, and the very existence of society. Jeannot, pull his coat and cravat off. *(The slaves obey.)* And string him up on that branch. At once.
VINCENT	M. Bullet, I protest.
BULLET	Colonel Vincent, I am responsible only to the Assembly. *(To the slaves.)* Go on.

(Baudière is dragged off stage. Bullet and Vincent stand watching. Baudière's slave starts forward, but one of the slaves pulls him back and signals for him to run. He hesitates for a moment and then escapes the opposite way.)

BULLET	Cut him down. Take his body to the stables. Strike off the head and parade it through the city tomorrow on a pike. *(Turns around.)* Where is his servant? Where is his servant, I say?
A SLAVE	He has gone, master.
BULLET	You let him escape? Find him. Until he is found, every day, starting tomorrow, one of you will dig his own grave. Do you hear?
SLAVES	Yes, master.
BULLET	Now go. And remember—with honey and molasses, and no stone-throwing allowed.

(Exit slaves.)

VINCENT	M. Bullet, I — I —

BULLET   Come, come, Colonel Vincent. *(The music begins again.)* There you are. The ladies are not disturbed. They are fascinated by the music of a new composer. One Mozart—a German. We intend to hear his operas in Paris this winter. Sit down. *(He pulls Vincent into a chair and pours out two glasses of wine.)* If for one moment we allowed these slaves to think that a man with slave-blood in his veins can aspire to equal rights with a white man, then the barriers are down and the hordes of blacks will overwhelm us. Against any attempts to break that barrier we act immediately. The Assembly will unanimously endorse my action tomorrow. It is the one subject on which you will find the planters united, except for such cranks as this de Baudière.

VINCENT   But these very scenes of violence, these conflicts over liberty and equality, with slaves looking on and taking part. Surely it puts ideas into their heads, and one day perhaps they will strike for liberty.

BULLET   Blacks strike for liberty! Such abstract notions do not enter into their heads. Some of you people in Europe think a Negro is a human being with a black skin. He is a sub-human type. In fact, scientists have proved that their sloping forehead prevents the full development of the brain. Be firm with them. That is all. Tomorrow morning I select a slave and set him to dig his own grave. If that runaway is not found in the afternoon, at six o'clock I assemble my thousand slaves in the field. There, before everyone, he buries himself up to the neck. This is a case where honey and molasses will be smeared on his face.

VINCENT   Why?

BULLET   So that the ants and flies will be at him almost immediately. Sometimes we allow the slaves to throw stones at him so as to put him quickly out of his misery. I'll not allow that tomorrow. And every slave looking on will know that perhaps it will be his turn the next day, or the next, or the day after that, as need be. I wager you that the runaway will be found before very long, Colonel Vincent. We have two hundred years of experience behind us. We know how to deal with them.

VINCENT	*(Walking again to the same spot on the verandah where he had stood at the beginning of the scene)* I have seen active service in many parts of the world, M. Bullet, but—
BULLET	It's a bit of a shock for strangers. It was for me when I came back from Paris as a young man. But it is the only way. Listen. *(Sound of drums.)* They are quite happy; dancing in the forest somewhere with their drums and making their heathen sacrifices. Let us leave them where they are. Two-thirds of the external trade of France comes from San Domingo. This island gives employment to a million Frenchmen. White San Domingo is with revolutionary France as long as it doesn't try to remove black men from the place intended for them by God. St. Paul said "Slaves, obey your masters." To our great Revolution, Colonel Vincent. Liberty, Equality, Fraternity.

(They drink.)

Curtain.

SCENE 2

August 6th, 1791. The depths of a forest. A little clearing is dotted with groups of Negro slaves. They, the Negro slaves, are the most important characters in the play. Toussaint did not make the revolt. It was the revolt that made Toussaint. The Negroes crowd close together, some carrying torches. Most of them are nearly naked, wearing either a loin-cloth or a shirt. All are dirty and unkempt. On a rough platform stand two of their leaders — Boukman (a gigantic Negro) and Jean-François — and on the step below them, Toussaint. As the curtain rises Boukman is addressing the crowd. All through the scene there is the steady beat of drums.

BOUKMAN	Liberty — Equality — Fraternity. The white slaves in France — they suffered like us — they've made a revolution. They killed the slave-owners — made every-body free. They divided the property, and now in France they have liberty, equality, and fraternity. *(There is cheering.)*

(Boukman turns to talk to the others. The crowd begins to talk excitedly. With considerable difficulty Boukman quiets them. Then he signals to Toussaint.)

| TOUSSAINT | Brothers, we suffer. I know how we suffer. All is ready and we are not afraid to fight. But before we kill let us make a petition and go one day to the Colonial Assembly. We'll tell them— |

(Out of the crowd leaps an almost naked figure. He clambers up to the platform and pushes his way to the front. The crowd hitherto quiet, is at once astir. The Negro is Dessalines, soon to be known as The Tiger, and afterwards first Emperor of Haiti.)

| DESSALINES | No petition—we have to fight! *(Stir in the crowd.)* Not tomorrow but today—now! *(Crowd responds.)* No more work, *(response from crowd)*, no more whip. *(There is almost a cheer.)* Black man eat bananas. Black man eat potatoes. White man eat bread. If white man want bread let white man work. *(There is a great laugh.)* If we kill the whites we are free. *(The drums are beating faster, as if quickened by Dessalines' speech.)* I, Dessalines, will work no more. Liberty! |

(With deep passion the crowd takes up the word: Liberty! Liberty! Boukman raises his hand. In the silence sounds clearly the quickened rhythm of the drum, and suddenly Jeannot forces his way through the crowd and onto the platform.)

JEANNOT	Today a white man, old man, with a white beard, came with petition to the master. He asked for rights.
TOUSSAINT	For who—for slaves?
JEANNOT	For slaves? No. For mulattoes.
TOUSSAINT	And what happened?
JEANNOT	Master hanged him—on a tree in the garden. His slave ran. Master say "Find him or tomorrow someone dig his own grave" *(the crowd groans)* "with honey and molasses" *(the crowd groans again)* "and without stone-throwing." *(There is an outburst of anger.)*
DESSALINES	A white man—see what they do, to their own people. We must fight.
BOUKMAN	Their hour has come.

(Dessalines leaps down from the platform and takes his place in front of the slaves. Toussaint walks down two steps and stands midway between the mass and the

leaders. Boukman extends his arm and a hush falls on the whole assembly. The drums cease.)

> The god who created the sun which gives us light, who rouses the waves and rules the storm, though hidden in the clouds, he watches us. He sees all that the white man does. The god of the white man inspires him with pride, but our god who is good to us orders us to revenge our wrongs. He will direct our arms and aid us. Throw away the symbol of the god of the whites who have so often caused us to weep, and listen to the voice of liberty, which speaks to us through our hearts.

(At the words: Throw away: he rips off a cross which hangs on a chain round his neck, and many Negroes do the same.)

(A Negro emerges from the darkness behind the platform. He carries a vessel which he hands to Boukman. Boukman receives it carefully and raises it high. The Negroes drop to their knees.)

(There is a great rattle of the drums. Again Boukman raises his hand. Again they crouch looking up at him in silence. Boukman hands the vessel round to those on the platform to drink. Jeannot drinks deeply, dipping both hands in. As he raises his face it is covered with blood which splashes down his dirty white shirt, the only garment he wears. Boukman turns to Toussaint and offers him the vessel. Toussaint hesitates.)

BOUKMAN   Drink, Toussaint.

(Toussaint remains motionless.)

JEAN-FRANÇOIS AND OTHERS ON THE PLATFORM
         Drink, Toussaint.

(Toussaint still hesitates. The kneeling Negroes call to him to drink. He takes the vessel into his hands and drinks.)

DESSALINES   *(Suddenly jumping to his feet)* Liberty! Liberty or death!

(The slaves take up the cry. The drums beat louder as the crowd goes off, and then begin to grow fainter. The slaves melt away in different directions. Liberty or death! is the password with which they bid each other farewell. Toussaint remains on the steps alone, his head bent. All go off except Dessalines and Toussaint.)

         (Taking him by the arm and leading him off) Come, Toussaint.

(The drums continue to beat fainter and fainter.)

Curtain.

SCENE 3

The slaves' encampment at La Grande Rivière. April 1793.

Under a tree are a magnificent Louis XIV table and chairs. At the table sit the leaders of the rebellion, Jean-François, Boukman and Jeannot, with silver flagons and drinking cups before them. They are fantastically dressed in silk and satin garments taken in the course of plunder. Epaulettes and multi-coloured bandoliers give a military touch. Their fingers are loaded with precious gems, but they wear no shoes. With them is another Negro, Macoya, who is perfectly attired down to the last button in the uniform of a Spanish general. At a distance sits Dessalines cleaning the blades of two or three rusty swords. He is, as before, half-naked except for a red sash in which are stuck two large gold-mounted pistols.

BOUKMAN	General Macoya, your news from the Spanish Governor is good. Jeannot, let's send for Toussaint.
MACOYA	Everyone talks of Toussaint. Who is Toussaint?
BOUKMAN	Physician to the forces, but now my secretary and aide-de-camp.
JEAN-FRANÇOIS	I do not trust that Toussaint.
JEANNOT	Neither me. He never wants to kill prisoners.
BOUKMAN	But he can write and read like a priest. He can put all this down on paper and then a week after read it out again just as how he put it down.
JEAN-FRANÇOIS	He is intelligent enough.
BOUKMAN	Let's have Toussaint. *(He shouts to Dessalines.)* Colonel Dessalines, I want Toussaint, my secretary and aide-de-camp.

(Dessalines comes up.)

DESSALINES	Very well, Viceroy.

(He blows one blast on a whistle and twenty men come marching in, four abreast. They are picked men, but in their arms are old muskets, cutlasses, spears, etc. They are as unkempt as they were on the night when the rebellion was decided upon, but they carry themselves with a new confidence. Dessalines blows three times and they halt. He blows twice, but as they attempt the about-turn there is a hitch in the manoeuvres. Three savage blasts on the whistle bring them to a stop.)

Captain Antoine!

(One of the men in the ranks comes up and salutes.)

DESSALINES You son of a slave, fit only to be a slave! One blast—march; two blasts—about-turn; three blasts—halt. Blast you! You can't learn—how you'll teach? I'll reduce you to the ranks. *(Dessalines raises his hand as if to strike him, but Antoine stands firm.)* Go and call Toussaint Breda. Quick.

(Antoine steps backwards and hurries off. Dessalines roars at him.) Salute, you swine, salute!

(Antoine salutes smartly and goes off.)

JEAN-FRANÇOIS What is this whistling business?

DESSALINES Toussaint says "Whistle. Don't shout." These fools can hear the whistle better during a fight.

JEAN-FRANÇOIS You've only twenty men.

DESSALINES Yes, but Toussaint says teach those and they'll teach the rest.

(Boukman picks up the whistle.)

BOUKMAN *(To the soldiers)* Come on—march.

(The soldiers march. Boukman blows uncertainly, but the soldiers continue to march. Dessalines pulls the whistle from him and blows twice. The soldiers turn about and march back. Dessalines blows three times and the soldiers come to a halt; he blows once and they march away. Macoya, Jean-François, etc., all applaud, and Dessalines, greatly pleased, salutes. As the soldiers march away Toussaint Breda enters and stands watching them go.)

Ah, here he is.

(Toussaint approaches the table and bows respectfully.)

TOUSSAINT   You sent for me, Viceroy?

BOUKMAN   Yes. General Macoya has come from Spanish San Domingo. He brings news and offers of help. Listen to him and then write it down.

MACOYA   (*Standing and drawing himself up to his full height*) I am the subject of three kings, the King of Congo, who is father of all the blacks, the King of France, who is my father, and the King of Spain, who is my mother.

BOUKMAN   Good.

MACOYA   And these three kings are the lineal descendants of the three wise men of the East who, guided by a star, came to adore the God-man at Bethlehem.

BOUKMAN   Very good.

(*Macoya pauses, and then continues with great emphasis.*)

MACOYA   If I array myself on the side of the revolutionaries and the colonies I may perhaps be obliged to fight against the friends of those three kings to whom I have sworn faith and allegiance.

(*Macoya sits down.*)

TOUSSAINT   You have brought terms of alliance from the Governor of Spanish San Domingo?

MACOYA   Yes.

TOUSSAINT   And these terms are — ?

MACOYA   The Governor of Spanish San Domingo says that those who are making revolution in France and these white colonists here who are sympathetic to them are enemies of God, enemies of the King of France, who loves his black children. The Governor of Spanish San Domingo says that it is because the King of France loves the blacks that the revolutionaries in France are fighting against him. In Europe the King of Spain is going to fight against the revolutionaries, and the Governor of Spanish San Domingo says that if you keep up the fight against these colonists here, who are wicked revolutionaries like those in Europe, he will give you arms and ammunition and large presents.

JEAN-FRANÇOIS That's what you say, but the Spanish Governor will deceive — the whites always deceive the blacks.

MACOYA *(Rising)* No. The King of Spain has made me, Macoya, a general of Spain. And if you promise to keep up the fight he will make all the leaders generals in the Spanish army like me, General Macoya.

(Macoya sits down.)

BOUKMAN Write it all down, Toussaint.

TOUSSAINT I shall, your Highness. . . . And what shall I write as the answer of the Brigadier-General and the Lord High Admiral?

JEAN-FRANÇOIS Wait until we tell you.

TOUSSAINT Pardon me, Admiral. I only wanted to make the record complete.

BOUKMAN What would you do, Toussaint?

TOUSSAINT Lord High Admiral, Viceroy, Brigadier, I would hear what the French Commissioner has to say. He may be here at any moment.

MACOYA What Commissioner is this?

TOUSSAINT One of the Commissioners whom the French Revolutionary Government have sent to govern the colony. His name is Roume. He has asked us to meet him in conference.

MACOYA You say he comes from the revolutionaries?

TOUSSAINT Yes.

MACOYA Then he is the enemy of my father, the King of France, and one of those who has put him in prison. *(Rising, and again with emphasis)* If I array myself on the side of the French revolutionaries I may perhaps be obliged to fight against the friends of those three kings to whom I have sworn faith and allegiance.

JEANNOT	Let's seize the Commissioner. We can hold him to ransom.
TOUSSAINT	No, we cannot do that. We have given them safe conduct.
DESSALINES	When a white man makes a promise to a Negro it's only to fool him. We must kill them or they'll kill us.
TOUSSAINT	You can't arrest the Commissioner. It would destroy all hope of peace.
DESSALINES	Peace! What peace? Peace when we go back as slaves. That is their peace. Jean-Francois, Admiral, give me the command.
JEAN-FRANÇOIS	No. They've got my wife a prisoner in Cap François, and if we seize the Commissioner they'll torture her.
BOUKMAN	No. We must accept the offer of the King of Spain. Let's capture the Commissioner and kill him. Jeannot, you'll get some more white blood to drink.

(Jeannot grins and rubs his hands.)

JEAN-FRANÇOIS	And what about my wife?
BOUKMAN	*(Pouring out a drink)* Oh, get another wife.
TOUSSAINT	Hear the Commissioner first, your Highness.
BOUKMAN	You are wrong this time, Toussaint. The Commissioner is coming here only to deceive us. The King of Spain has made Macoya a general and promises to make us all generals.
TOUSSAINT	You are greater than a general, Viceroy. Your Highness is Viceroy of the Conquered Territories. We need not decide now. Let us hear what the Commissioner has to say. He will not have come so far unless he has terms to offer. We can do what we like after.
BOUKMAN	No. We must help our Mother, the King of Spain, to fight for our Father, the King of France. Then we'll send for the King of Congo to come, and we'll all be happy and free.

(Suddenly there is the beating of a distant drum. All start. The rhythm is repeated.)

MACOYA	What's that?

TOUSSAINT   It is the Commissioner. I have had scouts on the lookout for him. No, Colonel Dessalines, you stay. I have arranged for Colonel Christophe to escort them here.

(Indecision is on every face. A soldier dashes in with a letter. He speaks to Dessalines.)

SOLDIER   This is for the Lord High Admiral.

DESSALINES   Salute, you swine, salute!

(Toussaint takes the letter and gives it to Jean-François. Jean-François handles it gingerly and shows it to Macoya. Macoya looks at it and passes it onto Boukman, who looks at it in turn and gives it back to Toussaint.)

BOUKMAN   Read it, Secretary.

TOUSSAINT   It is from Commissioner Roume. He will be here in a few minutes, and he is bringing one of the planters to represent the Colonial Assembly, a M. Bullet.

JEANNOT   Oh God! My old master!

TOUSSAINT   Your Highness, we must decide now. What shall we do?

(They are all silent.)

BOUKMAN   Say something, Jeannot.

JEANNOT   My master is a terror.

BOUKMAN   What do you think, Toussaint?

TOUSSAINT   Gentlemen, I have made a few notes here.

(He takes two books out of his pocket.)

MACOYA   What is that? The Holy Book?

TOUSSAINT   No, this is *Caesar's Commentaries*.

MACOYA   Humph. And the other one?

BOUKMAN   This is no time to talk about books. What is it, Toussaint?

TOUSSAINT   First — Free pardon for all who took part in the rebellion.

(He looks at them.)

	Second — All civil and political rights for the free mulattoes and the free blacks.
JEANNOT	But what about us?
TOUSSAINT	Third — the leaders of the rebellion and others to be mentioned by name to be free.
DESSALINES	No. Freedom for all. All fought for freedom, all must be free.
TOUSSAINT	*(Going up to Dessalines)* Dessalines, it is useless to ask for the freedom of all. The planters will never consent to it.
DESSALINES	Who wants them to consent? We shall drive them into the sea.
TOUSSAINT	Dessalines, as the slaves are —
DESSALINES	There are no more slaves. We are all free men. We shall remain free or die. Liberty or death, that's what we said.
TOUSSAINT	All of them are not fit to be freed suddenly. The whole country will be ruined. *(Drums again.)* We must decide quickly, gentlemen.
JEANNOT	If I am to be free, I agree.
BOUKMAN	And I too.
JEAN-FRANÇOIS	We shall hear what they have to say.

(Drums. Enter soldier.)

SOLDIER	*(Saluting)* The Commissioner is here, gentlemen.
JEAN-FRANÇOIS	Let him come in.

(Soldiers march in and march past, Colonel Christophe commanding, whistle in mouth. Then follow Commissioner Roume and M. Bullet. All except Macoya and Toussaint are still afraid of the white skin.)

ROUME	I am Commissioner Roume sent by the French Government to bring peace to San Domingo. With me is M. Bullet, representing the Colonial Assembly.

(Silence. Toussaint steps forward.)

TOUSSAINT	I wrote to you, sir. My name is Toussaint Breda. I am secre-

tary and aide-de-camp to Brigadier-General Boukman. This, sir, is our leader, Jean-François, Lord High Admiral of France and Chevalier de St. Louis. This is Brigadier-General Boukman, Viceroy of the Conquered Territories. This is Brigadier-General Jeannot.

BULLET So there you are, you scoundrel!

ROUME (*Hastily intervening*) Greetings to you from the Republic, Lord High Admiral. And to you, Viceroy, and to you, Brigadier. And this gentleman?

MACOYA (*Rising*) My name is General Macoya. I am the subject of three kings. The King of Congo, who is the father of the blacks; the King of France, who is my father; and the King of Spain, who is my mother. And these three kings are the lineal descendants of those three wise men of the East who came to adore the God-Man at Bethlehem. If I array myself—

TOUSSAINT This officer, Mr. Commissioner, is General Macoya. As you can see he is a general, a real general, of the Spanish Army. (*With emphasis*) He, Mr. Commissioner, is an envoy to the slaves from the Governor of Spanish San Domingo.

ROUME An envoy to the slaves from the Governor of Spanish San Domingo. I see. (*He bows slowly to Macoya.*) Gentlemen, I have come from France sent by the Revolutionary Government, which views with deep regret the unhappy differences which have arisen between the white and the black. The French Government loves equally its children, white and black, who are all equal in the sight of God. (*Dessalines speaks abruptly.*) And the Government of France wishes to have peace.

JEAN-FRANÇOIS What will the Government of France do about slavery?

ROUME The Government of France would like to hear what the Lord High Admiral and Chevalier, leader of his people, wishes for them.

BOUKMAN Read it from the paper, Toussaint.

TOUSSAINT I have terms drawn up here, Mr. Commissioner. First—A free pardon for all. Next—Political rights for all free men, white, mulatto, and black. And thirdly, freedom for those of us who are best fitted to benefit by it.

JEANNOT   Me.

BOUKMAN   And me.

TOUSSAINT   The leaders of the rebellion and a few others. It is not much that we ask.

ROUME   (*Obviously astonished at the moderation of the request, and looking at Bullet*) No, it is not much.

BULLET   The Colonial Assembly will make no terms with rebels. Get back to the plantations first.

TOUSSAINT   Sir, only a hundred to be free and to have political rights. If the planters will promise to treat the slaves more kindly they will go back to work and San Domingo will be at peace and prosperous again.

BULLET   Never. Unconditional surrender.

DESSALINES   I knew that.

TOUSSAINT   Sir, freedom for only fifty. And political rights like the other free blacks.

BULLET   Political rights for free blacks! That is the madness they talk in France, not in San Domingo.

TOUSSAINT   The French Government has passed a law which says that all persons who have lived in the colony for two years and paid taxes shall be entitled to meet for the purpose of electing and forming an Assembly.

BULLET   Persons of colour are not persons. Come back like the dogs that you are and beg our pardon.

JEAN-FRANÇOIS   We are not dogs. We are black but we are men.

BULLET   You are the property of the planters, bought and paid for and keep that always in your black skulls. The Assembly might pardon you if you repent and get back to work. Look at you, you have no arms, no ammunition, dressed up in stolen finery like the monkeys that you are. This is the last chance we are giving you.

DESSALINES   I told you so, Toussaint.

JEAN-FRANÇOIS   Silence, Dessalines. Sir, we have received offers of help from the Spaniards who will give us all the support we want.

BOUKMAN   And will make us generals in the Spanish Army.

TOUSSAINT   You know, sir, that the Spaniards hate the French Revolutionary Government and will support us. Here they have sent to us General Macoya—

MACOYA   (*Rising*) I am the subject of three kings, the King of the Congo, who is father of all the blacks—

BULLET   Then go to the King of Congo with your drunken rigmarole, you blabbering mounte-bank. General, indeed. The Spaniards are using you against the Revolution. As soon as you have served their purpose they'll drag that uniform off you and drive you back to the fields where you belong. You, do you know that to accept Spanish help against the Government of your country is treason?

JEAN-FRANÇOIS   But the Colonial Assembly offered the Colony to the English.

BULLET   That's a lie! How dare you?

(*Bullet strikes Jean-François across the face with his whip and Jean-François falls to the ground. Jeannot screams; Dessalines springs forward, sword in hand and blowing his whistle. Toussaint jumps in front of Dessalines. Roume helps Jean-François to his feet and supports him. Jean-François drops to his knees and kisses Roume's hand.*)

ROUME   Lord High Admiral, I shall place your requests before the other Commissioners and the Assembly, and the Government of France will decide.

MACOYA   I am the subject of three kings, and the Spanish Government will never help those who join the enemies of a king.

BULLET   The king! The king! You ignorant idiots, there is no King of France. They cut his head off two months ago.

(The slave leaders draw back from the Commissioner and Bullet in horror.)

JEANNOT   Has the French government cut off the head of the king, Mr. Commissioner?

ROUME   Yes.

MACOYA   Then I have lost my mother.

JEAN-FRANÇOIS   Then we can make no terms with you. From the beginning of the world the blacks have executed only the will of a king. We have lost the King of France. Peace be with his soul. But we are esteemed by the King of Spain who will give us succour.

ROUME   Do not decide at once.

JEAN-FRANÇOIS   We cannot deal with you until you've found a king.

BOUKMAN   We are for the king and the old order.

ROUME   But it is the king and the old order that will enslave you again. It is the Revolutionaries who will set you free. What freedom you will get you will get from the Revolution.

BOUKMAN / JEANNOT
            No.

JEAN-FRANÇOIS   No. The king loves his people. The king is for us.

BULLET   These monstrous fools! Why do you waste your time arguing with them?

ROUME   You, sir, Toussaint Breda, surely you must know that the king and the old order are against you, and that Robespierre, and Danton and Marat and all the French revolutionaries are on your side. Tell them.

(All hang on Toussaint's words.)

TOUSSAINT   We cannot join those who have killed a king.

BOUKMAN   That settles it. What do you say, Macoya?

MACOYA   I am the subject of three kings—

BULLET   Gr-r-r. I shall not stay here a moment longer, Mr. Commissioner. If you do not come I shall go without you.

ROUME	Gentlemen, I shall write to you. *(To Toussaint)* Are we safe?
TOUSSAINT	Go the way you came. Colonel Christophe, attend these gentlemen.
BULLET	And the next time we meet it shall be to deal with you as you deserve.
DESSALINES	When you catch us, Mr. Planter.

(Exit Bullet and Roume, escorted by Christophe.)

TOUSSAINT	Lord High Admiral and Viceroy, you were right to decide as you did. There is nothing to be gained from the planters. It will have to be war.
BOUKMAN	I said so at the start. Do you really think the King of Spain will make me a general and give me a uniform like that?
MACOYA	He will. I have two others besides this.
TOUSSAINT	Admiral-Viceroy.
BOUKMAN/JEAN-FRANÇOIS	Yes?
TOUSSAINT	May I form a company of my own?
BOUKMAN	Yes, if you wish. But you must still write.
JEAN-FRANÇOIS	Why do you want to form a company?
TOUSSAINT	It is war now. The time for letter-writing is over. I could give more help to the cause as a soldier.
JEAN-FRANÇOIS	I suppose you could.
BOUKMAN	I am going to be a general, Toussaint. So you can be a Brigadier.
TOUSSAINT	Thank you, General.

(Exit all except Toussaint. He stands silent, deep in thought. Then he sits down, takes a book out of his pocket, searches for a particular page, and is about to read when Boukman enters.)

BOUKMAN	Reading as usual.
TOUSSAINT	Yes, Viceroy.

BOUKMAN   What is that one?

TOUSSAINT   It tells about slavery.

BOUKMAN   Pst! Why read about that? There is no more slavery. *(He looks around.)* See, Toussaint, form your company quickly and drill them well—with the whistle. *(Looks around again.)* I'll need your help. That Jean-François calls himself admiral and he has never put his foot on a boat. We will be able to overthrow him, both of us, and you shall command in his place. I shall make you the admiral.

TOUSSAINT   Thank you, Viceroy. I shall remember it.

(Exit Boukman. Toussaint now sits disconsolate with his book open but unread. Enter Jean-François from the other side.)

JEAN-FRANÇOIS   Toussaint, will that grey be ready for tomorrow? I am going to Mass with General Macoya in the carriage, and I want the six grey horses.

TOUSSAINT   I shall work on her tonight, Admiral.

JEAN-FRANÇOIS   And Toussaint, when you form your company, you will be under the command of Boukman.

TOUSSAINT   Yes, Admiral.

JEAN-FRANÇOIS   He's a drunken scoundrel, and thinks only of women and his belly. Form your own company and then together we can surprise him. I'll make you Viceroy in his place.

TOUSSAINT   Thank you, Admiral. I shall remember it.

(Exit Jean-François.)

(His head in his hands) Oh God! These are the men on whom the fate of the black race depends. What future is there for us!

(He opens his book again. He reads, scarcely looking at the page, so often has he read the passage.)

"A courageous chief only is wanted. Where is he? That great man whom Nature owes to her vexed, oppressed, and tormented children. Where is he? He will appear, doubt it not.

He will come forth, and raise the sacred standard of liberty. This venerable signal will gather around him the companions of his misfortune. More impetuous than the torrents, they will everywhere leave the indelible traces of their just resentment. Everywhere people will bless the name of the hero, who shall have re-established the rights of the human race. Everywhere will they raise trophies in his honour."

White men see Negroes as slaves. If the Negro is to be free, he must free himself. We have courage, we have endurance, we have numbers. . . . "Where is he? That great man whom Nature owes to her vexed, oppressed and tormented children?" Thou hast shown me the light, oh God! I shall be that leader.

Curtain.

SCENE 4

Early 1794. The mountain retreat of Toussaint's wife and two sons. Madame Louverture is sitting sewing. Enter Mars Plaisir.

MARS   Where is the master?

MADAME L   The guards came and said someone had the password, but they were suspicious and wouldn't let them pass. So Toussaint himself has gone to see.

MARS   How do you find him, Madame?

MADAME L   More worried than I have ever seen him before, Mars. Even when he is playing with the boys he is preoccupied. And I have never known that to happen before. Good God! When will all this end? Mars, sometimes I think that when Toussaint was a coachman, and he and I and the boys went to the fields together, we were happier.

MARS   But Madame, the boys would have grown up to be slaves.

MADAME L   Yes. I shouldn't have said that. God forgive me. But this fighting never stops. Fighting, fighting, fighting—and there seems no end to it. That is what is worrying Toussaint. *(There is a knock at the door.)* Here they are.

(Exit Madame L and Mars. Enter Toussaint in a colonel's uniform accompanied by Bullet and General Maitland, both in civilian clothes.)

BULLET   Colonel Louverture, this is General Maitland.

TOUSSAINT   The Commander of the English Expedition!

BULLET   Yes.

TOUSSAINT   But I told Commissioner Roume that only he or any agent of his should ever come to see me here.

BULLET   I am an agent of Commissioner Roume's. At least—

TOUSSAINT   Mars. *(Enter Mars.)* Tell Captain Dessalines to double the guard, and allow absolutely no one to pass except Commissioner Roume himself.

MAITLAND   There is no treachery, Colonel Louverture. M. Bullet will explain.

BULLET   Colonel Louverture, that day when Commissioner Roume and I came to interview you at Grande Rivière I was deeply impressed by the moderation of your views.

TOUSSAINT   You did not show it at the time, and much has happened since then. The Commissioner himself has had to abolish slavery completely in the island.

BULLET   That measure has not been ratified by the government in France.

TOUSSAINT   Exactly.

BULLET   Commissioner Roume acted beyond his powers. He himself knows that freedom for all the slaves will ruin the island. All civilisation today is trembling in the balance. The revolution in France began well, but it has gone too far and is carrying the country to destruction.

MAITLAND   All over the world authority realises at last what sort of monster this French revolution is. Britain, Prussia, Russia, half Europe

	has formed a coalition against it. And the Spanish Government is one of its foremost supporters.
BULLET	We want you to help the forces of law and order in San Domingo. The white colonists have abandoned the Revolution.
TOUSSAINT	Does Commissioner Roume know this?
BULLET	*(In a burst of temper)* No—but he will know soon. And we shall not spare him.
MAITLAND	But meanwhile M. Bullet has certain propositions to put before you.
BULLET	The Colonial Assembly is seeking help from the British. The terms you will know later. But we swear to you that those mulattoes and blacks who join us will have their freedom and equal political and social rights with the whites. All of us who have, or will have, property and responsibility must join together to defend this island from anarchy.
TOUSSAINT	In other words, you want me to help you to restore slavery in this island.
MAITLAND	Not for all the blacks, Colonel Louverture. You have an army of four thousand men, all proved and tried soldiers. No man has so much influence with the blacks as you have. We know you as not only an able soldier and influential with your people, but as a man of moderate views. You and your soldiers and any whom you care to name, the friends and relations of your officers, all will be free. You will be equal to any white man. The British Government has consented to take over the island, and we guarantee the rights and privileges of all those who fight with us.
BULLET	With your help, Colonel Louverture, and that of your soldiers, we shall destroy Roume and his so-called Revolutionary Government, a band of cut-throats and regicides. You will have with you the white colonists and the British Government, the most powerful in the world.
TOUSSAINT	And the slaves?
BULLET	The planters realise today that they will have to treat the slaves better.

MAITLAND	The best guarantee that they shall do so is the fact that you, a Negro, with your black army will be one of the chief forces in the State.
TOUSSAINT	For how long? M. Bullet, there was a time when I would have consented to this. But not today. Even if I wanted to, I could not. Nothing on earth will make the blacks of San Domingo submit to slavery again.
MAITLAND	The British are sending ten thousand men, and we shall be well supplied with funds. With your co-operation, we can re-establish law and order—
TOUSSAINT	By shooting down those who do not agree to go back into the fields under the lash of the whip.
MAITLAND	You will be able to persuade them, Colonel Louverture. And what are the alternatives? If you join Roume you join a sinking ship. No help can come to him from France. The British fleet will see to that. And the Spaniards will support you only until the French Revolution is crushed.
BULLET	As soon as France is defeated in Europe they will forget all you have done for them and destroy your army.
TOUSSAINT	They will not find that so easy.
MAITLAND	And even if they do not break off relations with you? Have they abolished slavery in their dominions?
TOUSSAINT	Have the British?
MAITLAND	No, but the matter has been raised in the House of Commons. The Prime Minister is sympathetic and the whole subject of slavery is under review by His Majesty's Government. Mr. Pitt has appointed a committee to go into the question. Meanwhile we offer you a substantial instalment. You are a man of energy, talent, and ambition. Join us. You will be achieving security for yourself and your friends, and will be helping those of your people best able to benefit by freedom, besides being able to protect the rest.
TOUSSAINT	I cannot. My army, my officers, all are fighting for freedom, not only for themselves but for all.

BULLET	Only four thousand.
TOUSSAINT	I could make it forty thousand tomorrow if I had arms. Why do you think we win victory after victory? Because, wherever we go the whole population is on our side, welcome us, give us food, take the clothes off our backs, and give them to us, lead the enemy into traps for us. It is true I cannot trust the Spaniards, but can I trust you? Which are the slave-owners whom any slave can trust?
BULLET	Colonel Louverture, do you think you and your men, brave as you are, can withstand the soldiers and resources of the British Empire?
TOUSSAINT	It will be easier for me to do that than to join with the British to drive our people back to slavery. *(Rising)* Gentlemen, the interview is over. It ought never to have begun.
BULLET	You damned Negro. You dismiss us — You think —
MAITLAND	No, M. Bullet. Colonel Louverture is thinking of the interests of his people. And if he decides against us it is because he is not sufficiently convinced of our sincerity. Give me a few moments alone with him.
TOUSSAINT	Mars. *(Enter Mars.)* Take him out and keep guard over him. *(Exit Bullet and Mars.)* This is the way all these planters think of us now. He can barely be civil now. Once the ancient regime is restored, what use will he have for me and such as me?
MAITLAND	Colonel, we are both soldiers and we understand each other better than these civilians. Have I your permission to speak quite frankly to you?
TOUSSAINT	I owe no allegiance to the French Government. You can say what you please.
MAITLAND	Colonel Louverture, my Government can appreciate a man at his true worth. Bullet makes promises for the future. My Government has authorised me to act immediately. The British Expedition is well-equipped with arms for your soldiers and money for the expenses of you and those of your officers who will join us. Not as an inducement, but as a pledge of good

	faith. I can send to you in three days £100,000, a million francs in French money.
TOUSSAINT	A million francs!
MAITLAND	I merely mention that, but any sum that you care to name—
TOUSSAINT	General, you are nearer to having a bullet through you than ever you have been on the battlefield.
MAITLAND	I am sorry that you should misunderstand my motive, Colonel Louverture. I hope you don't think I am trying to bribe you.
TOUSSAINT	Mars. *(Enter Mars.)* Instruct Corporal Verny to march these two along the ravine—not the tracks. Tell him not to leave them until they are a mile outside the lines. And if either of them gives the slightest cause for suspicion they are to be shot without hesitation.

(Exit Mars and Maitland. Enter Madame Louverture.)

MADAME L	Toussaint, what has happened?
TOUSSAINT	Bullet has turned traitor to Roume. He's joined the English, and brought an Englishman here who tried to bribe me. God! Is there no honesty among men? Those boys of ours, Suzanne— what will they grow up to be?

(He walks over to an alcove, pulls the curtain aside, and the two stand looking at a bed where the boys are sleeping.)

MADAME L	Calm yourself, Toussaint.
TOUSSAINT	I have been calm, very calm. But when I looked at those two and knew that if they get the chance they will drive us and our people back into the fields, I could have sprung at their throats and torn their eyes out. If the rest of them in Europe are like those who come out here, then it is a wonder they have not torn each other to pieces already.
MADAME L	Perhaps they will one day, and then the blacks will have peace. *(There is a knock.)* Who is that now?
TOUSSAINT	It is Commissioner Roume. I had arranged to meet him. Let him in and don't go. I shall finish with all this tonight.

(Enter Commissioner Roume and Colonel Vincent. They bow.)

ROUME   Colonel Louverture, this is Colonel Vincent.

(Toussaint bows.)

VINCENT   I hope you are well, Colonel Louverture.

TOUSSAINT   Thank you. Mr. Commissioner Roume, what proposals have you brought to me this evening? You have a witness with you. My officers, my army, and I have nothing more to say than what I have told you and your agents before. These interviews are now useless. They must come to an end.

ROUME   Why this sudden hostility, Colonel Louverture? My position has always been plain. When I came here I didn't believe in the abolition of slavery. After ruling here for some months I decided that nothing else could ever restore this island to peace. On my responsibility I abolished slavery.

TOUSSAINT   You could not help yourself. It was an emergency measure.

ROUME   Granted. But I did it and have stuck to it. I have asked you many times to leave the Spaniards and join us, to fight for the Revolution and for the defence of the liberty of your people. You have refused, but at least we have understood one another. No man in my position and with the responsibility I have had to bear could have done more for your people. Why this sudden wish to break off all negotiations?

TOUSSAINT   You have abolished slavery here. But it exists in Martinique, in Guadeloupe, in every French colony. You have shown me letters from the French Government approving your decree, but slavery is still on the statute book of even your boasted Revolutionary Government.

ROUME   Is that all?

TOUSSAINT   Isn't it enough?

ROUME   It is. Well, Colonel, the Convention has ratified my decree. Slavery is abolished in every department and colony of France. That is the news I have brought.

(Madame L grips her husband's arm.)

TOUSSAINT   The Convention has abolished slavery?

ROUME   The Convention has abolished slavery. I sent Colonel Vincent to Paris, urging that it should be done. He was present at the sitting. He brought the dispatches this morning, and we set out to see you at once. Colonel Vincent.

(Madame L, deeply moved, walks over to the end of the room where the alcove is. Toussaint follows her, and the others follow them.)

VINCENT   I went with three deputies from San Domingo, a black man, a mulatto, and a white man. When the session began, the Chairman of the Committee on Decrees rose —

(The inner curtain rises and shows the President in his chair and a section of the Convention in session. [This is an almost verbatim report of the sittings of the 3rd and 4th February, 1794.] Vincent's voice dies away.)

CHAIRMAN OF THE COMMITTEE ON DECREES

   Citizens, your committee on decrees has verified the credentials of the deputies from San Domingo. I move that they be admitted to the Convention.

CAMBOULAS   Since 1789 the aristocracy of birth and the aristocracy of religion have been destroyed; but the aristocracy of the skin still remains. That too is now about to collapse. A black man, a yellow man, are about to join this convention in the name of the free citizens of San Domingo. *(Applause.)*

(The three deputies of San Domingo enter the hall. The black face of Bellay and the yellow face of Mills excite long and continuous applause.)

LACROIX (OF EURE-ET-LOIR)

   The Assembly has been anxious to have within it some of those men of colour who have suffered oppression for so many years. Today it has two of them. I demand that their introduction be marked by the President's fraternal embrace.

(The motion is carried amidst applause. The three deputies of San Domingo advance to the President and receive the fraternal kiss. The hall rings with fresh applause.)

BELLAY   Mr. President, in no part of France or her dominions are there such ardent defenders of the Republic as the black people of San Domingo. I implore the Convention to vouchsafe to the colonies full enjoyment of the blessings of liberty and equality.

LEVASSEUR (OF SARTHE)
         In drawing up the constitution of the French people we paid no attention to the unhappy Negroes. Posterity will bear us a great reproach for that. Let us repair the wrong—let us proclaim the liberty of the Negroes. Mr. President, do not suffer the convention to dishonour itself by a discussion.

(The Assembly rises in acclamation.)

(The two deputies of colour appear on the tribune. They embrace. Applause. Lacroix leads them to the President who gives them the presidential kiss. Applause.)

CAMBON   A citizeness of colour, who comes regularly to the sittings of the Convention, has just felt so keen a joy at seeing us give liberty to all her brethren that she has fainted. *(Applause)* I demand that this fact be mentioned in the minutes, and that this citizeness be admitted to the sitting and receive at least this much recognition of her civic virtues.

(The motion is carried. On the front bench of the amphitheatre, to the left of the President, the citizeness is seen, drying her tears. Applause.)

LACROIX   I demand that the Minister of Marine be instructed to despatch at once advices to the colonies to give them the happy news of their freedom, and I propose the following decree: The National Convention declares slavery abolished in all the colonies. In consequence, it declares that all men, without distinction of colour, domiciled in the colonies are French citizens and enjoy all the rights assured under the Constitution.

(The Assembly rises, and amidst enthusiastic applause and shouts of "Long live the Republic—Long live Liberty," the inner curtain falls, leaving Toussaint and the others alone on the stage.)

VINCENT   *(Continuing)* I was there. I saw it. Colonel Louverture, I am a white man, and have never felt nor feared the burdens of slavery, but at no moment in my private or public life have I been so much moved as by this spontaneous recognition of the rights of your oppressed and suffering people.

TOUSSAINT   Colonel Vincent.

(*They embrace.*)

ROUME   Colonel Louverture, this is the decree; this is the proclamation which I am authorised to make to the people. Here is the official account in the *Moniteur*. And here is the formal letter to you which the Minister of the Colonies has sent asking you to join us. We have little to offer you. We have neither money nor army. The Republic is in danger. In Europe the ancient monarchies are attacking us on all our borders, determined to crush this first great uprising in the whole history of mankind. More than our bullets and guns they fear the words liberty, equality, and fraternity, which tear the veils of tradition from the minds of all the oppressed who hear them. Tyranny the world over is trembling. In this very San Domingo of ours, Bullet and the white colonists are plotting against us and are seeking to restore the ancient regime.

TOUSSAINT   So you know.

ROUME   Of course I know. But the Revolution will triumph, if all the sons of liberty, white, black, and brown fight for it wherever they are. Here I have a gift from the Republic, a sword, and your papers made out as a Brigadier-General in the revolutionary army of France. I have only to sign them. Say the word, Colonel Louverture, and together we shall destroy the enemies of liberty in these islands.

TOUSSAINT   Mr. Commissioner Roume, I am at your service and the service of the French Republic. But it is not for your gifts nor for your titles, dearly as I shall prize them. It is because I feel that the only European government which will do its duty by the Negroes is the Government of the Revolution.

(*Toussaint and Roume grip hands.*)

ROUME   I swear that I shall be as faithful to you and to your people as to the Government which I serve.

VINCENT	Colonel, this will be happy news for the French Republic, threatened as it is on all sides.
TOUSSAINT	You have given me your confidence. Let me give you mine. Here are my two sons, whom I treasure most on earth. My army and all my influence are now yours, and as a guarantee of my good faith I shall hand my sons over to you to be sent to France to be educated in the true principles of liberty. My wife and I can only hope that if Providence spares us to see them return, they will be soldiers as brave and bear themselves as well as Colonel Vincent here.
ROUME	The Republic will treat them as its own children, Colonel Louverture. And now I have to return at once. But before I leave — Colonel Vincent, buckle on this sword. (*He writes on one of his documents.*) Here are your papers, General. Goodbye.

(*Roume and Toussaint embrace. Vincent salutes. He and Toussaint embrace. Vincent salutes again.*) Goodbye, Madame Louverture (*They bow low. Exit Roume and Vincent.*)

MADAME L	The boys — to grow up free — never to be slaves. I used to dream of it at nights.

(*Toussaint catches her as she falls.*)

Curtain.

Act II   SCENE 1

Five years later. A room in the Government buildings in Port-au-Prince. At the back is a window, closed. The curtain rises on Commander Hédouville and General Pétion, leader of the mulattoes.

PÉTION	Will General Maitland agree to the terms of peace?
HÉDOUVILLE	If he doesn't General Louverture will sweep him and his army into the sea. All Maitland can do now is to leave trouble behind for the French. He wants to use our difficulties. With the co-operation of you and the mulattoes, General Pétion, we can use him.

PÉTION Commissioner Roume has always supported Toussaint and his blacks.

HÉDOUVILLE Commissioner Roume is my subordinate. The Government in France which appointed me is different from the Government which appointed him. We stand for freedom, yes, but "ordered" freedom. Liberty, yes, but not license. We do not intend to restore slavery. But those blacks must be kept in their place. Commissioner Roume will do what I decide. If not, I shall send him back to France, and Colonel Vincent with him.

PÉTION Commissioner Hédouville, our people will need strong assurance that the French Government will never seek to restore us to the indignities and injustices we suffered before the Revolution. We are rebels against your authority. General Louverture is your general, carrying out your orders against us. If we fight your battles we do so hoping that the mulattoes will never again be subjected to the domination of these upstart slaves.

HÉDOUVILLE You can judge the position for yourself, General Pétion. We had to depend on Toussaint and the blacks against the British. But now that the British have been defeated we have as much reason as you for ending this black domination.

PÉTION We are in desperate straits. The town is starving. You are sure of General Maitland?

HÉDOUVILLE We have sounded him through the American Consul, Mr. Tobias Lear. Maitland will make his offer I am sure. He would have made it to Toussaint, but he is afraid of the Negro spreading revolution among the slaves of the other islands. *(Rises)* Goodbye, General Pétion. You will get back safely?

PÉTION Yes. No one dare touch the Commissioner's cutter, and after dark I swim ashore.

HÉDOUVILLE These are difficult times, General Pétion, for you and for me, but we shall come through. Hold out, relief is near.

PÉTION It is only food and ammunition we want. The town itself is impregnable.

(Exit Pétion. Hédouville rings bell. Enter attendant.)

HÉDOUVILLE   Commissioner Roume.

(Exit attendant. Hédouville paces the room. Enter Commissioner Roume.)

ROUME   I am at your service, Mr. Commissioner Hédouville.

HÉDOUVILLE   Commissioner Roume, I hope you have re-considered your views, and recognise the difficult situation in which the French Government is placed.

ROUME   I have nothing to add. I think if we trust General Louverture as we have done in the past, the French Republic will not suffer. Any other course is dangerous.

HÉDOUVILLE   General Louverture is aiming at independence.

ROUME   I have known him for six years. He has always been a faithful servant of the Republic.

HÉDOUVILLE   Maitland will be here in a few minutes. He will make the offer of supporting Pétion. I shall accept it, with reservations, of course, but I shall accept it.

ROUME   And then?

HÉDOUVILLE   Once the British are away, mulattoes under Pétion and blacks under Toussaint will tear each other to pieces. Peace is near in Europe. Let them keep each other occupied until our government at home is ready to restore its authority in this rebellious island.

(Enter attendant.)

ATTENDANT   General Maitland and Mr. Tobias Lear.

HÉDOUVILLE   You will let Colonel Vincent know as soon as possible that I expect a strict conformity with my policy. I would not like to have to send anyone back to France.

(Enter General Maitland and Mr. Tobias Lear.)

MAITLAND   Gentlemen, my staff and I have carefully considered the terms of the truce. We think it fair to both sides, and in a few days the final draft will be ready.

HÉDOUVILLE   I am sure that our respective governments will be very satisfied with our negotiations, General Maitland.

MAITLAND   May this be merely the preliminary to peace in Europe. And now, gentlemen, I want to speak to you of a matter which concerns all of us who rule in these colonies. I am speaking now, not as an Englishman, not as an enemy of France, but as a white man and one with the same colonial interests as yours. This General Toussaint Louverture, at the head of his black army, is a danger to us all.

HÉDOUVILLE   We see that as clearly as you, but the Government of San Domingo has no force by which it can assert its authority.

LEAR   *(Speaking with a strong American accent)* As consul for America, of course, I have no concern with all these matters. But if it were not for the black general and his black army San Domingo would be Spanish or English, but it would not be a French colony.

ROUME   That's true.

HÉDOUVILLE   Still the question before us is what General Maitland has said. The mulattoes under Pétion are holding out against Toussaint at the town of Jacmel. They are rebels against our authority, but if he conquers them, although nominally our servant, this Negro will be virtually master of the island. And the problem then is no longer French but concerns all who rule in these colonies, French, British, and Dutch.

MAITLAND   Gentlemen, as long as General Louverture continues the way he is going, the prestige of the Europeans in these colonies is in grave danger. And we rule as much by prestige as by arms. See what he calls himself now, "Louverture"—opener of a way for his people. At whose expense?

HÉDOUVILLE   But how to check him?

MAITLAND   There is only one way in colonial countries.

HÉDOUVILLE   And that is?

MAITLAND   Strengthen some local power against him—now. General Pétion is besieged with his mulattoes at the town of Jacmel. If Jacmel falls to Toussaint then the mulattoes are doomed; and Toussaint's road is open. Fortunately, Jacmel is almost impregnable —

LEAR   I wouldn't be too sure of anything being impregnable where Toussaint is concerned. Since I have been in San Domingo he has opened some doors that seemed pretty tightly closed.

MAITLAND   He is a good soldier, but not of such exceptional ability, Mr. Consul.

LEAR   He forced you to surrender, General.

MAITLAND   That is true, but the climate — we have been decimated by the fever, and he and his soldiers know every inch of the country. But we needn't go into that.

HÉDOUVILLE No, we need not.

MAITLAND   But, Mr. Commissioner, General Pétion needs help. Arms, ammunitions, military supplies of all sorts, and above all food.

HÉDOUVILLE Toussaint's army bars the way.

MAITLAND   Only by land — there is the sea. And if by sea why not from our British colony of Jamaica, which is only a few miles away? The Consul can secure the co-operation of America, in return for trade concessions. If we move quickly, not only Toussaint will never take Jacmel, but Pétion, properly strengthened, may be able to organise from there a counter-attack and break the power of this audacious and all-conquering Negro.

LEAR   My government is not interested in colonial complications, gentlemen. George Washington always told us to keep out of foreign entanglements and we shall keep out of them. If a substantial amount of trade can be promised to our men of business in New York then you can be sure my government will look with sympathy upon any measures you may take to guarantee the dominance of the white race.

MAITLAND   Of my good faith in this matter, Mr. Commissioner, you need have no fear. As soon as our treaty is signed I and all my men embark for home.

HÉDOUVILLE   Thank you, Brigadier-General, and you, Mr. Consul.

(At this moment a trumpet sounds. Roume and Hédouville, startled, jump to their feet.)

MAITLAND   What is that?

ROUME   That is Toussaint.

HÉDOUVILLE   But that is impossible. *(Trumpet sounds again.)* Yes, it's he. There he is at his tricks again. His letter said that he was leaving Dessalines in front of Jacmel and setting off himself for Port-au-Prince. Now he will come with a flawless excuse.

(Enter Mars Plaisir.)

MARS PLAISIR   The Commander-in-Chief, General Toussaint Louverture, Brigadier-General Christophe, and Brigadier General Dessalines.

(Almost on the announcement Toussaint walks into the room. He is just from horseback and even carries his riding whip.)

TOUSSAINT   Good-evening, Mr. Commissioner Roume. Good-evening, Mr. Commissioner Hédouville. Brigadier-General Maitland. *(Bows.)* Mr. Consul. *(Bows.)* Mr. Commissioner Hédouville, I have to announce that San Domingo is now under your undisturbed command. Jacmel is taken.

HÉDOUVILLE   Jacmel taken!

TOUSSAINT   Jacmel is taken. The last stronghold of the mulattoes is destroyed, and finishing Pétion off is merely a matter of days.

(Experienced diplomats as they are, the news has them all confounded.)

MAITLAND   *(Stepping forward)* Hearty congratulations on your success, Commander-in-Chief. You go from strength to strength. You and your army of blacks will soon be as famous in these parts as General Bonaparte and his army in Europe. Happy the Commissioners who have such a general and such soldiers to fight their battles.

HÉDOUVILLE   The Republic owes you a great debt, Commander-in-Chief.

	The French Government will be happy to know that once more you have served her so faithfully.
ROUME	No servant of France is more worthy of her gratitude. I say this from the bottom of my heart.
LEAR	Some said you couldn't take Jacmel, General, but I always knew that Pétion was no match for you. We discussed that, didn't we, General Maitland?
MAITLAND	We did, Mr. Consul.
TOUSSAINT	I thank you, gentlemen. It is not often that a general fresh from the field of battle can receive at the same time the congratulations not only of his own country, but of such great countries as England and America.
MAITLAND	We were just arranging the terms of my evacuation, General.
TOUSSAINT	Then the general whom I had left in command should be here.
HÉDOUVILLE	You are the Commander-in-Chief of the Army, but I am the head of the civil administration. It is always the civil authority which signs terms of peace, and I had already discussed all details with you.
MAITLAND	This puts me in an awkward position, gentlemen . . .
TOUSSAINT	General Maitland, would your government consider a treaty signed with me valid?
MAITLAND	We would have to in as much as you are in command of the Army which lies in front of us.
TOUSSAINT	Then I shall sign the treaty.
MAITLAND	But what about the Commissioner?
TOUSSAINT	When the treaty is being signed, the Commissioner will not be here.
HÉDOUVILLE	Of course I will be here. No treaty signed would be valid without my sanction.
TOUSSAINT	San Domingo is a department of France and has representatives in the Council of Five Hundred in Paris. In a week's time

an election takes place. By the law of France, whoever is asked to serve is bound to do so. I have good reason to know that General Hédouville will be elected as one of the representatives.

HÉDOUVILLE   But that is impossible! I am the Commissioner. I have not been nominated. I cannot be nominated.

TOUSSAINT   You can be nominated, and you will be, General Hédouville. And you will be elected, unopposed. Three days after a boat will leave for France, and it will be necessary for you to hasten to your legislative duties.

HÉDOUVILLE   But this is an outrage. General Louverture, there is no trick you have not tried, to undermine the Republican authority in this colony. You claim to work only for the liberty of your people, but it is your ambition that drives you. Peace will soon be declared in Europe and once the French Government is undisturbed by war it will make you pay for your crimes.

TOUSSAINT   Let the French Government punish me for my crimes, so long as it rewards me for my services.

HÉDOUVILLE   You have received enough rewards. What more do you want? You are Commander-in-Chief of a French army. Has any Negro ever reached as far as you?

TOUSSAINT   What has that got to do with it?

HÉDOUVILLE   You shall not have full command of this island. I go, but I appoint Commissioner Roume as my successor with full power until instructions arrive from Paris. You shall submit yourself to his authority in all matters. Commissioner Roume, you are now responsible to the Government of France for the colony of San Domingo.

TOUSSAINT   Commissioner Roume is already responsible to the Government of France for another colony. Mr. Commissioner Roume, by the terms of the treaty of Basle between France and Spain, the Spanish portion of the island was ceded to France. You were appointed Commissioner and ordered to take immediate possession.

ROUME I attempted to do so but failed.

TOUSSAINT You attempted? You sent General Agé and General Chanlatte to arrange for the formal transfer of authority but at the same time you wrote to Don Joachim Garcia, the Spanish Governor-General, telling him to refuse to hand over the colony. I have a copy of your letter.

HÉDOUVILLE We did it because we had grown to distrust your intentions. Had you and your soldiers got possession of Spanish San Domingo you would have been master of the whole island and it would have been still more difficult to control you.

TOUSSAINT That Commissioner Roume will explain to the French Government. Meanwhile, Brigadier-General Dessalines will supply him with two carriages and a safe escort to the village of Dondon where he will remain until the French Government recalls him to render an account of his administration. I do not think, gentlemen, that these arrangements about the treaty concern you any further. *(They hesitate.)* Unless perhaps Mr. Commissioner Hédouville would like to consult further with Mr. Commissioner Roume under the escort of General Dessalines.

HÉDOUVILLE You have trifled with many French Governments. But your time is short. General Bonaparte, the First Consul, will deal with you.

(Exit Hédouville and Roume.)

TOUSSAINT I take it that the terms of peace which you arranged, General Maitland, are the same we exchanged.

MAITLAND Yes, General. We evacuate every position we hold but we go with all our guns, ammunition, and baggage.

TOUSSAINT This, I hope, means the beginning of a long peace between the English and San Domingo.

MAITLAND I am sure of it, General. A great future lies before you and these people you have raised from slavery into prosperous and enlightened freedom. I remember when you insisted that it could be done and we doubted you. You have been proved right.

LEAR	Every Englishman will be heart and soul with them in their struggle for liberty.
MAITLAND	That, Mr. Consul, is the British tradition. But now that peace is near in Europe, General Louverture, the French Government may wish to re-establish slavery here.
TOUSSAINT	San Domingo is loyal to France, General. But there is no Negro who will not die in defence of his freedom.
LEAR	I told you so, Mr. Brigadier. Liber-r-rty or death.
TOUSSAINT	Liberty or death, Consul. It is no laughing matter. Thousands of our people have died with those words on their lips.
MAITLAND	Your victories and the exploits of your soldiers have earned the confidence and respect of the King of England and his ministers. In the name of His Majesty, King George III, I shall have pleasure in presenting you with a silver dinner service, a token of His Majesty's respect and regard. It shall be here tomorrow morning.
TOUSSAINT	The people of San Domingo, General Maitland, will deeply appreciate this mark of favour and recognition from His Britannic Majesty.
MAITLAND	I shall not fail to inform His Majesty. General Louverture, the friendship between San Domingo and Britain can be made still closer. France can do nothing against the British fleet. We are the masters of the ocean. If, perhaps, as I have heard it whispered you have thought of doing, if, General Louverture, you should decide to declare the colony independent and make yourself King of San Domingo, we would welcome it and give you our fullest support. King of San Domingo. You have only to say the word, King George would welcome his royal brother and England will become your firm ally. Then, General, with our fleet you can bring twenty thousand blacks from the Congo, arm them with guns and ammunition from America and make them into such soldiers as you have made the slaves. Think of what an army you could have. And not only England will support you. The Consul here promises you the support of America.

MAITLAND (CONTINUED)	have earned the confidence and respect of the King of England and his ministers. In the name of His Majesty King George III, I shall have pleasure in presenting you with a silver dinner service, a tok en of His Majesty's respect and regard. It shall be here tomorrow morning.
TOUSSAINT	The people of San Domingo, General Maitland, will deeply appreciate this mark of favour and recognition from His Brittanic Majesty.
MAITLAND	I shall not fail to inform His Majesty,.General Louverture, the friendship between San Domingo and Britain can be made still closer. France can do nothing against the ~~English~~ *British* fleet. We are the masters of the ocean. If, perhaps, as I have heard it whispered you have thought of doing, if, General Louverture, you should decide to declare the colony independent and make yourself King of San Domingo, we would welcome it and give you our fullest support. King of San Domingo. You have only to say the word, King George will welcome his royal brother and England will become your firm ally. Then, General, with our fleet you can bring 20,000 blacks from the Congo, arm them with guns and ammunition from America and make them into such soldiers asyou have made the slaves. Think of what an army you could have. And not only England will support you . The Consul here promises you the support of America.
LEAR	*of San Domingo* If a substantial portion of the trade can be diverted from France to us, Commander-in-Chief, then you can be sure that my Government will look with sympathy upon any measures you may take to guarantee the independence of the blacks.
TOUSSAINT	General Maitland, I must thank you for your offer, but I cannot accept it. God knows that in my dreams sometimes I see not only an independent black San Domingo. I see all these West Indian Islands free and independent communities of black men reaping the rewards of the long years of cruelty and suffering which our parents bore.
LEAR	This is your chance, General Toussaint.

"Toussaint Louverture." Hull History Centre (DJH/21), p. 54.

LEAR	If a substantial portion of the trade of San Domingo can be diverted from France to us, Commander-in-Chief, then you can be sure that my government will look with sympathy upon any measures you may take to guarantee the independence of the blacks.
TOUSSAINT	General Maitland, I must thank you for your offer, but I cannot accept it. God knows that in my dreams sometimes I see not only an independent black San Domingo. I see all these West Indian islands free and independent communities of black men reaping the rewards of the long years of cruelty and suffering which our parents bore.
LEAR	This is your chance, General Toussaint.
TOUSSAINT	No, the time is not yet. As long as the French do not try to re-establish slavery in San Domingo, we shall be loyal to France — we must be.
MAITLAND	But are you thinking of yourself? If even France does not seek to re-establish slavery, do you think she will allow you to arrest and dismiss her representatives as you have done this evening? Now that peace is to be declared your future with France is doubtful.
TOUSSAINT	That, General, the future will show. There are more urgent tasks before us now.
DESSALINES	Toussaint.
TOUSSAINT	Yes, General Dessalines?
DESSALINES	Take the offer, Toussaint. Take it. Make yourself king. The people fought to be free. You are the leader. They trust you. They will fight for you and for themselves. Make yourself king. A country of blacks and a black king—let the people see it. They will say: "This is our country." Nobody will be able to take it away again.
MAITLAND	This is exactly what I think. But your Commander-in-Chief trusts France.
DESSALINES	Don't trust France, don't trust any of these whites. Take their ships, take their guns, whoever offers take; and then let the

French come and the British *(He glares at Maitland.)* and even the Americans *(He glares at Lear.)* . . .

(Toussaint holds him by the arm.)

TOUSSAINT Dessalines. *(After a pause.)* What do you think, General Christophe?

CHRISTOPHE Commander-in-Chief, ten years ago you, and Biassou, Boukman, and Jean-François were negotiating with the French Commissioners and M. Bullet. I remember when Dessalines said "Freedom for all," and you said "No, all the slaves are not fit to be free." Dessalines was right then. Perhaps Dessalines is right now.

(As he utters the last words there begins a roar which grows into shouts: "Toussaint! Toussaint! Jacmel! Toussaint! Jacmel!")

DESSALINES You—it's you they want, Toussaint. They have heard that Jacmel is taken. They call for you.

(Toussaint goes to the window and throws it open, letting in a great burst of cheering. He waves his hand—the cheers redouble. With a wave of farewell he closes the window and, deep in thought, walks slowly back.)

TOUSSAINT General Maitland, San Domingo is a French colony and it must remain French. What you suggest cannot be. Consul, I shall be glad for supplies of arms and ammunition, and shall consider a trade agreement with you.

MAITLAND Good-night, General Louverture. And, remember, England is always your friend. Good-night, General Christophe. Good-night, General Dessalines. General Louverture, tomorrow morning at ten o'clock I am reviewing my troops. We shall be glad to have the honour of your presence.

TOUSSAINT Thank you, General. I shall come.

MAITLAND Thank you. If you do decide to accept our offer the bargain will be faithfully fulfilled. Good-night.

LEAR Good-night, Generals.

(Exit Maitland and Lear. The three stand silent.)

TOUSSAINT	*(Seating himself)* King of San Domingo! Well, Christo̶
DESSALINES	He and his dinner service and his king.
TOUSSAINT	Christophe, I shall give you the silver dinner service. I know you like that sort of thing.
CHRISTOPHE	If you don't want it certainly I shall have the present from His Majesty.
TOUSSAINT	I am sorry about Roume — he has been a good friend, but he has to go.
DESSALINES	Toussaint, you are too soft with these people. You will pay for it one day. What are you going to do now?
TOUSSAINT	Educate and train the people — reorganise our defences — get arms from America — be ready for any attempt against our liberty.
CHRISTOPHE	What Dessalines means is — what is our relation to France?
TOUSSAINT	I do not know. We shall be loyal to France, but we must be in a position to defend ourselves.
CHRISTOPHE	What do you think, Dessalines?
DESSALINES	I've told you a thousand times. Declare the island independent. It is ours. Our blood and our sweat have made everything that is here.
CHRISTOPHE	That will bring an expedition against us.
DESSALINES	It is coming in any case. Toussaint says he is loyal to France. France is one thing today and another thing tomorrow. At one time they abolish slavery, and execute the white planters. Today that General Bonaparte has all the white planters at his court — our bitterest enemies.
CHRISTOPHE	Bullet, the traitor, is there now. He has made his peace with the Republic.
TOUSSAINT	I know.
DESSALINES	You know and yet you talk of loyalty to France. The people know too. They are restless, confused. All we want is freedom.

all this loyalty, Toussaint. They will fight for free-
, last man.

n—yes—but freedom is not everything. Dessalines,
the state of the people. We who live here shall never see
a again—some of us born here have never seen it. Lan-
age we have none—French is now our language. We have no
ducation—the little that some of us know we have learnt from
France. Those few of us who are Christians follow the French
religion. We must stay with France as long as she does not seek
to restore slavery.

DESSALINES   Education—religion—Toussaint, always the white man's religion, the white man's education. When the white planters put
the slaves in prison and they call for food they cut off his flesh
and give it to him to eat. I, Dessalines, was born on the Congo
and lived there, but never saw such things. It is the white men
in San Domingo that show them to me.

TOUSSAINT   We cannot remember these things always. White men have
knowledge that we need. We must forget the past.

DESSALINES   Forget! Look at my skin—marks of the whip. You have not
got them. I shall carry them to my grave. Every slave in San
Domingo carries marks like these. Who gave them to us? White
planters—men with your white religion. You forgive them,
Toussaint. You say come back to work for San Domingo—they
salute you—General Louverture, Commander-in-Chief—they
say, "How are you, General Dessalines? Come to dinner." But
Toussaint, in their hearts they hate us. We were the slaves—
now we are the masters. You think they like it? For every white
man a Negro is only fit to be a slave.

TOUSSAINT   The English do not care anything for us. They want to use us—I
know that. But if we join them against France we are isolated
from everything that could advance us. Of the half million
Negroes in this country three hundred thousand were born in
Africa. They can fight, but apart from that they are barbarous
savages. We must stick with the French as long as possible. I
shall govern the country now. When things are more settled
I shall make a new constitution. I shall appoint myself First

	Consul for life, and shall send it to France. I shall ask Colonel Vincent to present it to the First Consul.
DESSALINES	You have arrested Roume and will leave Vincent? If you send him to Paris he will betray our military secrets.
TOUSSAINT	I have confidence in Vincent.
DESSALINES	Confidence in a white man. Take the offer, Toussaint. Make yourself king—take the island. If we had depended on education and religion we would never have got our freedom. Education and religion, but freedom first.
TOUSSAINT	We shall keep our freedom. I shall arm the population—give every peasant a gun and ammunition—tell them that whoever wishes to take the guns away from them wishes to restore slavery. That is all we can do at present. We need the French as much as they need us. If they keep faith with us, we shall keep faith with them.

(*Exit Dessalines and Christophe, leaving Toussaint standing alone, deep in thought.*)

Curtain.

SCENE 2

Nearly two years later. Bonaparte's apartment in the Tuileries. The stage is divided into two parts, one small ante-room, to the left, and a large room. When the curtain goes up, only the ante-room is lighted.

There are soldiers and an orderly. Colonel Vincent is walking to and fro in the background. Those who come in do not attempt to speak to him.

Enter M. Bullet and General Pétion.

PÉTION	I don't think the campaign will be long.
BULLET	The campaign long? No, sir. The blacks are docile by nature. They have been stirred up by unscrupulous agitators like this Toussaint. It is the Revolution in France which caused all this.
PÉTION	But the Revolution has been the salvation of France.

BULLET	Of course. Not so much the Revolution as the killing of the king. We had almost come to terms with them, but when they heard that the king had been guillotined, it ruined everything. That was a fatal mistake. Europeans should remember this. Have a revolution by all means, but never kill the king.
PÉTION	Sh! Here's one who will not agree with you.
BULLET	Who is that?
PÉTION	The Commander of our expedition. Leclerc, the First Consul's brother-in-law, with his wife.
BULLET	Ah, the sister who is more to the First Consul than Josephine.
PÉTION	Sh! You forget where you are.

(Enter Leclerc and his wife. Pétion salutes.)

LECLERC	Ah, M. Bullet. Madame Leclerc, allow me to present to you M. Bullet, one of the leading representatives of the exiled colonists. And this is General Pétion, the leader of the mulattoes.
PAULINE	I have seen General Pétion at a levee.
PÉTION	It is a distinction to be remembered by you, Madame. I look forward to a short and successful campaign under so accomplished a soldier as your husband. I am sure your army will fight all the more bravely because you accompany it.
BULLET	Your husband will not be long in putting those dogs back in their kennels. San Domingo was a beautiful place in the old days. We would have loved to entertain you there before those black barbarians took charge of the country. Balls, receptions, theatres—
LECLERC	We appreciate what you have suffered, M. Bullet. As soon as law and order are restored we shall form some sort of society there. Madame is looking forward to it.
PAULINE	I am indeed. Of course, one is sorry to leave Paris. But the Republic demands it. I think we shall be very dependent on the officers of the army, and the colonists too. You will do your duty on the field, and we shall strive to do ours off it. I am taking my

own musicians and artists, and my husband promises me that after these brigands have been crushed the first thing he will build is a good theatre.

BULLET   Madame, we had all those in the old days. Cap François was the Paris of the Antilles.

LECLERC   And will be again before very long, M. Bullet.

(An orderly comes up to Leclerc.)

ORDERLY   General Leclerc.

(Leclerc goes into the other room.)

PAULINE   The officers of the army must take care of themselves in battle, General Pétion.

BULLET   Madame, have no fear. With sixty grenadiers I could capture that black monkey, and without Louverture the blacks are a mob.

PAULINE   Are you a member of my husband's staff?

PÉTION   Yes, Madame. Formerly it was an honour to serve him. Now it will be a pleasure.

PAULINE   If you fight as well as you speak, General, you are a brave soldier.

PÉTION   The knights of old fought better at tournaments than on the field of battle, Madame.

(Bullet, neglected, wanders off and speaks to a soldier. Vincent continues his pacing.)

PAULINE   Who is that officer over there?

PÉTION   That is Colonel Vincent, *the* Colonel Vincent.

PAULINE   Ah! He is the officer who has brought Toussaint's constitution. But he looks a gallant soldier!

PÉTION   The gallant soldiers are either coming from San Domingo, Madame, or going there.

(The orderly goes up to Pauline and she gives her hand to Pétion who kisses it with pretended passion.)

ORDERLY   Madame Pauline Leclerc.

(Pauline goes in.)

ORDERLY   M. Bullet.

(Bullet goes in.)

ORDERLY   Colonel Vincent.

(Colonel Vincent goes in.)

(Enter Isaac and Placide, Toussaint's two sons, eighteen and nineteen years of age, respectively, and their tutor, Father Coignon.)

ORDERLY   This way please, gentlemen. *(Leads them offstage.)*

(After a distinct pause the lights go up on the large room. Bonaparte stands to one side. Behind him are grouped Leclerc, etc. Vincent stands solitary at the other end of the room.)

VINCENT   First Consul, God raised this Toussaint Louverture to govern. Not only does he read the hearts of his subjects but he masters affairs, and re-organises the administration of San Domingo with a boldness and success that astonish all men.

BONAPARTE   What miracles has he performed?

VINCENT   No miracles, sir, but he was a slave and rules a half-barbarous people. First among the rulers of the world he has introduced into his country the economic system of free trade, so that the commerce of the country leaps beyond all expectation.

LECLERC   Does the trade of France leap forward too?

BONAPARTE   Quiet, Leclerc. What else, Vincent?

VINCENT   Not only in commerce, but also in social relationships, this extraordinary Negro shows the breadth of his outlook and the elevation of his mind. He has introduced into San Domingo full religious toleration. He plans vast schemes for the education of his people. He sends Negroes to France to be trained at the public expense, to learn from us, in order to go back and teach.

BONAPARTE   To teach what? To teach blacks to rule over whites?

VINCENT	No, Consul. He appoints to a post whoever is fit for it, white, black or mulatto. All he asks is that they serve the country. And the planters are coming back and taking up their estates again, for they feel that they can trust him.
BONAPARTE	Trust him? With half a million black savages roaming wild on the countryside.
VINCENT	First Consul, Toussaint has pacified the labouring classes by a scheme as simple as it is bold. They are not paid in wages but they get a quarter of whatever they produce. If they are left in peace they will never revolt again.
BONAPARTE	You, Colonel Vincent, a French officer, dare to sponsor this document to me, not only to present it but to speak in its favour. General Louverture, Consul for life! A Negro who used to drive a coach daring to call himself Consul for life. His next step will be to proclaim the colony independent.
VINCENT	First Consul, the constitution does not claim independence. It swears allegiance to France. The Commander-in-Chief—
BONAPARTE	Do not speak to me of Commander-in-Chief—I shall not leave an epaulette on the shoulders of a single nigger in the colony.
VINCENT	First Consul, he means good faith. He has sent his sons here to be educated.
BONAPARTE	His sons! As if men let sons stand in the way of their ambition.
VINCENT	The English offered to make him King of San Domingo if he would form an alliance with them. He refused.
BONAPARTE	How do you know that?
VINCENT	Toussaint told me himself an hour after General Maitland made the offer.
BONAPARTE	He lied. The English made him no such offer. Would any man in his sense have refused that chance? You will be telling me next that the Americans offered him support and he refused that too.
VINCENT	He did, Consul.
BONAPARTE	He did, and perhaps, Colonel Vincent, both the British and

Americans offered him an alliance and he refused that too, out of loyalty to France, I suppose. Colonel Vincent, when the British Cabinet learnt of my plans it wanted to oppose them. I merely stated that I would clothe Toussaint with unlimited powers and recognise the colony's independence. That stopped their objections. They dare not have an independent black state so near their own slave colony of Jamaica.

VINCENT   If I may venture to say it, First Consul, there is a difference between a black state which they control, and a French colony to which the French government has given independence.

BONAPARTE   It does not matter. Toussaint shall have independence neither from the English nor from me. Leclerc will drive those black vagabonds into the mountains and in three months' time we shall have Toussaint here to account for his crimes and his impertinence.

VINCENT   Consul, I crave your indulgence. It is out of love for France that I speak. Toussaint was a slave and he leads an army of men who were slaves, but they are not to be despised.

LECLERC   They have no arms, they fight with sticks and stones.

VINCENT   Today they are well armed, they have large supplies of ammunition from America — they drill ceaselessly.

LECLERC   What leadership have they? Half the officers cannot read.

VINCENT   That is true. But they have been trained and seasoned by the almost continuous fighting of the last ten years.

BULLET   With sixty grenadiers I could capture that —

(*Bonaparte's gaze freezes Bullet into silence.*)

VINCENT   And at the head of these men, First Consul, is a man, the most active and tireless you can imagine. He is everywhere, and always at the spot where his presence is most needed. He is a man of extreme temperance, never needs rest, can resume the labours of the Cabinet after the most tiresome journeys, and his skill and power in mystifying everyone make him a man so superior to all around him, that most of the Negroes worship him like a god.

PÉTION	I know those blacks. At the first defeat they will leave him.
VINCENT	Not today. No man living has acquired over an ignorant mass such boundless power as General Toussaint over his people in San Domingo. He is the absolute master of the island. Nothing can counteract his wishes. An expedition from France, however powerful, will — will not have an easy task.
BONAPARTE	Colonel Vincent, you think that Toussaint and his black rebels can defeat the soldiers of Marengo?
VINCENT	Not that, First Consul. In Europe they could not stand before us. But the character of the country is difficult. These blacks know every inch of it. Then there is the climate — the yellow fever —
BONAPARTE	Tsk! The yellow fever. You suffer from a black fever, Vincent. So the English fleet, the country, the climate, and the yellow fever, all help these blacks and are leagued together to defeat my expedition? You forget, Colonel Vincent, that neither the sands and the burning sun of Egypt nor the snows of the Alps have been able to stay the victories of my army. You, a French officer, frightened at some black savages in gaudy uniforms. Officer! A guard!

(A guard of four soldiers comes in and forms behind Vincent. Meanwhile Pauline Leclerc has been whispering to her husband who refuses her entreaties by shaking his head decisively. She, Bonaparte's much too favourite sister, steps coquettishly forward.)

PAULINE	Brother, he talks stupidly, but he is a brave soldier and bears himself well. He knows San Domingo, he may be useful to us. He is only doing what he considers to be his duty, out of love for France.
BONAPARTE	His duty? He seems to think that his duty is to those rebel slaves who have been allowed to run riot too long. Do not meddle in these matters, sweet.
PAULINE	I leave you in a fortnight, brother. I shall not ask another favour of you for a long time. Do not arrest him. He will acknowledge that he is wrong.

(She plucks at Bonaparte's coat lapel.)

LECLERC   (*To Vincent*) There is one chance for you. Say that you did not wish the First Consul to underestimate the strength of the blacks. Ask to be allowed to serve on my staff. Say that you will be able to render valuable service to France and the expedition.

(*Pauline walks across to Vincent.*)

PAULINE   Colonel, speak to the Consul, confess your mistake.

(*She walks back to Bonaparte.*)

BONAPARTE   Well, Vincent.

VINCENT   (*After a look around*) First Consul, it is by your permission that I speak. I have served you and France faithfully and I request of you one last favour. Sir, delay this expedition for a few months.

(*Leclerc starts forward. Bonaparte restrains him with a gesture of the hand.*)

BONAPARTE   Go on, Vincent. Say all you have to say.

VINCENT   First Consul, if only you could see, as I have seen, the changes that he has wrought in one short year of power. Do not attack him. Give him a few years to consolidate his work. It may be the beginning of a new kind of colony. He is loyal to France and to you.

BONAPARTE   And at the same time intrigues with Britain and America.

VINCENT   Only for necessary supplies, Consul, which we couldn't send. If you refrained from sending an expedition against him, if instead you wrote him a few simple words of help and encouragement, in five years, Consul, there would be a new France in the Antilles, black in skin, but speaking French, thinking French, loving us because we have recognised their freedom and helped them out of the degradation of slavery into the enlightenment of liberty and civilisation.

LECLERC   What use will they be to us?

VINCENT   They will be French and yours, nothing will take them from you. And we shall have a colony, an army and generals which will make France the queen of the Antilles and break the power of Britain in those waters.

BONAPARTE   Give up San Domingo, abandon the fairest and richest prize of all the colonies to this upstart coachman. Those black devils have bewitched you. With such ideas you are not fit to serve in my army. You will know your fate soon. Take him away. The audience is finished. Leclerc, remain.

(Exit all except Bonaparte and Leclerc.)

Do not court-martial Vincent. We do not want too much publicity just at present. Banishment will be enough.

(He knocks on the table. Enter the orderly with Father Coignon and the two sons of Louverture.)

(Bonaparte rises to greet them.)

How are you, Father Coignon? And these are the two sons of our brave General Louverture.

(Father Coignon presents them.)

(With his hand on Isaac's shoulder) I have always had the most admirable reports of you, and I am glad to see you before you leave for home. Are you happy to return to San Domingo?

PLACIDE   Yes, sir. We have been away for over six years.

ISAAC   But we are sorry to leave France where everyone has been so kind to us.

BONAPARTE   They do you great credit, Father Coignon.

COIGNON   And themselves also, First Consul. I have never had better pupils.

ISAAC   And we could not have wished for a better tutor. We are glad that he is going to San Domingo with us.

BONAPARTE   You are anxious to be home as quickly as possible. I also often wish for my island home. Take the first possible boat. I shall give you a letter for your father. Take with it my warmest personal greetings to him and Christophe and Dessalines, all our brave brother officers in San Domingo.

ISAAC   We shall, sir.

BONAPARTE	And assure him that he must pay no attention to rumours that the expedition is directed against him. It is to make him stronger against the enemies of France.
ISAAC	We know that, First Consul.
BONAPARTE	Well, goodbye. Goodbye, Father Coignon. I shall try to see you again before you leave. I have ordered special uniforms for you as a personal gift from myself.
ISAAC	You overwhelm us with your kindness, First Consul.
BONAPARTE	No, it is too little. I wish I had time to do more. France will never forget what your father has done for her. A pleasant journey and a happy homecoming.

(Exit Coignon and the two Louvertures.)

BONAPARTE	These are your final instructions. Roughly the campaign will be divided into three periods. In the first, Toussaint shall be treated well, while you occupy the principal positions. In the second, gain over the black generals by bribes and promises, and then order Toussaint to come to Cap François and deliver himself.
LECLERC	I shall need much money.
BONAPARTE	Take it from the rich in San Domingo. In the third period arrest all the black generals and send them to Paris. If Toussaint is taken in arms shoot him as a rebel within twenty-four hours. Disarm the population, and then, but only then, restore slavery. Do you understand?
LECLERC	Restore slavery?
BONAPARTE	Of course. Do you think we went to the Congo and rooted out these blacks in order to make them into French citizens? That is a doctrine for priests and professors, not for officers in my colonial service. The Chamber of Commerce is pressing for the renewal of the slave trade. The country needs it.
LECLERC	Yes, First Consul.
BONAPARTE	Draft a letter to Toussaint, which I shall sign, and give it to

those boys. Address him with great honour. Tell him that he has served France faithfully. Tell him that the Constitution contains a few extravagances but that we recognise the difficult conditions under which he has produced it. In the letter, Leclerc, whenever possible, talk about religion and about God.

LECLERC   Yes, First Consul.

BONAPARTE   This expedition consists of thirty thousand men and sixty ships.

LECLERC   Yes, First Consul.

BONAPARTE   And the reserve?

LECLERC   Ten thousand men and twenty-six ships, First Consul.

BONAPARTE   Vincent is no fool, and those blacks are perhaps stronger than we think.

LECLERC   I don't think they are so strong.

BONAPARTE   Vincent spoke with conviction. Leclerc, take the reserve with the expedition. I shall have a reserve of equal strength prepared. That gives you forty thousand men and eighty-six ships. Toussaint has no ships and only sixteen thousand men, and black rebels at that. If you play your cards well, six weeks after you land San Domingo will be French and yours.

Curtain.

Act III   SCENE 1

Toussaint's hut in the mountains. Early 1802. Madame Louverture is sitting between her sons and General Christophe and Father Coignon.

COIGNON   Madame Louverture, you are thrice fortunate in such a husband and such sons.

MADAME L   General Louverture and I will always be grateful to you, Father Coignon. Oh, I wish Toussaint could come.

ISAAC   If he could come and hear our message all this trouble would

	be over. General Christophe, the First Consul spoke not only of father, but of you and General Dessalines and all his brave brother generals of San Domingo.
CHRISTOPHE	Yet his brother-in-law is devastating the country and calling on all of us to give up our arms and be shot as traitors.
COIGNON	It is all a misunderstanding, General. When you burnt Cap François General Leclerc had no alternative.
ISAAC	You might have waited, General Christophe.
CHRISTOPHE	General Leclerc should have waited. I carried out the orders of the Commander-in-Chief. He instructed us to tear up the roads with shot; throw corpses and horses into all the fountains; burn and destroy everything rather than surrender.
MADAME L	My sons, what a homecoming this is for you!
ISAAC	Only let father meet General Leclerc. The General will easily convince him of the love of the First Consul and of all France for San Domingo.
PLACIDE	Why does he tell his generals to destroy the country, General Christophe—his own country, our country?
CHRISTOPHE	Because he and all of us agree rather death than slavery.
PLACIDE	Slavery!
COIGNON	Do not mention the word, my son. The First Consul does not for one moment—
MADAME L	He is coming.

(Enter Toussaint.)

TOUSSAINT	My sons. *(Embraces them.)* Suzanne. *(They embrace.)*

(He stands holding Isaac; Madame L. holds Placide.)

	But your tutor. *(He turns to Coignon and stretches out his arms to him.)* Father.
COIGNON	Wait, General Louverture. The father should remember that he is in arms against the very Government which has educated

	his sons and now sends them back to him. Let them plead with their father for the cause of peace.
TOUSSAINT	My sons to plead with me for Leclerc!
COIGNON	Isaac, speak to your father.

(Isaac hesitates.)

TOUSSAINT	Speak, my son.
ISAAC	Father, General Leclerc has not come to San Domingo to bring war. He is waiting anxiously to see you, to welcome you and bring this unhappy strife to an end.
TOUSSAINT	Who brings peace with an army of forty thousand men?
ISAAC	Father, it is because General Christophe treated him as an enemy, opposed his landing, and burnt Cap François rather than let him occupy it.
CHRISTOPHE	I asked him for time to let me inform the Commander-in-Chief. He refused.
TOUSSAINT	Christophe obeys my orders.
ISAAC	Father, he means peace. If only you would see him, he will prove it to you.
COIGNON	You have read the First Consul's letter, General Louverture?
TOUSSAINT	Yes, breathing peace, while General Leclerc's cannon bellows war.
PLACIDE	Father, declare a truce and see General Leclerc.
TOUSSAINT	Only generals in danger of defeat declare a truce. In the face of an attacking army I cannot forget that I carry a sword.
PLACIDE	The First Consul feels only goodwill and gratitude to you.
TOUSSAINT	He shows it in a strange way. Why did I not receive this letter before?
PLACIDE	There was no boat. We had to wait and come with General Leclerc.

COIGNON	From the first hour of landing General Leclerc has been striving his utmost to get into touch with you. He wants you to hold the office of Lieutenant-General by his side.
TOUSSAINT	Even before he meets me I am declared a traitor to my country, unless I place myself and my army in his power.
PLACIDE	Father—
TOUSSAINT	Wait, my son. I, a traitor, who delivered my country from the Spaniards and the British, restored it to prosperity, established order and justice. And now the First Consul sends my sons to lure me to my downfall.
COIGNON	To be the ambassadors of reconciliation.
TOUSSAINT	If Leclerc means peace, let him cease trying to capture the strategic points of the colony.
ISAAC	Father. Unless you submit, it will mean ruin for all of us.
TOUSSAINT	If he gets me into his power it will mean slavery for all San Domingo. This huge expedition can mean nothing else. Your First Consul insults me while I still have power; what would he do to me when my hands are tied?
COIGNON	Take care, General Louverture, lest from personal ambition, you lead your family and your country to destruction.

(He looks at Christophe.)

TOUSSAINT	I have no future without the trust and confidence of the people of San Domingo. It is they who have made me what I am, and not the First Consul. My sons, today when I see you for the first time after all these years of separation, a day that should be all gladness and rejoicing, I have to put a bitter choice before you. You are my sons, I can keep you. But I shall not.
MADAME L	Toussaint—

(He signals silence to her.)

| TOUSSAINT | Here is San Domingo, your father, your mother, your own people. There is France which has educated you and made you what you now are. You seem to think that the First Consul and |

Leclerc mean peace and goodwill. I shall resist them for I know that their victory over us means slavery. You are now men. You must trust to your own judgement. Choose, my sons, choose freely. Whatever you decide I shall always love and cherish you.

MADAME L   Toussaint, declare a truce for two days only and go and meet Leclerc.

ISAAC   Father, go and see him. The First Consul assured us of his love and regard for you.

PLACIDE   If you had been there, Father, all this would not have happened. If we set out now we shall meet him by tomorrow evening. Think of what it will mean, not only to us, but to the soldiers and the whole population.

COIGNON   General Christophe, add your entreaties.

CHRISTOPHE   I shall do what the Commander-in-Chief decides.

TOUSSAINT   No, my sons. You must choose. Have no fear. Whatever you decide, you shall always remain my deeply loved children.

ISAAC   Father, I think you are wrong. I am a faithful servant of France, as you taught me to be. I believe that she is just. I shall never take up arms against her without good cause.

(Madame L sobs. Toussaint puts his arm around her.)

TOUSSAINT   I could have wished that you, Isaac, had chosen otherwise. And you, Placide?

PLACIDE   I am yours, father. I fear the future—I fear slavery—I am ready to fight to oppose it. I no longer know France.

TOUSSAINT   Tonight you shall be appointed a commander in my own guards. Father Coignon, I shall give you a letter to General Leclerc in which he shall know my decision.

MADAME L   Isaac.

TOUSSAINT   No, Suzanne, come.

(Exit Toussaint, Madame L, and Placide.)

ISAAC   Father, what have I done?

COIGNON	You have acted according to your conscience and your duty as a citizen of France.
ISAAC	But if the First Consul does try to restore slavery after he has trapped Father?
COIGNON	You will then be absolved from any oath you have sworn and will be free to act as you please.
CHRISTOPHE	It might then be too late.
COIGNON	You need have no fear. The First Consul is ruler and representative of the great state of France and his word is his bond. General Christophe, I have heard much of you, and General Leclerc regrets that he was not able to procure an interview with you before you burnt Cap François.
CHRISTOPHE	He could have waited.
COIGNON	It was an act which I am sure you regret. General Leclerc was anxious to meet you. He knows your reputation—not only as a soldier, but as one accomplished in the arts of peace—by far the most cultured of all the black generals, and the one most devoted to French civilisation.
CHRISTOPHE	Not when it seeks to take away our liberties.
COIGNON	There you follow your general. For eight years slavery has been · abolished. Is the First Consul a madman to seek to reimpose that yoke on all these thousands? Such an attempt would be doomed to failure.
CHRISTOPHE	Toussaint is convinced that once the army is defeated the attempt will be made.
COIGNON	General Christophe, your Commander-in-Chief is a great man who has rendered valuable services to France, but he has drunk deep of unchecked power. And unchecked power corrupts and destroys. Unconsciously he has identified his own position with the safety of his people. His personal domination of San Domingo is threatened. But the liberties of the people are not. To preserve the one he may sacrifice the other and bring down all who blindly support him in a common ruin, men per-

haps who, if they resisted his disloyalty, and continued to serve France, might rise to the highest honours under the First Consul and be themselves the guardians of their people's liberty. Think well, General Christophe. The future of this beautiful island, the lives of thousands of its inhabitants, rest with you. If at any time you should wish to see General Leclerc, he would welcome you with open arms. (*He takes one of Christophe's hands in his.*) My blessing on you, my son. I know that it is a difficult decision for you to make. But God, I am sure, will not deny you his guidance.

(*Christophe sits staring in front of him.*)

Slow curtain.

SCENE 2

March 24th, 1802. About six o'clock in the evening. The fortress of Crête-à-Pierrot in San Domingo. On a rampart, running diagonally across the stage, stands Toussaint. During the first part of the scene he walks from one side to the other. At one end of the rampart is a flag-staff. In the courtyard are soldiers, cannon, etc.

Enter Capt. Verny, aide-de-camp to Toussaint, with writing materials in his hand. He climbs up to the ledge below Toussaint.

VERNY   Ready, General.

TOUSSAINT   (*Speaking half to himself, and with his eyes glued to the glasses*) How long will he wait? It is time for the retreat. He should have started—at least ten minutes. (*He consults a watch and again looks long through the glasses.*) It is time. It is time.

VERNY   But didn't he begin to give way five minutes ago?

TOUSSAINT   Yes. He is giving way, but too slowly. Faster, faster, give way faster and then run. I told him: Run early. That will bring them on. Then stop and pretend to make a stand. (*He continues to look through the glasses.*) Turn and run—turn and run. If he fights them too hard they will not follow fast enough and all will be ruined.

(He turns round to Verny, but keeps looking through his glasses at short intervals. There are distant sounds of firing.)

A letter to General Christophe, copy to General Dessalines. Tell him that this is the twenty-first day of the siege. Tell him that we are reduced to seven hundred men. Tell him that we can make our food and water last three or four days, perhaps a week. Ah, they are giving way now, but still not fast enough. Does Antoine think I sent him there to enjoy himself? *(To Verny)* Tell Christophe that in seven days we have beaten off three attacks. *(Sounds of musket-shots.)* Ah! We are running at last. Tell him that they have begun to pound the fortress with heavy artillery. They are coming now. I cannot see Antoine.

TRUMPETER   He is behind, sir.

TOUSSAINT   He should be in the front leading the retreat. Tell Christophe that the men suffer, but they will die rather than surrender. Tell him that every day Leclerc sends messages to me promising everything if only I will declare a truce and join him. I've told him that I shall hang the next messenger who comes. Tell him that we shall leave the fortress only when it falls to pieces around us. Give warm greetings to Christophe and to Dessalines. Tell Christophe I know he will hold Mornay as we shall hold Crête-à-Pierrot.

(Exit Verny.)

Ah, here they come. How eagerly the fools follow. Not too fast, blacks. They may suspect. Antoine should stop and—Ah! he does it. *(Volley of shots. Toussaint puts down his glasses.)* Brave Antoine. Now run again. Trumpeter! Sound the attention.

(The trumpeter sounds a call.)

Brave blacks! Into the ditch, blacks, into the ditch. *(To the trumpeter)* Sound the ready. In, in, in. Down, you stragglers, down. *(To the trumpeter)* Sound the fire.

(The trumpeter sounds a call, and there is a roar of musketry from the fortress. Toussaint seizes a gun himself and fires. Hands the gun to the trumpeter to reload and fires another.)

TOUSSAINT They scatter like flies.

(There is the continuous rattle of musketry from the fortress.)

Good shooting. Rake them down — rake them down. How they run. Trumpeter, sound the cease-fire and then the counter-attack. Run up the red flag. No quarter.

(The red flag goes up.) (He shouts below:) The Third Regiment by the north-west door. Ladders and planks for those in the ditch. Ladders and planks.

TRUMPETER Ladders and planks.

(There is great activity below.)

TOUSSAINT How they run! Ah, if I had a division here, how many of you would get back home?

(Enter Verny.)

Verny, they are in full retreat. Four hundred dead at least. Put it in the letter. And be quick — it will be dark in half an hour. This is the time for the messenger to go.

(Enter Captain Antoine, followed by a bedraggled soldier.)

Ah, Antoine. *(To Trumpeter, handing him the glasses.)* Keep guard. *(He descends and embraces Antoine.)* Good work, Antoine. You should have started the retreat before. But all is well. How they fell into it.

Who is this?

ANTOINE He comes from Christophe with dispatches.

(Antoine hands them to Toussaint, who gives them to Verny, and Verny begins to read.)

TOUSSAINT General Christophe still holds Mornay?

SOLDIER Yes, General.

TOUSSAINT Good. And he is well?

SOLDIER Yes, General.

TOUSSAINT	Good. When did you get through the French lines?
SOLDIER	Last night, sir. I've been hiding all day, waiting for dark.
TOUSSAINT	Brave Negro. Give him food and water.

(There is an exclamation from Verny.)

What is it, Verny? Read it.

VERNY	*(After a brief hesitation and a glance at Toussaint)* "19th March 1802. To General Louverture, Commander-in-Chief. From General Christophe. Greetings. For many weeks now I have been receiving letters from General Leclerc, asking me to begin negotiations with him-"
TOUSSAINT	Yes—
VERNY	"After many requests and repeated pledges of good faith from him I consented to have an interview with the Captain-General—"
TOUSSAINT	What!
VERNY	"—And I have agreed to enter his service as the last means of safeguarding our liberties."
TOUSSAINT	Give it to me. Then it is a trick. Ah, you dog! *(He catches the messenger by the throat.)* The Frenchman bribed you. You said Mornay was safe. You said Christophe was well. *(He lets go the throat, but holds the man and shakes him.)* Answer. *(The messenger cannot reply. Toussaint lets him go and he falls to the ground.)* But it is a trick Christophe is playing—to take him unawares and surprise him and massacre his soldiers.
VERNY	No, General. There are letters also from General Christophe's secretary. General Christophe is still at Mornay with all his soldiers, but there are French regiments there now, and he holds the town for General Leclerc.
TOUSSAINT	Go, all of you—leave me. Take this carcass away.

(Exit all. Toussaint mounts the ladder.)

Christophe gone—deceived by the Frenchman. Ah God! That

I had them both in my hands. They would never deceive again. Ah, Christophe! Christophe! To join the Frenchman. But it is not true — it cannot be true. It is a trick. The lying Frenchman tries to deceive . . . If Mornay is gone then the armies are lost and Negroes slaves again.

(The guns begin to boom. Toussaint climbs to the top of the ledge and stands silhouetted against the night sky dotted with stars.)

Ay. Shoot — shoot. You have taken Mornay but you will not take Crête-à-Pierrot. You will not take Limbé. You will not take Dondon. *(Gun sounds.)* Ay. Shoot. We burnt Cap François. We shall burn Port-au-Prince. We shall destroy San Domingo — make it a desert. Our bones will be your slaves. Yes, you deceived Christophe, but you will not deceive Dessalines — you will not deceive Maurepas. If Mornay is gone than the armies are lost and Negroes slaves again.

(Enter Verny.)

VERNY   Sir, we have questioned the messenger. Limbé, Dondon — all are gone. Our soldiers hold them, but they have all entered Leclerc's service.

TOUSSAINT   Mornay! Limbé! Dondon! All gone.

VERNY   All, sir.

TOUSSAINT   Then we are cut off. The whites will never leave us — never. Black skin cursed by God — white God, black God. Same flesh, same blood, but black skin — born to be slaves. Oh, my people! To sweat in the sun in the white man's field — to cook the white man's food — to groom the white man's horse — to clean the white man's shoes. They will never leave us — never. Oh, Christophe! Christophe! If Mornay is gone the armies are cut off, and Negroes slaves again.

VERNY   If we go on we shall be destroyed. If we accept his terms at least we shall have arms to defend our liberty.

TOUSSAINT   Surrender! — and have others decide our fate.

Curtain.

SCENE 3

Late in 1802. Leclerc's villa on the outskirts of Cap François. Sitting on the balcony are Madame Leclerc and Suzanne, her mulatto companion. Pauline, like Suzanne, is dressed in the local costume.

Enter Pétion and General Lemmonier-Delafosse.

PAULINE   General Pétion, thank heaven the war is over. I am going to give a grand ball to celebrate the peace. Now what will this ball be? It must be either a linen ball or a muslin ball.

SUZANNE   Let us have another Creole ball, Madame.

PAULINE   No, I have been wearing Creole for the past week. What do you think, General Pétion? It must be either linen or muslin. Now which shall it be? Suzanne, get me a fan.

(Suzanne goes out.)

PÉTION   *(Moving close to Pauline)* It depends on the one you are wearing at the time.

PAULINE   Flatterer! We shall have a muslin ball.

PÉTION   Or better still, two balls, Madame. A muslin ball and then a linen ball.

PAULINE   Pétion, you are marvellous. But which shall we have first? Ah, I know who will help us. General Delafosse, where is that young officer who danced so well last Saturday? You remember him? He has a mole on his right check.

DELAFOSSE   His regiment is burying him this afternoon, Madame.

PAULINE   Burying him? Good God!

DELAFOSSE   The yellow fever does not respect anyone, not even those who can decide whether the first ball should be linen or muslin.

PAULINE   What a dreadful place this is. Anyway, we shall be able to overcome the disease now that the war is over.

DELAFOSSE   The war is not yet over, Madame.

PAULINE	But it is. My husband told me that Toussaint is coming to sign the terms of peace today. Isn't that so, Pétion?
PÉTION	Not exactly to sign, Madame, but to discuss signing.
PAULINE	But he has no soldiers, no army, and his best men have left him—Christophe and many others.
PÉTION	If the Captain-General promises not to re-establish slavery, Toussaint will sign. That is why Christophe came.
PAULINE	Of course the General will promise.
DELAFOSSE	Christophe told the Captain-General that if he or any other general thought for one moment that slavery would be restored they would all join those bands of brigands who swear that they will never give up their arms. . . . But I bore you, Madame, with these matters. Toussaint is certainly coming and you may be sure that you will be able to give your ball next week.

(Suzanne rushes in.)

SUZANNE	Madame, Toussaint is coming. His bodyguard is with him. They are marching through the city with swords drawn.
PAULINE	With swords drawn!
DELAFOSSE	There is no need to be afraid, Madame.
PAULINE	I am not afraid. But people who come to sue for peace do not come with drawn swords.
SUZANNE	Madame, may I go? The whole city is out to see him come in. He rides at the head of the troops and the band is playing the *Ça Ira* and the *Marseillaise*.
PAULINE	*(Slightly hysterical)* The *Marseillaise*? That is the song of the Republic.
SUZANNE	But it is our song, too, Madame.
PAULINE	Your song?
SUZANNE	But, yes, Madame. When we fought for freedom we sang those songs. The revolutionaries in France sang them and we sang

them too. We made our songs but always our soldiers march to the *Marseillaise*.

PAULINE   But that is impertinence. They have no right, the black savages.

DELAFOSSE   Do you think that if they were savages we would have so much trouble to subdue them? I have seen a column torn by shot from four pieces of cannon march on a redoubt and not make a single retrograde step.

(In the distance, faint but growing stronger, is the sound of music and a low murmur. Only Suzanne seems to hear, however.)

They advanced singing. Three times they approached, arms in their hands but not drawing a shot, and each time, repulsed, they retired, leaving hundreds of men on the field. The song they sang was thrown into the air by two thousand voices singing in unison, and the roar of the cannons formed the bass.

SUZANNE   This was the song.

(Suzanne steps forward and sings, and the music in the distance faintly present hitherto comes through clearly to accompany her.)

To the attack, grenadier!
Who gets killed, that's his affair,
Forget your Pa, forget your Ma,
To the attack, grenadier!

(Suzanne sings it through twice.)

DELAFOSSE   That was the song. None who fought against them that day, Madame, thinks of them as black savages.

(The Marseillaise *continues, growing louder. The band and soldiers are approaching.)*

That masses square! Marching to death! Gaily singing! Lighted by the magnificent sun! Years have passed, but today as always, that imposing and grandiose picture returns to my imagination as vividly as in the first instant.

(The music is now quite near. The company on the balcony retires, and Toussaint and his soldiers march in, the band off stage coming to a great climax. The soldiers draw up on both sides of the steps where they remain with swords drawn. Toussaint

walks slowly up the steps, followed by Placide and Verny, and is met by Delafosse. A few seconds later Leclerc rushes out and throws himself into the arms of Toussaint.)

LECLERC   Welcome, General. This is a great day for me, for both of us. Let me say how your coming here impresses me as a proof of your good faith and your magnanimity. I see you have your guard with you.

TOUSSAINT   I was coming alone. They refused to leave me.

(Toussaint stands silent, looking at Leclerc.)

LECLERC   General, this reconciliation which you now ratify will restore prosperity to the Colony. We shall consolidate the present institutions of San Domingo, for these institutions are the fundamental basis of the liberty and the happiness of all.

TOUSSAINT   General Leclerc, when the people of San Domingo fought in a war for the benefit of France, they never thought that they would ever have to resist their natural protector.

LECLERC   Let us forget the past. All shall be repaired. General, let us rejoice at our union. My wife, the generals and officers of the army who are here, must be witnesses of our common gladness.

(He throws open the folding doors. Enter Pauline with Suzanne, Delafosse, Pétion, and two French officers.)

            My friends, this is General Toussaint Louverture. This, General, is my wife, Pauline, sister of the First Consul. She has long wished to meet the famous soldier of San Domingo whose fame and exploits are household words in France. The others—the others you know. *(Bowing, etc.)* General, we cannot but praise and admire you when we think how well you have borne the burden of the government of San Domingo. Yet after all these years you must require some help. I propose that you hold the office of Lieutenant-General of the island.

TOUSSAINT   I shall hold no office. The moment this matter is settled I go into retirement.

LECLERC   But, General—

TOUSSAINT   Nothing will change my mind.

LECLERC	As you say. I swear to employ your officers according to rank. I shall appoint the brave General Dessalines as head of the police department in the North. *(Applause)* And the equally brave General Christophe head of the police department in the West. *(Applause. Toussaint stands waiting. There is a pause. Then Leclerc continues.)* And I swear before the face of the Supreme Being to respect the liberties of the people of San Domingo.
TOUSSAINT	General Leclerc, I have come to terms with you because to continue the war means only a further destruction of my country. I am, as you know, still powerful enough to burn, ravish, and lay waste, but it is my own country that I destroy, the country which we Negroes have fought so hard to set on its feet again. You have sworn a solemn oath to respect the liberties of my people.
LECLERC	I swear it on the honour of a French Officer.
TOUSSAINT	That was all I was fighting for. I withdraw, but if at any time those liberties are threatened, I hold myself free to break my oath, and I know that those brave and honest men whom you have taken into your service, and who will serve you faithfully, will never forget the watchword of every son of San Domingo — liberty or death. Tomorrow night I sleep in my own plantation at Ennery where I shall be if at any time you require me.
LECLERC	And your son — he will have a bright future with us.
PLACIDE	I go with my father.
TOUSSAINT	I must leave now.
LECLERC	Surely, General, you can stay with us for a while.
TOUSSAINT	It is impossible. My army is awaiting the signal for ratification. I am anxious for peace and to be relieved of the cares of state.

(He walks over to his soldiers.)

Let the messengers go to Mornay at once. Take this. *(Gives a ring. Two soldiers leave.)*

Soldiers, I address you for the last time. Slavery will not be restored in San Domingo. The General has sworn in the name of the Supreme Being to respect the liberties of our people. Every officer will be re-employed without loss of rank. For myself, I go into retirement of my own free will.

Soldiers, it is now ten years since we have been comrades on the battlefield. We have done many great things together. I must thank you for the courage, love, and devotion which you have always shown me. Now I have nothing more to give you. I leave with you the best of myself — our common memories. Nothing can take those from us.

(Toussaint descends the remaining steps to the courtyard, and stands looking at the men. An officer sheathes his sword and steps forward, taking off his hat, showing a grey head. Tears roll down his cheeks.)

OFFICER   General, is it over?

(He and Toussaint embrace. Toussaint embraces another officer.)

TOUSSAINT   Tell the others what I have told you. Farewell.

(Toussaint salutes. The band strikes up "To the Attack, Grenadiers," and the soldiers march off.)

(Enter servants with wine. Isaac enters.)

PAULINE   General Louverture, you will take some refreshment with us before you go?

TOUSSAINT   Thank you, Madame. I will have a glass of water.

(They drink. Leclerc, etc., go inside, leaving Delafosse, Toussaint, and his two sons.)

ISAAC   It is all settled, father?

TOUSSAINT   I hope so, Isaac. I am going to Ennery. You will come and see us there, my son?

ISAAC   Of course, father.

DELAFOSSE   How will you spend your retirement, General?

TOUSSAINT   Farming. I shall superintend the work in the fields, repair buildings, cultivate the land, and improve the plantation. I shall have time now to entertain my friends, exchange visits, pay some attention to the domestic side of life — enjoy the company of my family. I have not had much time during the last ten years.

(While he is speaking French soldiers with fixed bayonets begin to appear in various parts of the courtyard, and advance slowly towards him. Toussaint, unsuspecting, continues.)

I shall be happy to entertain you and your friends.

(He catches sight of the soldiers; he and Placide draw their swords.)

ISAAC   General, what is it?

DELAFOSSE   General Louverture, we are not making an attempt on your life. Nor shall we do you any injustice or indignity. We merely have orders to safeguard your person.

TOUSSAINT   For what purpose?

DELAFOSSE   To send you to France. You are too dangerous to stay here.

ISAAC   Father!

PLACIDE   You French traitors!

(Soldiers surround Toussaint, separating him from his two sons. Others seize Placide and Isaac.)

DELAFOSSE   Your own black generals have told us that they cannot guarantee the peace of the country as long as you are in it.

TOUSSAINT   My own officers!

DELAFOSSE   Your own officers. How else could we dare to arrest you?

TOUSSAINT   They hope to save their properties and their rank. Fools! You can deceive them, General. But you cannot deceive those hundreds of thousands who have won their freedom. Do with me what you will. In destroying me you destroy only the trunk. But the tree of Negro liberty will flourish again, for its roots are many and deep.

Curtain.

SCENE 4

Late in 1802. Toussaint's cell in a prison in the Alps. Toussaint is in the far corner. Before the curtain rises Toussaint is heard singing hymns with Mars Plaisir.

MARS	Master, it's getting very cold.
TOUSSAINT	Here! Put this on, Mars.
MARS	No, master, you must feel it too.
TOUSSAINT	No, come here. Put it on.

(As Toussaint wraps the coat around Mars, Mars weeps.)

TOUSSAINT	Come my good Mars, no tears.
MARS	Master, they gave us no news.
TOUSSAINT	They give no news because they cannot crush the revolution.
MARS	But, master, the mistress and the children.
TOUSSAINT	God help them. I shall never see them again — perhaps never hear from them. But if I could only hear one word from San Domingo! Here they come. Be brave.

(Enter Governor Baille and two assistant-gaolers.)

BAILLE	Here is your food.
TOUSSAINT	Thank you.
BAILLE	Get on with it at once. Quickly. There is much to be done today.
TOUSSAINT	Is there any news for me?
BAILLE	Come on. Eat first.
TOUSSAINT	Commandant, if there is news of my wife and children, will you let me know? Has the First Consul sent a reply to my petition?
BAILLE	I have had instructions from the First Consul. But eat your food first.
TOUSSAINT	I do not want any food.
BAILLE	Very well. You, come on.

(One gaoler produces chains.)

TOUSSAINT What has he done?

BAILLE Everything. Treason and rebellion. He must leave you today. He is going to another prison.

(Mars begins to weep.)

MARS Master!

TOUSSAINT Mars, you must submit.

(Toussaint and Mars embrace.)

TOUSSAINT But why the chains?

BAILLE I cannot answer any more questions.

(The chains are put on Mars.)

TOUSSAINT Goodbye, Mars. We may never meet again. If perhaps you see my wife and children, carry my last farewells to them. I wish I could console you. I shall always remember your services and your devotion. *(He holds Mars by both shoulders.)* And know, Mars, that we have not suffered in vain. Our cause will conquer in the end. If you get a chance to send it, that is my last message to our people.

MARS Goodbye, Master.

BAILLE Take him away. *(Exit gaolers with Mars.)* And now you are to have a visitor.

TOUSSAINT A visitor! From the First Consul? He brings news—

BAILLE How can I know what news he brings? But he comes from the First Consul. He is General Caffarelli, the First Consul's aide-de-camp.

(Toussaint is not listening to him. Trembling though he is his spirits have risen, and he stands waiting.)

(Enter General Caffarelli.)

BAILLE This is the prisoner, General. Toussaint, this is General Caffarelli, aide-de-camp to the First Consul.

(Toussaint bows.)

CAFFARELLI   General Louverture, I bring you a message from the First Consul.

TOUSSAINT   General, before everything, I implore you, give me some news of my wife and sons. I have been here many months and have never heard a single word about them.

CAFFARELLI   I am sorry. I know nothing about your family, but I daresay I may be able to find out something later. I come on an errand of special importance.

TOUSSAINT   What is it? I am willing to answer all questions and I can prove my innocence.

CAFFARELLI   The First Consul has learnt from many sources that just before General Leclerc's arrival you secreted forty million francs in the Cahos Mountains in San Domingo. He wants you to tell me where that treasure was hidden.

TOUSSAINT   Is that all?

(He turns away. His head falls and he goes slowly to his seat by the fire and sinks into it.)

CAFFARELLI   Tell me the hiding place, General. And I shall do my utmost to help your cause with the First Consul.

TOUSSAINT   *(Shivering)* I hid no treasure.

CAFFARELLI   General, didn't you shoot the six Negroes who had carried the treasure into the mountains?

TOUSSAINT   It is a slanderous lie.

CAFFARELLI   What secret negotiations did you make with England about independence?

TOUSSAINT   I made none.

CAFFARELLI   General, this obstinacy will do you no good. The First Consul has charged me to get the information from you. If I go back without it things will go bad with you.

TOUSSAINT   They could not go worse.

BAILLE	He is as cunning as an old fox. He quarrels about his wife and his children and his money and his watch, but as soon as you ask him one word about politics he becomes dumb. What you want is a whipping, you old snake.
TOUSSAINT	(Rising, and for a moment recovering all his strength) This is too much. I have incurred the wrath of the First Consul, but as to fidelity and probity, I am strong in my conscience. Among all the servants of the state none is more honest than myself.
CAFFARELLI	You were a traitor.
TOUSSAINT	Would a traitor have saved the colony from Spain and Britain? I was one of his soldiers and the first servant of the Republic in San Domingo; I could have been king of a free island—now I am ruined, dishonoured, wretched, a victim of my own services.

(As he speaks Toussaint becomes gradually exhausted. He finally staggers to his chair and crumples into it, mumbling to himself.)

BAILLE	That is the end. You will get nothing more from him today. Sometimes he sits like that for days.

(Goes to Toussaint and shakes him.)

Toussaint! Toussaint! General Louverture! I have some news about your wife and children.

(Toussaint makes no response.)

It's no use.

CAFFARELLI	How long has he been like this?
BAILLE	For weeks now. He comes and goes. But he won't die. We have cut down his food, cut down his fuel. But he won't die. He is as tough as leather. Every week messages from the First Consul come saying that he must not escape, and pressing for more rigorous treatment. We must see him eat his food. We must watch him perform his natural functions. We must spy on him. The old black is beginning to get on my nerves too. I dream of the black devil and wake at night and cannot go back to sleep

for thinking of him. It would be easier for everybody if he were murdered outright.

CAFFARELLI But I must take some sort of answer back to the First Consul. (*Going over to Toussaint and shaking him.*) Pull yourself together, man, and speak. If you don't tell me where those francs are you will never see your wife and children again. And the First Consul will restore slavery in San Domingo.

(*Toussaint slowly raises his head.*)

Yes. The First Consul will restore slavery in San Domingo. Do you hear? Slavery.

TOUSSAINT (*Still sitting on his chair but slowly recovering*) Slavery in San Domingo? No. The First Consul can never restore slavery in San Domingo. No one will ever do that again.

CAFFARELLI The army is defeated; only a remnant remains.

TOUSSAINT You can defeat an army, but you cannot defeat a people in arms. Do you think an army could drive those hundreds of thousands back into the fields? You have got rid of one leader. But there are two thousand other leaders to be got rid of as well, and two thousand more when those are killed.

CAFFARELLI Whom do you think you are talking to? I shall put you in chains.

TOUSSAINT I wouldn't wear them long. You have tried to break my spirit and use me against my own people. But the more you tortured me here, the more I was certain that you were failing there. There is little you can do to me now. (*His voice sinks.*) Slavery in San Domingo? Never — never —

(*He sinks back exhausted into his chair.*)

CAFFARELLI (*To Baille*) You are right — it's no use. Go away for four days and forget to leave the key. Come.

(*They go off. The clock strikes three. The stage goes dark, and gradually lightens again. Toussaint is still huddled in his chair. After a few moments the clock strikes three again. At the first stroke he holds up his head. By the third he has risen to his feet.*)

TOUSSAINT	(*Loudly and clearly*) Oh, Dessalines! Dessalines! You were right after all!

(*He falls to the floor.*)

Curtain.

SCENE 5

May 1803. The large dining hall in the semi-official Hotel de la République, Cap François. Leclerc, Pauline, Pétion, Lemmonier-Delafosse, and a young French officer. Leclerc is nervous and on the verge of a breakdown. He wipes his forehead often.

LECLERC	It is the guns. If they did not have the guns I could make the attempt. But the whole population is armed. You can defeat an army, but how can you defeat a people in arms?
PAULINE	But can't you get the guns away?
DELAFOSSE	We have tried, Madame. But they repeat like parrots: "Whoever wants to take our guns away wants to restore slavery." Toussaint told them that, and nothing can get it out of their heads.
LECLERC	The First Consul is too impatient.
DELAFOSSE	To call for this decree now — in the position we are.
LECLERC	We shall have to destroy all the mountain Negroes, and half the Negroes of the plains. Without these measures the colony will never be at peace.
PAULINE	But haven't we won all the battles? Haven't all the leaders made peace?
LECLERC	For every leader who comes to us a hundred spring up elsewhere.
PAULINE	That General Dessalines — he would murder us all if he got the chance. I can see it in his eyes. Why not arrest the two of them tonight the moment they come, Captain-General? My brother wouldn't hesitate.

LECLERC   No, we cannot do that at present. We lack money and reinforcements.

(Leclerc falters and leans on the table.)

PAULINE   What is it?

LECLERC   Nothing—the heat. A glass of water.

(The young officer hastily pours a glass and hands it to him. Leclerc drinks and stands upright, obviously trying to take control of himself.)

> I saw the doctor's returns this morning. In seven regiments two-thirds of the men are down with the fever. To have it means death in almost every case.

(Enter Servant.)

SERVANT   General Dessalines and General Christophe.

(Enter Dessalines and Christophe. Greetings are exchanged.)

CHRISTOPHE   I trust that the Captain-General is well.

LECLERC   Quite well, I assure you.

(Wine is served. Dessalines tosses off his glass almost at a mouthful, and before he can hand it back the young officer fills it again. Dessalines drinks a second time.)

DESSALINES   Captain-General, I hear that the First Consul has restored slavery in Martinique and Guadaloupe. Have you heard that?

LECLERC   Some faint rumour has reached me.

DESSALINES   *(Looking at Pétion)* And that mulattoes are to lose all social and political rights.

PÉTION   That is not true.

(He looks at Leclerc.)

LECLERC   Of course not.

(The young officer again attempts to fill Dessalines' glass. Dessalines turns and in sudden fury dashes the decanter from the officer's hand. Meanwhile Pétion has slipped quietly away.)

DESSALINES   You little white worm! Make me drunk and I shall drink your blood and your general's too.

LECLERC   General! You are insolent. Do you wish to be arrested?

DESSALINES   Call your guard. My guard is here and Christophe's, both under arms. With one word I can make you, all of you, prisoners.

PAULINE   You traitors! General Pétion!

(She turns to look for him.)

LECLERC   Where is Pétion?

PAULINE   But he was here—

LECLERC   Another traitor.

DESSALINES   Treachery! You—Captain-General—you speak of treachery. Listen. Toussaint said "Stay with the French." I stay. But make the attempt to restore slavery in San Domingo, and in that hour I call on every black in the country, and we sweep every Frenchman into the sea.

(Leclerc tries to speak, but staggers and falls fainting. There is a rush towards him, and cries of "Water!" Dessalines forces himself among them, takes a long look at Leclerc and laughs.)

He has it, Christophe. He will not govern this island for forty-eight hours more.

PAULINE   What do you mean?

DESSALINES   Look at his eyes. Thousands of you have died from it—thousands more will. Go back to your own country or your flesh will rot before you fall!

(Leclerc has staggered to his feet, supported by the others. He stares at Dessalines, and as he finishes speaking, Leclerc collapses again. He is borne off, and Dessalines and Christophe remain alone.)

(As Dessalines begins to speak, soldiers start to crowd into the room.)

We move tonight. We shall have the mulattoes against us, but we cannot wait. God, if only Toussaint was here!

(Enter Captain Verny.)

VERNY   There is news, General—news for all San Domingo.

DESSALINES   *(His hand on his sword and speaking almost in a whisper)* What is it?

VERNY   Toussaint is dead.

(There is a groan from the crowd. Dessalines and Christophe look at each other.)

DESSALINES   Did he die in prison?

(Verny, unable to speak, nods his head. There is open lamentation.)

What else?

VERNY   This letter came by the boat this morning.

DESSALINES   Read it.

(By this time the crowd is pressing round in a solid mass. In dress and bearing they are a civilised people.)

VERNY   *(Reading)* "I have to tell you that General Louverture died a week ago in his prison at Fort de Joux. His gaolers found him stiff in his cell where he had been dead, so it is reported, for three or four days. It is given out that he died from apoplexy, but the circumstances are very suspicious. The prison doctor has refused to sign the certificate. This is all I know at present. Meanwhile, accept my sincere sorrow, and the sorrow of all our friends at the bitter fate of our great master."

(Dessalines dashes the tears away from his eyes.)

DESSALINES   See, Christophe, see what awaits us.

VERNY   There is also a postscript, General.

DESSALINES   Well—quick!

VERNY   *(Reading)* "Official information is difficult to get now since money no longer comes, but from reliable sources we learn that the First Consul intends to restore slavery immediately in Guadeloupe, Martinique and San Domingo."

DESSALINES   Over my dead body, and the body of every son of San Domingo!

(Dessalines jumps on to the dinner table, smashing and scattering crockery. The room is now filled with a throng of excited people.)

Friends, you have heard. Toussaint is dead, who fought for our freedom. He made San Domingo our own country—the country of the blacks. . . . Those whites said: "Negroes are stupid, fit only to be slaves." But Toussaint ruled. In one year he made San Domingo prosperous. Leclerc, he swore by the Supreme Being to respect the liberties of San Domingo. That made us join him—we wished to stop the strife. And now see what the treacherous dogs have done. See what they want to do. But we shall avenge Toussaint. French blood in torrents shall flow. I, Dessalines, swear it. Toussaint died for liberty. We shall keep that liberty. Let their Consul himself come. . . . We shall keep it or we shall die defending it. Liberty! Liberty or death!

(The crowd takes up the cry "liberty or death!" The soldiers draw their swords. Suddenly there is a stir and Pétion forces his way through. He approaches the table.)

What do you want here? Mulattoes are no friends of Negroes. The bastards, they follow behind the whites like dogs.

PÉTION   I come as a friend. The First Consul has ordered that the ancient regime is to be restored in San Domingo. Leclerc told me; but he didn't say it was for mulattoes too. His army is already falling to pieces. I and my division will join you. Liberty is ours if only we unite.

(Dessalines stretches out his hand and pulls Pétion on to the table. He pulls Christophe up on the other side.)

DESSALINES   To arms, friends! No rest, no sleep till we drive every Frenchman into the sea. From this minute San Domingo is a free country—no. San Domingo no more. Haiti! The old name the island had before these Europeans came to bring slavery and degradation. Haiti!

(There is wild cheering.)

Haiti no colony, but free and independent. Haiti, the first free and independent Negro state in the new world. Toussaint died for it. *(He grips Pétion and Christophe on either side.)* We shall live and fight for it! Bring me that flag.

(Verny steps forward and hands him the flag on his sword. Dessalines is about to rip it vertically, when he changes his mind. Instead he rips the white off and throws it on the table.)

> *(Pointing to the black)* This is for the blacks, and this *(pointing to the red)* is for our mulatto brothers. Black and red. But this *(pointing to the white)* I trample under my feet. *(Frenzied cheering.)* Henceforth, this, our flag! And now, friends, to the attack!

(The crowd breaks into the song "To the Attack, Grenadiers.")

Curtain.

(*Until a copy of the final 1936 script is discovered, Act II, Scene 1, originally published in* Life and Letters Today, *is the only scene available to compare with the original published playscript contained herein.*)

ACT II, SCENE I, FROM *TOUSSAINT LOUVERTURE* (1936)

C. L. R. James is a Negro writer, born in the West Indies in 1901. After teaching and miscellaneous journalism, he came to England in 1932. He writes for the *Manchester Guardian* and other papers. He hopes to publish next year a political study of Toussaint Louverture and the Haitian Revolution.

[Note by the Author.—In July 1789, the French portion of San Domingo (today Haiti) was the richest and most valuable colony in the world. Thirty thousand whites and a similar number of mulattoes controlled the production of vast wealth by the ruthless exploitation of half a million slaves. In August 1791, the slaves, stirred to action by the conflict between whites and mulattoes, rose in revolt against their masters. They encamped in the mountains and waged a guerrilla warfare against the French colonial government, which was torn by its own dissensions and the bewildering sequence of events in revolutionary France. In the early years of the revolution, the various Commissioners sent out by the French government (of whom Roume was one) might have come to terms with the revolted slaves, then undisciplined and unorganised. But all such attempts were foiled by the treachery *and* intransigence of the local ruling class. Out of the turmoil of revolution and civil war arises a powerful Negro army led by three outstanding figures, Dessalines, Christophe, and, incomparably the greatest of them all and the undisputed chief, Toussaint Louverture. Freedom is the watchword of commanders and soldiers alike. The mulattoes meanwhile have organised themselves and seized the south of the colony. The French planters, in despair, invite the British government to conquer the colony and re-establish slavery. The British send an expeditionary force. In this confusion the Negroes steadily become the most powerful force in the country and Toussaint's army is officially recognised by the government in France. After long and arduous years of campaigning, the British find themselves in a position where they must come to terms with Toussaint or be driven into the sea. Here Act II begins.]

Act II   SCENE 1

A room in the Government Buildings in Port au Prince. At the back is a window, closed.

MAITLAND   Gentlemen, I have spoken, not as an Englishman, not as an enemy of France, but as a white man and a representative of a colonial power with the same interests as yours.

ROUME   General Maitland, no one can appreciate more than I the truth of what you have said. I saw Toussaint Louverture for the first time eight years ago. He was Toussaint Bréda then, one of a horde of savages, not even a leader, some sort of secretary to one of the leaders. When the slaves joined the Spaniards Toussaint made a regiment, then an army, and in a few months none of our soldiers could stand before him. Luckily for us the Convention abolished slavery completely. He joined us at once and drove the Spaniards out of all the French territory he had conquered for them. We have been blamed for appointing a Negro Commander-in-Chief of a French army. But what could we do? The British invaded the island. It was he and his army who kept them at bay. Every rebellion, every conspiracy against the government, it was he who put it down. Our government in Europe was busy with revolution and with war. We could get no help from them. Were it not for Toussaint and his black army, General Maitland, you would be signing a very different sort of peace with us now. Commissioner Hédouville was sent specially to reorganise the government of the island and hold Toussaint in check. But what can diplomacy do against an always victorious army?

LEAR   *(Speaking with a strong American accent)* Officially, of course, I have had no concern with all these matters. But during my stay here as Consul for America I have followed Toussaint's career pretty closely and Mr. Commissioner Roume is right. If it were not for the black general and his black army, San Domingo would now be Spanish or English, but it would not be a French colony.

HÉDOUVILLE   Still, the question before us is what General Maitland has said. The mulattoes under Rigaud and Pétion are holding out against Toussaint at Jacmel. If he conquers them, then this Negro is nominally our servant, but virtually master of the island. And the problem then is no longer French but concerns all who rule in these colonies, French, British, and Dutch.

MAITLAND   That, Mr. Commissioner, is now the main consideration of the British government which I represent. As long as General Toussaint continues the way he is going, the prestige of the Europeans in these colonies is in grave danger. And we rule as much by prestige as by arms. See what he calls himself now, "Louverture," opener of a way for his people. At whose expense?

HÉDOUVILLE   But how to check him?

MAITLAND   There is only one way in colonial countries.

HÉDOUVILLE   And that is?

MAITLAND   Strengthen some local power against him. Now! General Pétion is besieged with his mulattoes at the town of Jacmel. If Jacmel falls to Toussaint then Pétion's commander, Rigaud, with the main mulatto force is doomed; and Toussaint's road is open. Fortunately, Jacmel is almost impregnable —

LEAR   I wouldn't be too sure of anything impregnable where Toussaint is concerned. Since I have been in San Domingo he has opened some doors that seemed pretty tightly closed.

MAITLAND   He is a good soldier, Mr. Consul, but not of such exceptional ability.

LEAR   He forced you to surrender, General.

MAITLAND   I admit. But the climate has been very enervating for my men; and then he and his soldiers know every inch of the country. But we needn't go into that.

HÉDOUVILLE	No, we need not. And I agree with you, General Maitland, that though Toussaint has performed many miracles, he will not soon perform the miracle of taking Jacmel.
MAITLAND	But, Mr. Commissioner, General Pétion needs help. Arms, ammunition, military supplies of all sorts, and above all food. It cannot be given to him by land. Why not by sea? And if by sea why not from our British colony of Jamaica, which is only a few miles away? The Consul here can secure the co-operation of America, in return for trade concessions. That should not be difficult to arrange. If we move quickly, not only Toussaint will never take Jacmel, but Pétion, properly strengthened, may be able to organise from there a counter-attack and break the power of this audacious and all-conquering Negro.
HÉDOUVILLE	General Maitland tells us that he has discussed this question with you, Consul.
LEAR	My government is not interested in colonial complications, gentlemen. George Washington always told us to keep out of foreign entanglements and we shall keep out of them. It is trade my government is interested in. If a substantial amount of trade can be promised to our men of business in New York then you can be sure my government will look with sympathy upon any measures you may take to guarantee the dominance of the white race.
ROUME	It seems the only way. Yet Toussaint is a terrible man to cross. If he discovered anything, there is no saying what he might not do. To all parties concerned.
HÉDOUVILLE	We shall consider your suggestion, gentlemen, and shall communicate with you quickly. You will of course remember that we are representatives of the French government and we shall have to consider the proposal from many points of view.
MAITLAND	I realise your responsibilities, Mr. Commissioner. Of my good faith in this matter you need have no fear. As soon as our treaty is signed I and all my men embark for home. Yet the matter is urgent, and we shall hold ourselves ready to go into further details with you at any time you may appoint.

HÉDOUVILLE   Thank you, Brigadier-General, and you, Mr. Consul. At any rate, Pétion cannot be dislodged for weeks to come.

(At this moment a trumpet sounds and Roume and Hédouville, startled, jump to their feet.)

MAITLAND   What is that?

ROUME   That is Toussaint.

HÉDOUVILLE   But that is impossible. *(Trumpet sounds again.)* Yes, it's he. There he is at his tricks again. His letter said that he was leaving Dessalines in front of Jacmel and setting off himself against Rigaud. Now he will come with a flawless excuse.

(Enter Mars Plaisir.)

MARS PLAISIR   The Commander-in-Chief, General Toussaint Louverture.

(Almost on the announcement Toussaint walks into the room. He is just from horseback and even carries his riding whip.)

TOUSSAINT   Good-evening, Mr. Commissioner Roume. Good-evening, Mr. Commissioner Hédouville. Brigadier-General Maitland. *(Bows.)* Mr. Consul. *(Bows.)* Mr. Commissioner Hédouville, I have to announce that San Domingo is now under your undisturbed command. Jacmel is taken.

HÉDOUVILLE   Jacmel is taken!

TOUSSAINT   Jacmel is taken. Pétion cut his way out and has escaped with a few troops. Rigaud's last stronghold is destroyed, and finishing him off is merely a matter of days.

(Experienced diplomats as they are, the news has them all confounded.)

MAITLAND   *(Stepping forward)* Hearty congratulations on your success, Commander-in-Chief. You go from strength to strength. You and your army of blacks will soon be as famous in these parts as General Bonaparte and his army in Europe. Happy the Commissioners who have such a general and such soldiers to fight their battles.

HÉDOUVILLE   The Republic owes you a great debt, Commander-in-Chief.

The French government will be happy to know that once more you have served her so faithfully.

ROUME   Victory always attends your arms, Commander-in-Chief. No servant of France is more worthy of her gratitude.

LEAR   Some used to say that you couldn't take Jacmel, General, but I always knew that Rigaud and Pétion were no match for you. We discussed that, General Maitland, didn't we?

MAITLAND   We did, Mr. Consul.

TOUSSAINT   I thank you, gentlemen. It is not often that a general fresh from the field of battle can receive at the same time the congratulations not only of his own country, but of such great countries as England and America.

MAITLAND   We were just arranging the terms of my evacuation, General.

TOUSSAINT   Where is General Maurepas?

HÉDOUVILLE   We did not think it necessary for General Maurepas to be here, Commander-in-Chief. I had discussed the terms with you on your last visit from the front.

TOUSSAINT   General Maitland, when the truce was declared, it was with me and my officers that you arranged the preliminary terms of peace.

MAITLAND   True, Commander-in-Chief, but in your absence I thought that I would deal with the representatives of the French government, the civil authority.

TOUSSAINT   General Hédouville —

(He awaits an answer.)

HÉDOUVILLE   You are the Commander-in-Chief of the army, but I am the head of the civil administration. It is always the civil authority which signs terms of peace, and I had already discussed all details with you.

MAITLAND   This puts me in an awkward position, gentlemen —

TOUSSAINT   General Maitland, would your government consider a treaty signed with me valid?

MAITLAND	We would have to, inasmuch as you are in command of the army which lies in front of us.
TOUSSAINT	Then I shall sign the treaty.
MAITLAND	But what about the Commissioner?
TOUSSAINT	When the treaty is being signed, the Commissioner will not be here.
HÉDOUVILLE	Will not be here? Of course I will be here. No treaty signed would be valid without my sanction.
TOUSSAINT	San Domingo is a department of France and has representatives in the Council of Five Hundred in Paris. In a week's time an election takes place. By the law of France, whoever is asked to serve is bound to do so. I have good reason to know that General Hédouville will be elected as one of the representatives.
HÉDOUVILLE	But that is impossible! I am the Commissioner. I have not been nominated. I cannot be nominated.
TOUSSAINT	You can be nominated, and you will be, General Hédouville. And you will be elected, unopposed. Three days after a boat will leave for France, and it will be necessary for you to hasten to your legislative duties.
HÉDOUVILLE	But this is an outrage. General Louverture, there is no trick you have not tried, to undermine the Republican authority in this colony. General Laveaux, Commissioner Sonthonax, Commissioner Raymond, you have manoeuvred them all out of the island by one means or another. You claim to work only for the liberty of your people, but it is your ambition that drives you. Peace will soon be declared in Europe and once the French government is undisturbed by war it will make you pay for your crimes.
TOUSSAINT	Let the French government punish me for my crimes, so long as it rewards me for my services.
HÉDOUVILLE	You have received enough rewards. What more do you want? You are Commander-in-Chief of a French army. Has any Negro ever reached as far as you? You shall not have full com-

mand of this island. I go, but I appoint Commissioner Roume as my successor with full power until instructions arrive from Paris. You shall submit yourself to his authority in all matters. Commissioner Roume, you are now responsible to the Government of France for the colony of San Domingo.

TOUSSAINT   Commissioner Roume is already responsible to the Government of France for another colony. Mr. Commissioner Roume, by the terms of the Treaty of Basel between France and Spain, the Spanish portion of the island was ceded to France. You were appointed Commissioner and ordered to take immediate possession. You sent General Agé and General Chanlatte to arrange for the formal transfer of authority but at the same time you wrote to Don Joachim Garcia, the Spanish Governor-General, telling him to refuse to hand over the colony. I have a copy of your letter in my possession.

ROUME   I did it because I have grown to distrust your intentions. Had you and your soldiers got possession of Spanish San Domingo you would have been master of the whole island and it would have been still more difficult to control you.

TOUSSAINT   That, Mr. Commissioner, you will explain to the French government. Meanwhile, Brigadier-General Dessalines will supply you with two carriages and a safe escort to the village of Dondon where you will remain until the French government recalls you to render an account of your administration. I do not think, gentlemen, that these arrangements about the treaty concern you any further. (*They hesitate.*) Unless perhaps Mr. Commissioner Hédouville would like to consult further with Mr. Commissioner Roume under the escort of General Dessalines.

(*Exeunt Hédouville and Roume.*)

TOUSSAINT   General Maitland, I arrived not ten minutes ago. I heard that you gentlemen were in conference and I came straight to you. I thought that my news and my presence here would be of some value to the discussion. There is other business. But General Dessalines and General Christophe are not yet here. Neither is as well mounted as I am.

MAITLAND	Nor so fine a rider, Commander-in-Chief. I have heard of your skill in horsemanship. If I may suggest it, Commander-in-Chief, you certainly need a few minutes to refresh yourself. Pray take them. The Consul and I will chat pleasantly together until you and your officers are ready.

(Toussaint bows and exits.)

MAITLAND	This puts an entirely different complexion on affairs, Mr. Consul.
LEAR	That it does, Mr. Brigadier. That darkie has more brains than you gave him credit for.
MAITLAND	He certainly is a remarkable Negro. This is the fault of the early Commissioners who promoted him. He should have been kept in his place from the beginning. The question is, which side are we going to support now?
LEAR	That is only for me to decide, Mr. Brigadier.
MAITLAND	I do not understand you, Mr. Consul.
LEAR	As soon as you agreed to sign the treaty with Toussaint, of course it meant that Hédouville and Roume had nothing to fall back on.
MAITLAND	Put yourself in my place, Mr. Consul. Suppose General Louverture had refused to listen to them and pressed on the attack against me?
LEAR	Maybe, Mr. Brigadier. But for a man who thought that the Negroes and this black general were the greatest danger to the whites in these islands, you seem to have come in on his side mighty quickly.
MAITLAND	I had to think of my army, Consul. I am a general first and an ambassador after.
LEAR	Perhaps it will help you to know that you weren't deceiving those Commissioners with your scheme about supporting Rigaud. They had long ago written to the government at home who had sanctioned the plan of using Rigaud as a countercheck to Toussaint.

MAITLAND	How do you know that?
LEAR	Because they told me so themselves, and asked me to sound you on the point. Are you quite sure, Mr. Brigadier, that it is white prestige you wish to protect?
MAITLAND	I shall be frank with you. It is true that Louverture is a bad example to these thousands of blacks, and we should prefer to see Rigaud and his mulattoes holding the power. All these mulattoes want is to have the privileges of whites. Once we agree to that they will be as savage with the blacks as any white man. To-day, Mr. Consul, Britain's chief object in these waters, is to checkmate the power of France. Now that peace is declared, France is sure to send an expedition. If a strong native power can be established here before the French expedition comes, then France will bleed to death in this island.
LEAR	What if the black becomes too strong? He is strong enough already.
MAITLAND	By that time he would have lost the support of the French and then the British fleet could always crush him.
LEAR	It is trade my government is interested in, Mr. Brigadier.
MAITLAND	Mr. Consul, in any agreement that we may come to, it shall be stipulated that the fullest opportunities will be given to the traders of your nation. Do we understand one another, Mr. Consul?
LEAR	I think we do at last, Mr. Brigadier.
MAITLAND	He is a long time in coming. I have been warned to be careful. You know, Consul, in dealing with Orientals and men of colour, white men can never have that full confidence that we can have in one another, for instance.
LEAR	Quite so. But you need not be afraid of General Toussaint. I wouldn't trust myself within reach of that tiger Dessalines for five minutes. But though Toussaint is mighty cute he wouldn't be guilty of treachery. He is a nigger by accident.

(*Enter Mars Plaisir.*)

| MARS PLAISIR | The Commander-in-Chief, General Toussaint Louverture, Brigadier-General Dessalines, Brigadier-General Christophe. |

(Enter Toussaint, Dessalines, and Christophe.)

| MAITLAND | I am indeed delighted and honoured to have the pleasure of meeting the two chief officers of so distinguished a commander who are themselves so famous for their exploits in the field. |

| CHRISTOPHE | You do us too much honour, General Maitland, the pleasure is ours. |

(Dessalines says nothing, merely nods awkwardly.)

| TOUSSAINT | I take it that the terms of peace which you arranged, General Maitland, are the same we exchanged. |

| MAITLAND | Yes, General. We evacuate every position we hold but go with all our guns, ammunition, and baggage. |

| TOUSSAINT | This, I hope, means the beginning of a long peace between the English and San Domingo. |

| MAITLAND | I am sure of it, General. And you can be assured that henceforth His Majesty's Government will be your truest friend. General, a great future lies before you and these people you have raised from slavery into prosperous and enlightened freedom. Every Englishman will be heart and soul with them in their struggle for liberty. But now that peace is near in Europe, the French government may wish to re-establish slavery here. |

| TOUSSAINT | San Domingo is loyal to France, General. I am loyal to France — none more loyal than I. But there is no Negro who will not die in defence of his freedom. |

| LEAR | I told you so, Mr. Brigadier. Liber-r-rty or death. |

| TOUSSAINT | Liberty or death, Consul. It is no laughing matter. Thousands of us have died with those words on their lips. |

| MAITLAND | Commander-in-Chief, I admire your spirit and the spirit of your people. Your victories and the exploits of your soldiers have earned the confidence and respect of the King of England |

and his ministers. In the name of His Majesty, King George III, I shall have pleasure in presenting you with a silver dinner service, a token of His Majesty's respect and regard. It shall be here tomorrow morning. General Louverture, the friendship between San Domingo and Britain can be made still closer. France can do nothing against the English fleet. We are the masters of the ocean. If, perhaps, as I have heard it whispered you have thought of doing, if, General Louverture, you should decide to declare the colony independent and make yourself King of San Domingo, we would welcome it and give you our fullest support. King of San Domingo. You have only to say the word, King George will welcome his royal brother and England will become your firm ally. Then, General, with our fleet you can bring twenty thousand blacks from the Congo, arm them with guns and ammunition from America, and make them into such soldiers as you have made the slaves. Think of what an army you could have. And not only England will support you. The Consul here promises you the support of America.

LEAR   My government is not interested in the rivalry of colonial powers, Commander-in-Chief. All that we ask for is a fair share of the trade of San Domingo. If a substantial portion of that trade can be diverted from France to us, then you can be sure that my government will look with sympathy upon any measures you may take to guarantee the independence of the blacks.

TOUSSAINT   (After a long pause) General Maitland, I must thank you for your offer, but I cannot accept it. God knows that in my dreams sometimes I see not only an independent black San Domingo. I see all these West Indian islands free and independent communities of black men reaping the reward of the long years of cruelty and suffering which our parents bore. But the time is not yet. As long as the French do not try to re-establish slavery in San Domingo we shall be loyal to France. We are no longer Africans. We who live here shall never see Africa again, some of us born here have never seen it. Language we have none. French is now our language. Your English language we do not speak. We have no education, the little that some of us know we have learnt from France. France must teach us more. Those few of us who are Christians follow the French religion. Your English religion is different. Our future is with France, General. As long as she does not seek to re-establish slavery.

MAITLAND   But are you thinking of yourself? If even France does not try to re-establish slavery, do you think she will allow you to arrest and dismiss her representatives as you have done this evening? Now that peace is to be declared your future with France is doubtful.

TOUSSAINT   That, General, the future will show. There are more urgent tasks before us now.

DESSALINES   Toussaint.

TOUSSAINT   Yes, General Dessalines?

DESSALINES   Take the offer, Toussaint. Take it. Make yourself king. The people fought to be free. You are the leader. They trust you. They will fight for you and for themselves. Make yourself king. A country of blacks and a black king—let the people see it. They will say: "This is our country." Nobody will be able to take it away again. Do not trust France, Toussaint, trust your own people. You say education, Toussaint, religion. What is the use of that? These white planters, they go to France for education; they go to church to the priest for religion. We know those priests, Toussaint. And what then? When the cook don't bake the meat well, the mistress say: "Put him in the oven." And they put him in the red oven. They, the white planters, when they put the slave in prison and he call for food they cut off his flesh and cook it and give it to him to eat. I see white planters beat women big with child. I, Dessalines, was born on the Congo and lived there, but never saw such things. It is the white men in San Domingo that show them to me. Look at my skin. *(He tears his uniform open.)* The marks of the whip, I shall carry them to my grave. Every slave in San Domingo carries marks like these. Where we got them? White planters, men with this white education, men with this white religion. You forgive them, Toussaint. You tell them "Forget, come back. Work for San Domingo." And they come back because they want their plantation. They salute you, General Louverture, Commander-in-Chief. They say, "How are you, General Dessalines? Come to dinner." But Toussaint, in their hearts they hate us. We were the slaves, now we are the masters. You think they like it? For all white men black men only fit to be slaves. He, the Englishman, talk nice to you, offer you presents, say it is from his king. Why? Because you have guns, because you have power. But the English have slaves, too. They treat them just as the French. This Englishman offer you help, not because he love you, but because he want something from you. Toussaint, trust the people. Education and religion, but freedom first. Don't trust the French. Don't trust the English. Don't trust the Americans. Trust the people. For freedom they will fight to the end. Take his English ships. Bring the men from Congo. They have not this white education, they have not this white religion, but bring them and give them to me and Christophe while you govern the country. I, Dessalines cannot read, cannot write. Christophe here cannot read, he cannot write. But give us our grenadiers behind our back and let the French come and the British too *(He glares at Maitland.)* and the Americans.

(He turns to Lear.) Let them all . . .

(Toussaint grips him by the shoulder.)

TOUSSAINT   Dessalines! *(There is a long silence, Toussaint holding Dessalines while he buttons his tunic and recovers himself.)* What have you to say, General Christophe?

CHRISTOPHE   Commander-in-Chief, ten years ago you, and Biassou and Jean-François were negotiating with the French Commissioners and M. Bullet. I remember when Dessalines said: "Freedom for all," and you said: "No, all the slaves are not fit to be free." Dessalines was right then. Perhaps Dessalines is right now.

(As he utters the last words there begins a roar which grows into shouts: "Toussaint! Toussaint! Jacmel! Toussaint! Jacmel!")

DESSALINES   You. It's you they want, Toussaint. They have heard that Jacmel is taken. They call for you.

(Toussaint goes to the window and throws it open, letting in a great burst of cheer-

ing. He waves his hand — the cheers redouble. With a wave of farewell he closes the window and, deep in thought, walks slowly back.)

TOUSSAINT   General Maitland, I cannot accept your offer. San Domingo is a French colony and it must remain French. As long as the French are faithful to us we shall be faithful to them. What you suggest cannot be. Consul, I shall be glad for supplies of arms and ammunition, and shall consider a trade agreement with you.

MAITLAND   For the present, as you say, General Louverture. But remember that England is always your friend. Goodnight, General Christophe. Goodnight, General Dessalines. Goodnight, General Louverture. I must thank you for your kindness and courtesy. If you accept our offer the bargain shall be faithfully fulfilled. Goodnight.

LEAR   Goodnight, Generals.

(Exeunt Maitland and Lear. The three stand silent.)

TOUSSAINT   *(Seating himself)* King of San Domingo! Well, Dessalines.

DESSALINES   He and his dinner service and his king. Toussaint, you are too soft with these people. You will pay for it one day. Land for plantations — and slaves to work. That is their word, that is their God, that is their education, that is their religion.

TOUSSAINT   I know that as well as you, Dessalines. White men preach but they expect only Negroes to practise. If the rest of them in Europe are like those who come out here, then it is a wonder they have not torn one another to pieces already.

DESSALINES   Perhaps they will some day and then the blacks will have peace.

TOUSSAINT   Perhaps, but we have to negotiate with them meanwhile, and we must prepare for the worst. Once only did they show any friendship to us, and that was for those few months when Robespierre, Danton, and Marat ruled. Since then — . If we had five years. Not five; three. If we only had three years to educate and train the people a little more.

DESSALINES   We can but die. But we must protect ourselves against the treacherous dogs. What will you do with Vincent?

TOUSSAINT	I am sending Vincent to France. I have made a new constitution for San Domingo and Vincent will present it to the First Consul.
DESSALINES	Why let him go? He will betray our military secrets.
TOUSSAINT	No, I have confidence in Vincent. What do you think, Christophe?
CHRISTOPHE	White men never keep faith with Negroes. But yet I do not think Vincent will betray.
DESSALINES	He will betray. Arrest him and keep him here.
TOUSSAINT	It is already arranged. Vincent goes and I entrust him with the constitution. He may be like the rest. What does it matter? Every peasant has a musket, and nothing will deceive them. *(Rising.)* Dessalines and Christophe, remember this. What the future holds for us I do not know. These whites are stronger than us, but they fight so much with one another that we can have hope for the future. I have entrusted the six million francs to Gérard. If we consolidate ourselves in the West Indies we shall establish a base in Africa and from there fight the slave-trade, that curse and degradation of our people. We had great civilisations in Africa before the whites came. But two hundred years of the slave-trade have wrecked everything and now they reproach us with the ruin they have made. The six million francs is not much. But it is a beginning. That is in the future. For the present we shall have to manoeuvre between British and French, between French and Americans, between British and Americans.
DESSALINES	All are the same. Plantations and slaves.
TOUSSAINT	I know. But of all European peoples the French will least be able to re-establish slavery here. The British, the Spaniards, the Americans, will all try to ensnare us into alliances. They hope that when they have broken us away from France they will have us at their mercy. Do not give France that excuse. I am nearly sixty, I may be murdered at any minute, I may be killed the next time the army takes the field. You two will have to carry on. The people have arms. That and only that will save them from

slavery. But you must help them. Let your guiding policy be: Stick to the French. The blacks have fought under the French flag; under that flag they have driven out the Spaniards and driven out the British. They have received their freedom from the French Parliament, ratified by one hundred proclamations, oaths, and pledges. Any European nation that attempted to impose its will upon San Domingo would find us ready to resist. Our black soldiers are the bravest in the world. But should the French, of all people, attempt it, they will light a flame which will consume them in its fury. This evening, when I looked at those three and knew that if any of them got the chance he would drive us and our people back into the fields, I felt that I could spring at their throats and tear their eyes out. But people with our responsibilities must keep their tempers. Keep yours, Dessalines, and never forget. Manoeuvre, manipulate, but remain with the French.

Curtain.

LIFE AND LETTERS TODAY, 14, NO. 3, SPRING 1936

THE PRODUCTION AND
PERFORMANCE OF
TOUSSAINT LOUVERTURE

| | | | |

**Negro's Play about Negro Hero. Biography of a Genius.
Man who Defied Napoleon. Revolution in Haiti**

The oldest and most eminent play-producing society in England, the Stage Society, enters on its thirty-seventh season this autumn. Miss Flora Robson, the actress, who has just become a member of the council and executive committee of the society, expounded the new season's programme to me last week.

"We are doing three plays this year," said Miss Robson. "A new comedy by Elmer Rice; a biographical play on one of the most remarkable geniuses in history, the negro General Toussaint L'Ouverture; and a French adaptation of Aristophanes' 'The Peace' . . . [The biographical] play is about the negro General Toussaint L'Ouverture who lived about one hundred and twenty years ago. In some ways he must have been one of the most remarkable, and civilised, men who ever lived. He raised a revolt among the negroes of Haiti, fought off the English troops, and French troops sent by Napoleon, who came to subdue him. He then established in the island not a dictatorship, but a Republic, with many extraordinarily original and advanced ideas.

"He had been greatly influenced by the French Revolution. In his youth he had read the works of the Abbé Raynal—that Napoleon had also read in *his* youth. Ultimately he was decoyed back to France, and finally starved to death in a Swiss prison. The play has been written by Mr. C. L. R. James, a negro living in London. It would provide a magnificent part for Mr. Paul Robeson, and we have written asking him to do it. But he is away in America at the moment, and we do not yet know if he will be able to accept." . . .

"Is the general policy of the society changing in any way this season?" I asked. "No," said Miss Robson. "We have had the luck to be exempted from Entertainment Tax, and this will help us a lot. We have been exempted on the grounds that we are 'educational' (which sounds dull, but needn't be), and also on the ground that the society is not out to make any profit."

"Do you get many English plays sent in for production?" I asked. "Yes," said Miss Robson. "And we would always rather do English plays in preference to foreign ones—if we could get them good enough. We got one the other day from Australia. It was very illiterate, and was accompanied with a letter saying: 'See if you can do anything with.' And the curious thing is that the dialogue, mostly taking place in Australian bar-parlours, was often extremely good!"

H[UBERT] G[RIFFITH], *THE OBSERVER*, 20 OCTOBER 1935

The Stage Society: A Negro Play

Mr Paul Robeson has been invited by the Stage Society to take the title part in a new biographical play about Toussaint L'Ouverture, the negro general and one of the liberators of Haiti. The play has been written by Mr. C. L. Jones [*sic*], a negro living in London. . . .

L'Ouverture claimed to be descended from an African chief. His first surname, Breda, was changed to L'Ouverture in token of his value in causing a gap in the ranks of the enemy. He obtained his master's confidence and was made superintendent of the other negroes on the plantation. After the insurrection of 1791 he joined the insurgents and acted as physician to the forces. His rapid rise is said to have aroused the jealousy of Jean-François, who had him arrested on the ground that he was too partial to the whites. He was freed by the rival insurgent chief, Baisson, but after the death of Baisson, he placed himself under the orders of Jean-François.

Subsequently he joined the Spaniards, whom he deserted for the French when the French Government ratified the Act declaring the freedom of slaves. In 1796 he was made Commander-in-Chief of the armies of St. Domingo. Soon he raised and disciplined a powerful army of negroes, made himself master of the whole country, removed the authority of France, and assumed the title of "Buonaparte of St. Domingo." Ultimately he was captured by the French, and finally starved to death in a Swiss prison on April 27, 1803. . . .

Thirty-six years have passed since the Stage Society in its opening season produced Mr. Bernard Shaw and other dramatists of independent mind. In 1930, after producing more than 150 plays, the existence of the society was imperilled, but fortunately a new Executive Council was formed to carry on the work. This year the Council has found a valuable recruit in Miss Flora Robson, who has already taken an active part in choosing the three plays announced for the coming season, a season which will be greatly helped through the society's recent exemption from entertainment tax.

THE TIMES, 22 OCTOBER 1935

Play by an I.L.P.er

One of three plays being put on by the Stage Society this season has been written by C. L. R. James, the chairman of the Finchley I.L.P. It is about the negro General Toussaint L'Ouverture, who lived about 120 years ago.

The *Observer* writes:

"In some ways he must have been one of the most remarkable, and civilised, men who ever lived. He raised a revolt among the negroes of Haiti, fought off the English troops, and French troops sent by Napoleon, who came to subdue him. He then established in the island not a dictatorship, but a Republic, with many extraordinarily original and advanced ideas."

NEW LEADER, 25 OCTOBER 1935

"Toussaint L'Ouverture." Mr. Paul Robeson to Play Title Part

Mr. Paul Robeson has accepted the Stage Society's invitation to play the title part in *Toussaint L'Ouverture*, the biographical play about the negro general and one of the liberators of Haiti. The play has been written by Mr. C. L. R. James, a negro living in England, and will be produced on March 15 and 16. . . .

THE TIMES, 25 OCTOBER 1935

Negro Play

Paul Robeson is to appear under the auspices of the Stage Society at the Westminster Theatre on Sunday, March 15, and the following afternoon in "Toussaint L'Ouverture," a play by C. L. R. James, a young negro dramatist. It deals with the only successful slave revolt in history, the action taking place in Haiti during the French Revolution.

Mr. Robeson plays the hero-victim, who was the subject of one of Wordsworth's sonnets, and with him will be a big negro cast. Some of the white characters are being acted by Geoffrey Wincott, Ivan Samson, Fred O'Donovan, Kynaston Reeves, and Helen Vayne. The play, described as a straightforward historical drama, is being produced by Peter Godfrey.

SUNDAY TIMES, 1 MARCH 1936

Mr. Paul Robeson as a Negro General

Mr. Paul Robeson will be seen at the Westminster Theatre on Sunday week as Toussaint L'Ouverture in a biographical play about the negro general and one of the liberators of Haiti, written by Mr. C. L. R. James. Mr. James is himself a negro. He hopes to publish next year a political study of Toussaint L'Ouverture and the Haitian revolution. . . .

Mr. Peter Godfrey has been engaged by the Stage Society to produce the play. It will be acted by a cast of English and negro players. There will be two performances, the first on Sunday afternoon and the second on the following afternoon.

THE TIMES, 2 MARCH 1936

Dramatis Personae

Mr. Paul Robeson is appearing in the Stage Society's production of "Toussaint L'Ouverture" at the Westminster today week [i.e., next Sunday—Ed.] and on the following Monday matinee. Mr. Robeson's personal popularity is immense, and there will probably be some hundreds of people who would like to join the Society (a private society) merely for the sake of seeing him in this remarkable play. The cheapest form of membership, which costs a guinea, includes two seats for "Toussaint L'Ouverture" and one seat for the last play of the season (or one for "Toussaint" and two for the last play of the season). Application should be made to the Secretary, The Stage Society, 32, Shaftesbury-avenue.

THE OBSERVER, 8 MARCH 1936

PAUL ROBESON
AS THE NEGRO NAPOLEON.

PAUL ROBESON, *the distinguished coloured actor and singer, took the name-part in the Stage Society's production of* "TOUSSAINT LOUVERTURE," *by C. L. R. James. The play deals with the tragedy of the great negro who led the revolt against slavery in San Domingo while the French rulers of the country were occupied with their own Revolution. Mr. Robeson will soon be seen in a new film,* "Song of Freedom," *in which he plays the part of a negro who, after having been a dock labourer, becomes a singer, and later discards fame and returns to his people in Africa.*

Paul Robeson as Toussaint Louverture (*The Sketch*, 25 March 1936, p. 613). © The British Library Board. All Rights Reserved, 19 August 2011.

THE STAGE SOCIETY.

Founded 1899.

AUTHORS WHO OWE THEIR FIRST PERFORMANCE ON THE ENGLISH STAGE TO THE STAGE SOCIETY.

(ABRIDGED LIST.)

1900 Gerhardt Hauptmann	Anton Chehov	1923 Ernst Toller
1901 Gilbert Murray	1912 August Strindberg	1924 Elmer Rice
1902 Granville Barker	Jacinto Benavente	1925 Stark Young
1903 Somerset Maugham	1913 { Dostoievski	1926 James Joyce
St. John Hankin	{ Jacques Copeau	D. H. Lawrence
Hermann Heijermans	1914 Anatole France	1927 Karl Schönherr
Maxim Gorki	1915 C. K. Munro	1928 Jean Jacques Bernard
1904 Leo Tolstoy	1916 T. Sturge Moore	John van Druten
1905 Joseph Conrad	1917 Revival of William Congreve	R. C. Sherriff
1906 Nikolai Gogol	1919 Harold Rubinstein	1929 Alexei Tolstoi
1907 Frank Wedekind	Herbert Trench	1930 Clifford Bax
1908 Arnold Bennett	1920 Georg Kaiser	1932 Fernand Crommelynck
1909 Ivan Turgeniev	Charles Vildrac	Alexander Afinogeniev
1910 Ashley Dukes	1921 Wilhelm von Scholtz	1933 Jean Giraudoux
1911 G. Lowes Dickinson	1922 Luigi Pirandello	1934 Eric Linklater

---

THE FIRST PERFORMANCES IN ENGLAND OF THE FOLLOWING PLAYS WERE GIVEN BY THE STAGE SOCIETY.

(ABRIDGED LIST.)

1899 You Never Can Tell	Bernard Shaw	1919 The Faithful ... ... John Masefield
1900 The Coming of Peace ...	Gerhardt Hauptmann	1920 From Morn to Midnight ... Georg Kaiser
Captain Brassbound's Con-		1921 At Mrs. Beam's ... ... C. K. Munro
version	Bernard Shaw	The Race with the Shadow ... Wilhelm von Scholtz
1901 Pillars of Society ...	Henrik Ibsen	1922 Six Characters in Search of an
1902 Mrs. Warren's Profession ...	Bernard Shaw	Author ... ... Luigi Pirandello
Monna Vanna	Maurice Maeterlinck	The Rumour ... ... C. K. Munro
1903 A Man of Honour ...	Somerset Maugham	1923 The Machine Wreckers ... Ernst Toller
The Good Hope ...	Hermann Heijermans	1924 Progress... ... ... C. K. Munro
The Lower Depths ...	Maxim Gorki	The Adding Machine ... ... Elmer Rice
1904 The Power of Darkness ...	Leo Tolstoi	Man and the Masses ... ... Ernst Toller
1905 Man and Superman ...	Bernard Shaw	The Man with the Load of
One Day More... ...	Joseph Conrad	Mischief ... ... Ashley Dukes
1906 The Weavers	Gerhardt Hauptmann	1925 Ivanoff ... ... Anton Chehov
The Inspector General ...	Nikolai Gogol	1925 Exiles ... ... James Joyce
1907 Waste	Granville Barker	The Mountain ... ... C. K. Munro
1908 Cupid and Commonsense ...	Arnold Bennett	1926 The Widowing of Mrs. Holroyd* D. H. Lawrence
1909 The Shewing-up of Blanco		1927 The Great God Brown ... Eugene O'Neill
Posnet	Bernard Shaw	1928 L'Ame en Peine ... ... Jean Jacques Bernard
1910 Pompey the Great	John Masefield	Young Woodley* ... ... John van Druten
1911 The Cherry Orchard ...	Anton Chehov	Journey's End... ... ... R. C. Sherriff
Esther Waters	George Moore	1929 After All* ... ... John van Druten
1912 Creditors	August Strindberg	1930 Socrates* ... ... Clifford Bax
The Bias of the World ...	Jacinto Benavente	1931 The Children's Tragedy ... Karl Schönherr
1913 The Brothers Karamazov ...	Dostoievski and	1932 Le Cocu Magnifique ... Fernand Crommelynck
	Jacques Copeau	Fear ... ... Alexander Afinogeniev
1914 The Dumb Wife	Anatole France	1934 Intermezzo ... ... Jean Giraudoux
Uncle Vanya	Anton Chehov	The Devil's in the News ... Eric Linklater
1916 The Toy Cart	Arthur Symons	1935 Days Without End ... ... Eugene O'Neill
1917 Good Friday	John Masefield	La Machine Infernale ... Jean Cocteau
1918 The Dead City...	Gabriele D'Annunzio	Other Selves ... ... Henri Krag
		Not for Children ... ... Elmer Rice

*Signifies: In conjunction with The Three Hundred Club.

THE INCORPORATED
STAGE SOCIETY

Founded 1899   *Incorporated 1904*

CLV: THE SECOND PRODUCTION
OF THE THIRTY - SEVENTH SEASON

SUNDAY, 15th MARCH, 1936, at 8.30
MONDAY, 16th MARCH, 1936, at 2.30

WESTMINSTER THEATRE

Kindly lent by Anmer Hall

COUNCIL OF MANAGEMENT

Mrs. C. Coventry	P. S. Long-Innes
O. Raymond Drey	Desmond MacCarthy
R. E. Enthoven	Matthew Norgate
R. H. Glen	Bertram Park
Mrs. R. H. Glen	Miss Flora Robson
Allan Gomme	Miles Tomalin
Anmer Hall	Ossia Trilling
Sir Cedric Hardwicke	T. St. V. Troubridge
J. Isaacs	Allan Wade
W. S. Kennedy	Emanuel Wax,
	Hon. Treas.

32 SHAFTESBURY AVENUE, W.1

Hon. Sec.: SHEELAGH HARTIGAN

Robeson a Success in Drama by Negro; London Applauds His Playing of Liberator of Haiti in "Toussaint Louverture"

London, March 15.—Paul Robeson appeared tonight in the role of the Haitian liberator in the Stage Society's Sunday night performance of "Toussaint L'Ouverture," a first play by a young West Indian Negro, C. L. R. James.

Although unevenly written and produced, the episodic drama of the rebellion of San Domingo slaves at the end of the eighteenth century nevertheless held an appreciative audience's attention throughout, receiving an ovation at the final curtain.

Mr. Robeson naturally outshone the large cast of Negroes and whites.

The play may be seen again if and when Mr. Robeson's hoped for Negro Repertory Theatre in London becomes a reality. He said tonight he particularly wished to encourage Negro plays by Negro playwrights, as heretofore such dramas have been almost exclusively written by whites.

Mr. Robeson managed to sandwich this play in toward the end of a long, successful concert tour of the British Isles begun immediately following his return from Hollywood after making the film "Show Boat." He will soon appear in a British film, "Song of Freedom," concerning a world famous Negro singer who returns to Africa. Thereafter may come his own Negro theatre here.

NEW YORK TIMES, 16 MARCH 1936 (SYNDICATED IN
JAMAICA'S *DAILY GLEANER*, 28 MARCH 1936)

Paul Robeson as Toussaint; Drama of a Liberator

Looked at as an easy lesson in a part of the world's history not generally known here, yesterday's Stage Society production, "Toussaint Louverture," has considerable interest. Looked at simply as a play, it has to be called artless and therefore dull.

Its author, C. L. R. James, is a West Indian, and this stage account of the chief liberator of Haiti is written from the heart. But Mr. James is a journalist (he writes about cricket for a great provincial newspaper) and not a dramatist. He knows his facts, but not how to marshall them for stage effect.

Thus he gives us a scene in which Napoleon instructs Gen. Leclerc how the Negroes of San Domingo are to be treacherously induced to submit and then reduced once more to slavery. Then, instead of following up this excellent piece of theatrical preparation by showing us how Leclerc carried out his orders, he plunges us into a quite unexplained battle in which Toussaint is beating some enemy impossible to identify, owing to the drowning of dialogue in the noise of conflict.

The result of this and similar technique is that much well-meant work and careful writing go for little. However, the character of Toussaint himself emerges as a man of greater capacity and a higher honour than the white men who contrived his downfall.

Paul Robeson brings his great sincerity and capacity for earnestness to the name-part, which is indeed the only important individual part in the play.

W. A. D[ARLINGTON], *DAILY TELEGRAPH*, 17 MARCH 1936

Mr. Paul Robeson's Thrilling Part; "Toussaint L'Ouverture"

In "Toussaint L'Ouverture," presented by the Stage Society at Westminster Theatre yesterday afternoon, Mr. Paul Robeson found a hero after his own heart.

The play is a dramatised biography, by Mr. C. L. R. James, of the founder of Negro freedom in Haiti.

Toussaint is portrayed as a model of all the virtues, besides a born ruler and military genius. When his schemes are ruined by Napoleon's treachery the reign of terror against white people in the island begins.

Worthy as this may be as propaganda, the theatre, alas, would give a more cordial welcome to the blood-and-thunder part of Haiti's history.

Still, it was good to see Mr. Robeson's wholehearted response to his part — his acting was thrilling at moments — and to note how the many less gifted players of colour in the cast were enjoying themselves.

M. WILLSON DISHER, *DAILY MAIL*, 17 MARCH 1936

Robeson in Play by Negro—Author Takes a Part

An actor who had played the part of Macoya stepped forward and took the applause as author yesterday afternoon. I am given to understand that R. E. Fennell is his real name. Like many others in the cast, headed by Paul Robeson, he is a negro.

Considering the difficulties of dealing with the life of the famous Haitian rebel and President, the author has made a very good job of his material.

The play must have been a great pleasure for Paul Robeson to act, for Toussaint's opinion on the necessity of black people being educated has always been a plank in his platform. Paul Robeson made a fine figure of a man as the famous Toussaint.

E. A. BAUGHAN, *NEWS CHRONICLE*, 17 MARCH 1936

Paul Robeson as Slave Leader

Thanks to the Incorporated Stage Society's special performance yesterday, we saw Paul Robeson in a magnificent role.

"Toussaint Louverture," by C. L. R. James, is all about the Negro of that name who became leader of the San Domingo slaves 140 years ago. It is a noble character nobly played with all the actor's resonance and dignity.

There is wonderful atmosphere in the intrigues between Spain, Britain and France and the simple Africans, who grope towards that liberty now embodied in the Republic of Haiti.

The play unhappily suffers from repetition, and the author has dodged showing any of the violence which surrounds the action. It is worth bold revision; for the monstrous treachery of Napoleon to his loyal islanders is such that the absence of romance and humour does not matter.

P. L. M[ANNOCK], *DAILY HERALD*, 17 MARCH 1936

Stage Society: "Toussaint Louverture" by C. L. R. James

Mr. James tells here the story of the great Negro who led a revolt against slavery in San Domingo while the French, rulers of his people, were occupied by their own revolution. The inadequacy of the black hordes when first they became their masters; Toussaint's transcendence of them and his power to discipline his followers as well as to inspire them with enthusiasm; his wish not to defy the French but to attain freedom within the sovereignty of France; his betrayal, capture and death in a French prison; and, finally, the opening of a second revolt under Dessalines which was to tear the white from the tricolour and lead at last to the substitution of Haiti for San Domingo — all these events are described in an episodic narrative which, though bare and sometimes ingenuous in treatment, is clear and continuously interesting. Mr. James's dialogue is informative rather than suggestive; it lacks suppleness, and too many of his scenes are at their best when they depend upon Mr. Paul Robeson's almost unsupported monologues; but the work as a whole is sincere and unpretentious. For this reason, and because the dramatist, having an interesting subject, sticks to it, the play, in spite of woodenness now and then, holds the stage at the Westminster Theatre.

What binds its episodes together is Mr. Robeson's individuality. There are useful performances in his support by Mr. John Ahuma as Christophe and Mr. Robert Adams as Dessalines; Miss Helen Vayne, as the only white woman in the cast, gives a personal value to unpromising material; but the action is genuinely vitalized by Mr. Paul Robeson alone. His method is unusual and its merit hard to define. By the rules that apply to others it is clumsy, but his appearance and voice entitle him to rules of his own, justifying the directness of his attack upon his audience. It brings him out of the frame and, in a play dependent on composition, would have to be modified; but this play is not a composed picture — it is almost exclusively a portrait of Toussaint — and Mr. Robeson's interpretation of him deliberately and rightly lays stress upon his dominance, and reduces his associates to the background. In a play concerned with slavery, it is much that the tone is neither of whining nor of hysterical defiance, but of reasoned determination. Toussaint is at once astute and guileless, preserving through all misfortune his personal integrity and through all triumph a cautious eye for political reality as he understands it. When he is trapped, one feels that he has been mistaken in his calculations but not in his ultimate purpose, and the sympathy evoked by Mr. Robeson in his prison cell is not for a tricked negro but for a statesman paying a price for his ideal. In brief, though the obvious characteristic of Mr. Robeson's acting is its gigantic vitality, it by no means depends upon this only, but has the special tension that springs only from disciplined emotion and balance of mind.

THE TIMES, 17 MARCH 1936

Mr. Paul Robeson as Toussaint: A Documentary Play

It is one of theatre's paradoxes that within its walls truth tends to become duller than fiction. Mr. C. L. R. James justly asserts that his play on Toussaint, performed this afternoon by the Stage Society, is substantially true to history. This faithfulness it must be which has made stirring events seem so static. The fault cannot be with the actors, since Mr. Paul Robeson is Toussaint and heads a willing horde of black players against a conscientious troupe of white ones. And it is certainly not with Mr. Godfrey's production, which, with deft handling of light and colour, makes the thing a rhapsody in black surmounted by the tricolour.

Perhaps the truth is that art has done its all for Toussaint with that rather laureatish sonnet Wordsworth addressed to him in his last years. Exultations, agonies, and love and man's unconquerable mind. These things, said the poet, should be his friends for aye. Mr. Robeson, in a Napoleonic hat, nobly suggests such emotions and such aims. He is particularly noble at the point where he realises his duty and thanks God for sending him light. And it was perverse of Mr. Godfrey to withdraw all light from the actor at this juncture.

The one dramatic event in the history is Toussaint's treacherous arrest by the French after they have promised emancipation to the whole of Haiti. The author makes the most of this, though it necessarily occurs very late in his play. The rest is a tale of revolt and insurrection which not even the gallantry of the Stage Society can nowadays make other than a cinematic matter.

A[LAN]. D[ENT], *MANCHESTER GUARDIAN*, 17 MARCH 1936

Robeson as Negro Leader

[There is] not a more forlorn figure than Mr. Paul Robeson in search of a play. "Toussaint L'Ouverture," his latest experiment, which the Incorporated Stage Society produced at the Westminster Theatre yesterday afternoon, is another doubtful venture.

The play tells of the Negro rising in San Domingo led by Toussaint L'Ouverture, and is written with great care and fidelity, but as a theatrical entertainment, it is ponderous to a degree.

Mr. Robeson was, of course, terribly in earnest, and his earnestness, as always, gave dignity and importance to whatever he did. But he was a little prone to force his voice in emotional climaxes: a great pity, for this spoils its lovely, luscious quality.

STEPHEN WILLIAMS, *EVENING STANDARD*, 17 MARCH 1936

Paul Robeson; Stage Society Show Does Not Give Him Great Part

Toussaint L'Ouverture, liberator and dictator of Haiti in Napoleonic times, was a great man, probably the greatest negro in history. His history ought to provide Mr. Paul Robeson with a great part, but Mr. C. L. R. James, the negro author of "Toussaint L'Ouverture," which the Stage Society presented at the Westminster Theatre, has not written such a part.

The weakness of this chronicle play, as of so many other chronicle plays, is that all the action happens "off." Toussaint has little to do but utter noble sentiments and gesticulate over the view of distant battles, concealed sufferings, invisible sieges and assaults.

GOOD CAMERA STORY

So Mr. Paul Robeson's noble voice and presence have nothing to bring to life and vivid reality. Even the hero's tragic end in a French prison, betrayed by the country to which he was so obstinately loyal, is robbed of grandeur by trivial detail.

The other parts are not important. All the negro parts were played by negro actors, among whom Mr. Hugh Charleson and Mr. Robert Adams were the most effective. Mr. Norman Shelley, as a white planter, and Mr. Wilfred Walter, as Toussaint's emissary to Bonaparte, were notably good.

If this piece has a future, it is probably on the screen. This is a fine story for the camera to tell.

J. G. B[ERGEL], *EVENING NEWS*, 17 MARCH 1936

Paul Robeson in Negro Play—A Dignified Study; Toussaint Louverture, by C. L. R. James

The great negro liberator of San Domingo — the present Haiti — from slavery could hardly have been better or more fitly played than he was yesterday at the Westminster Theatre in this dramatic tribute by a coloured author.

The play itself is hardly so great as its theme or as the power which Mr. Robeson himself could quite obviously have put into a fuller and more intimate study. Toussaint Louverture not only won freedom for his fellow-negroes, but kept them in order. Against his moderation and integrity, the execrable perfidy of Napoleon as First Consul, and sheer incompetence of General Leclerc suffer a comparison that hardly enhances the "Napoleonic Legend."

The future Emperor (Mr. Geoffrey Wincott) is represented as a merely unscrupulous political gangster. We see Toussaint laying down his arms in good faith, and being immediately arrested. We see his death in the alpine prison of Joux, and the curtain finally falls upon the threat of the massacre—which actually happened—of all the whites in Haiti by way of revenge.

So far as it was possible, Mr. Robeson gave us a magnificently simple, sincere and dignified presentment of Toussaint. But the language was too formal. A little "spiritual," beautifully sung by Mr. Robeson in the prison scene, gave a refreshing touch of naturalness.

A mixed black and white cast, in which Mr. Fred O'Donovan played Leclerc, with Miss Helen Vayne as Pauline—Leclerc's wife and Napoleon's sister—varied considerably in merit.

MORNING POST, 17 MARCH 1936

Our London Letter: Black Episode

Paul Robeson has made one of his far too rare appearances in performances this weekend of "Toussaint Louverture," presented by the Stage Society at the Westminster Theatre. The play is the work of Dr. [sic] C. L. R. James, himself a man of colour, and deals with twenty years of the history of Haiti, or San Domingo as it was then called. Louverture, the character played by Mr. Robeson, was a negro of breadth of outlook and elevation of character and something like [a] military genius. But he was too simple to be a match for the French, who tricked and manoeuvred him and his fellow natives out of the success that might otherwise have attended in Louverture's time, and did later attend their fight for autonomy.

Our own day has seen a coloured representative of the Republic of Haiti presiding over an Assembly of the League of Nations. Dr. James's play is episodic, not to say patchy, but it contains several fine scenes, and Mr. Robeson's acting has the dignity and power which characterises all his work. Mr. Peter Godfrey's production was interesting in conception.

LIVERPOOL POST, 17 MARCH 1936 [THIS REVIEW SEEMS TO HAVE BEEN SYNDICATED AND PUBLISHED ELSEWHERE: FOR EXAMPLE, SEE "PAUL ROBESON ON THE STAGE" BY "PLAYGOER" IN *THE MALTA CHRONICLE AND IMPERIAL SERVICES GAZETTE*, 1 APRIL 1936.]

Robeson as the Other Napoleon:
"Toussaint L'Ouverture" at the Westminster

Napoleons of different aspects and colours take the stage this week. Three of them — the kindly and philosophic Napoleon of "St. Helena," and in "Toussaint L'Ouverture" two — the dominant First Consul, making one of the biggest mistakes of his career, and Toussaint himself, the Negro slave who rose to be ruler of what was later the first independent Negro Kingdom in the world, and who was called "the Bonaparte of St. Domingo."

The play, written by a coloured author, C. L. R. James, was presented at the Westminster Theatre on Sunday evening and Monday afternoon by the Stage Society, with Paul Robeson as Toussaint. Physically, he was hardly suited to the role of the forty-seven-year-old ex-coachman, worn out with years of slavery, and, it is said, a man of small stature, but he played the part with quiet dignity, and, in one or two scenes, with a passionate intensity that gave his words a power they lacked in themselves.

Two thousand square miles of territory were flaming with uncontrollable and desperate passion. Whites were searched out from their hiding places and slaughtered in the most hideous fashion the slaves could conceive. But one of the slaves, Toussaint, remained loyal to a master who had shown him kindness and justice. For seventeen days he hid him among the mangoes, then put him on board ship with his family, and sent him to safety. Then, and only then, did he join his own people in their maddened fight for liberty. Two years later he was head of the black army. He turned from the Spanish, for whom he had been fighting, to "his natural protectors," the French, gave them his support and influence in the island, began to re-establish peace.

He wanted not independence then, but simple freedom. He ruled St. Domingo with wisdom, and with liberty, equality, fraternity as his watchwords. In his narrow scope he was as great, or greater than, Napoleon. He united both French and Spanish settlements under one rule. He gave the degraded and tortured Negroes spirit and hope. In the palace at St. Domingo things were working their way to a civilisation — there was free trade, religious toleration, plans for the education of the blacks.

But in Paris the First Consul, distrustful and infuriated, listened to the planters who had been driven out and who wanted their estates and slaves returned. He sent a vast fleet and an army of 46,000 men against Toussaint's 16,000. Unable to force an entry into St. Domingo, Le Clerc, Napoleon's brother-in-law, tried treachery. Under cover of a peace parley on friendly terms, he persuaded Toussaint to meet him. The Negro general was seized, shipped to a prison in the Juras, denied trial, justice, appeal. In the cold damp of the prison cell he died — the greatest soldier of his race, the loyal comrade-in-arms of the French, the saviour of one of France's most-prized possessions from her English and Spanish assailants.

But what he had won was kept. Hayti is now a member of the League of Nations, and its representative presided over the League's eighth assembly. The freedom bought through death and torture has been maintained. There is immense potential drama here, but though Mr. James has written with deep sincerity and earnestness, he needed more knowledge of the theatre and flair for the essential to make a good play. He shows the difficulties of governing a people still savage and ignorant, the contemptuous hatred of the whites, Toussaint's single-handed struggle for civilised rule instead of barbaric domination, but he does it too much by words and shows us too little of direct action.

Toussaint's meeting with his young sons, whom he had sent to France to be educated, and whom Napoleon dispatched back to him with tempting offers, which could have been a scene of tense significance and would have shown us a side of Toussaint's character almost untouched here, is omitted altogether; and of the negro intrigues around him at the beginning of his rise there is only a suggestion.

Still, there was a sombre feeling in the play that had its own meaning, and the acting of Robert Adams as Dessalines, the Negro general, of John Ahuma as Christophe, Toussaint's successor, and of Mr. Robeson himself, was very fine. The author appeared in a small part and the reverberant fullness of so many negro voices left a strange impression of solemnity and dark richness.

MARGERY ROWLAND, *THE ERA*, 18 MARCH 1936

"Toussaint Louverture"

One of the greatest figures in negro history was brought to life by Paul Robeson at the Westminster Theatre last night when he acted the leading part in "Toussaint Louverture."

This Stage Society production of C. L. R. James's play was sincere and reasonably interesting—considering the length of the monologues. These were well written and necessary, for the biography featured its subject with a kind of fierce admiration. Moreover, Mr. Robeson was always natural, and the action included a scene in which his fine singing voice was heard. The leading light's gifts gave the whole a unity that it would not have had otherwise, and lent interest to an old story.

Toussaint Louverture fought for the freedom of many a cause, notably the liberation of the people in San Domingo—the modern Haiti—who were enslaved by the French. The warrior eventually died in a French prison, but he left a cleaner record than some of his white contemporaries. In fact, even the mighty Napoleon did not show up too well.

At the Stage Society performance Mr. Robeson was supported by a black and white company, with Geoffrey Wincott as Bonaparte, Helen Vayne as Pauline Leclerc, John Ahuma as Christophe, Robert Adams as Dessalines, and Fred O'Donovan as Leclerc.

A tribute to a coloured conqueror by a coloured writer.

GLASGOW HERALD, 18 MARCH 1936

The Stage Society: "Toussaint L'Ouverture"

On Sunday evening, March 15, 1936, the Incorporated Stage Society produced at the Westminster Theatre a play, in three acts and eight scenes, by C. L. R. James . . . "Toussaint Louverture" deals in episodic fashion with the negro revolt in the West Indian island of San Domingo, now Haiti, and its period of action covers the years from 1791–1802. The incidence of the French Revolution and its bearing on Haitian affairs is shown, but the main interest of the play centres on the figure of the famous negro liberator who was the victim of French treachery. It is a page of history all but forgotten. François Dominique Toussaint called L'Ouverture, was the negro patriot of San Domingo who freed the island from slavery, released it from the British and the Spaniards, and rendered great services to the French Republic. A decree of Napoleon issued in 1801 declared slavery re-established in the French settlements, and Toussaint determined to resist it.

We see the beginnings of the trouble in a forest in the French part of the island, in a slave encampment, in the Government Buildings in Port au Prince, and in Bonaparte's apartment in the Tuileries after which there is a battle scene in the Fortress of Crête-à-Pierrot. The final scenes deal with the French occupation of the island, the imprisonment and mysterious death of Toussaint, and the tearing up of the French Tricolour by Dessalines, Toussaint's negro successor, who is determined to resist slavery.

All this carries with it a certain degree of excitement and movement in picturesque surroundings which might possibly be made more effective through the more expansive medium of the screen. As it is written, however, the play is altogether too propagandist. Propaganda—in this case the cause of the negro races—is all very well in its proper place, but it is not permissible in a play which purports to be substantially true to history. The coloured races have certainly been persecuted by the whites, but the author's bias in their favour would appear to deny the whites a shred of nobility of character or honesty of purpose. In his play the blacks are white and the whites are black.

Paul Robeson gave a fine dignified performance of Toussaint, and sang a little negro spiritual in the prison scene. In fact, his characterisation of the simple, noble-souled negro lifted the whole play to a plane it might not otherwise have obtained. The First Consul Bonaparte, here shown as a mean, treacherous political trickster and as obstinate as a mule, was admirably played by Geoffrey Wincott; while Wilfrid Walter put in sound work as an officer cashiered by this stupid Napoleon for speaking the truth. General Leclerc, that incompetent French officer, was cleverly played by Fred O'Donovan and Helen Vayne did well as Leclerc's wife, Napoleon's sister. Robert Adams, a coloured actor, was at his best as Dessalines when that implacable hater of the whites tore up the Tricolour.

Others who did good work in a cast which included quite a number of coloured players in subsidiary parts were Townsend Whitling (as an English general), Kynaston Reeves (as Hedouville, a French official), Charles Maunsell, Norman Shelley, Lilian Davies, Felix Irwin, George Cormack, Harry Andrews, Hugh Butt, and Lawrence Brown, the last named as Toussaint's coloured servant.

"Toussaint Louverture" which was repeated on Monday afternoon, was well produced by Peter Godfrey. Ormiston Miller was the Stage manager, assisted by Audrey Lake and Anne Jenkins. The musical effects were by Philip Thornton. The play was very well received.

Additional Notice: A discussion on "Toussaint Louverture," which was produced by the Incorporated Stage Society on Sunday, and is noticed elsewhere, is to take place this Thursday evening at 8.30 at Oddenino's Restaurant, 54 Regent Street. Hubert Griffith will open the discussion, and the author, C. L. R. James, will speak.

THE STAGE, 19 MARCH 1936

Revolt! Negroes Struggle for Freedom: A Play by C. L. R. James

Toussaint Louverture was a negro who led the slaves of the French colony of St. Domingo to freedom in the latter part of the eighteenth century. He became such a menace to the French that Bonaparte had him brought to Europe and incarcerated in the prison of Joux, where he died in 1803.

The struggle of these Negroes to free themselves is a dramatic theme round which C. L. R. James, whom I.L.P.ers know well, has written a striking play.

Paul Robeson takes the part of Toussaint the leader who builds up a powerful and disciplined army of Negroes behind him and at the same time negotiates with the representatives of white Governments with exceeding skill. The bribes of the white officials he contemptuously turns down, their promises he regards with scepticism, and he is feared by them as much as he is loved by his army.

The whole play cogently puts the problem of empire with its exploitation and slavery of the coloured people. The "civilising" missions of the Capitalist Governments, their promises solemnly made and lightly scrapped, their trickery, makes a pretty picture for an audience whose rulers have the largest empire in the world under their domination.

The production, with its minimum of scenery, is excellently done by Peter Godfrey, and the large cast, many of them Negroes, succeeds in convincing the audience that an Empire is nothing of which any white civilisation can be proud.

Can we hope that the play, produced by the Stage Society at two private performances, will be put on at one of London's theatres so that large numbers of people can see it?

NEW LEADER, 20 MARCH 1936

Toussaint l'Ouverture, at the Stage Society

Most of us know little of Toussaint l'Ouverture except Wordsworth's sonnet to him:

> Thou hast great allies;
> Thy friends are exultations, agonies,
> And love, and man's unconquerable mind.

So we were able to follow with some feelings of suspense Mr. C. L. R. James's chronicle play. The production as a whole was rough rather than ready, but we doubt if the play, respectable though it is, could ever be very impressive. The subject requires a power of imagination which Mr. James does not appear to possess. But he brings out effectively, though without exaggeration, the nobility of Toussaint's character and the treachery of the white men. As Toussaint Mr. Paul Robeson gave a most thoughtful performance: he is one of the most impressive actors alive. Mr. Hugh Charleson as Dessalines was remarkably good, and Mr. Geoffrey Wincott made a brilliant young Bonaparte. The play "ends happily," after Toussaint's death, with the proclamation of Haiti's independence. There is room for another play about the horrors which ensued under the tyranny of Christophe, who here is shown as quite an amiable man.

NEW STATESMAN, 21 MARCH 1936

Letter in Response to the *New Statesman's* Review from C. L. R. James

SIR,—In his notice of my play, *Toussaint L'Ouverture*, your dramatic critic found space for the following sentence: "There is room for another play about the horrors which ensued under the tyranny of Christophe, who here is shown as quite an amiable man." Doubtless there is room for many plays. This particular play which he suggests might, however, have an opposite effect to that which your critic envisages. For it would have to begin with the fact that the murder of all the whites in San Domingo (a tragedy from which the Haitians themselves suffered ultimately) was instigated by white men and Englishmen. Cathcart, the English agent, warned Dessalines that the English would neither trade with him nor support the independence of Haiti until every white man in the island was killed. They aimed at monopolising Haitian trade while the blacks at least were struggling to save themselves from the lash of the slave-whip. Your correspondent will find the necessary evidence on page 18 of *La Perte de Saint-Domingue*, by M. Camille Guy, a pamphlet republished from the *Bulletin geographique, historique et descriptive* No. 3, of 1898. I regret to have to bring this fact to the notice of your readers in this connection. Its proper place is in history or biography and not in a *tu quoque* of the blacks did this, but the whites did that. I could have put it into the play, but did not because these things in the long run tend to obscure instead of clarifying great political issues. The amiability or otherwise of Christophe has nothing to do with either the play or the history. All men do all things under certain circumstances, a lesson which your critic has not yet learnt, despite the steadily accumulating piles of evidence with which the post-war world has been furnishing him. I have written, therefore, not only because I consider his remark uncalled-for, but also to correct any false or misleading impressions which it might have given to the unwary.

C. L. R. JAMES, *NEW STATESMAN*, 28 MARCH 1936

Toussaint L'Ouverture

On Sunday and Monday last the Incorporated Stage Society presented *Toussaint L'Ouverture*, by C. L. R. James. The central character of the successful slave rebellion, which culminated in the establishment of the Republic of Haiti in place of the French colony of San Domingo, was played by Paul Robeson. How much the enthusiasm of the audience was due to sympathetic appreciation of the story of the hard-won emancipation of a down-trodden race rather than to the place which Robeson has gained in London's affection is hard to gauge. Nevertheless the play was worth producing and worth seeing. Perhaps a braver production, with the necessary emphasis on the incredible duplicity of the whites (more particularly Napoleon) and, in the acting, greater sophistication in their assumption of superiority, would have increased the dramatic value of this very sincere and appropriately salutary play.

TIME AND TIDE, 17, NO. 12, 21 MARCH 1936

Two Great Negroes

Paul Robeson, who remains one of the world's great artists, showed last week another side of his marvellous versatility. When the Stage Society put on "Toussaint L'Ouverture," a play written by C. L. R. James, a West Indian coloured man, a brilliant young journalist and an orator, we saw told in all its pitiful majesty the story of a great Negro. Although offered the crown of San Domingo by the British Government, who wanted to use him as a pawn Toussaint preferred allegiance to a France which tricked and betrayed him, and allowed him to die in prison.

Even today, although he died well over a century ago, his memory survives and his teachings go on. Robeson played, of course, the part of the Negro leader. During a meeting of Negroes which I attended as a protest against Italy's invasion of Abyssinia, I heard speakers refer with pride to the inspiring life of Toussaint, a great man of colour.

PLEA FOR THE COLOURED

"It is only our skin that is different," is the cry of James's dramatised narrative. "Underneath we are all the same." Well, to my mind, it is a great romance that at a time when Italy is crushing out Abyssinia with gas bombs and aeroplanes and tanks, there has been produced in London, by a stage society because of which we first heard of Shaw and a score of world-famous playwrights, a play by a coloured man in which he pleads for his people.

And Robeson was, as always, magnificent. He is greater than almost anything in which he acts.

HANNEN SWAFFER, *THE PEOPLE*, 22 MARCH 1936

Stage Society: "Toussaint L'Ouverture" by C. L. R. James

Wishing to confirm the opinions about Toussaint expressed in Wordsworth's sonnet, I consulted a work of reference, which informed me, among other things, that "Toussaint's defection was followed by the surrender of Marmalade." For the less advanced students of West Indian history, I should add that this does not refer to a gentleman going on a diet, but to the interminable intrigues of Franco-Spanish planters and their slave-driver politics from which that one decent and angry son of African liberty may defeat a dozen jobbing Latins and even, when the British intervened, some heads as well as hearts of oak. Toussaint's magnificent stand for his people was over-thrown in the end by the abominable duplicity of the French, and Mr. James has no hesitation in portraying Napoleon in his true colours, that is as an un-generous bully whose main concern was finding jobs for his family as keepers of the graveyards which his policy created.

Mr. James's play is a careful prose-record of Toussaint's tremendous struggle against the remorseless toughness of the European exploiters and the weakness and flightiness of his own hard-driven people. The pulse of righteous indignation beats strongly, and sometimes the narrative needs trimming and tightening. The play, however, manages to be continuously interesting because Toussaint himself is interesting. Probably poetry would better have honoured the great and magnanimous figure of ebony which Mr. Paul Robeson presented like some tremendous tree defying hurricanes and finally overwhelmed by the small, mean blade of French dishonesty. If Mr. [W. H.] Auden had been part author, we might have ended with a real Hymn of Haiti to voice what triumph the Negroes retained; as it was, the surge of emotion came through in Mr. Peter Godfrey's production, to which the coloured actors contributed far more of value than the white. With the exception of Mr. Geoffrey Wincott's Napoleon, the white men, as enacted, were something of a burden, whereas the simplicity of the insurgent blacks, while it did not involve great performance, had its own natural humour and charm.

IVOR BROWN, *OBSERVER*, 22 MARCH 1936

"Toussaint Louverture," a Play by C. L. R. James

It was Mr. Paul Robeson who held the interest at this Stage Society produc-tion. The play proved to be a somewhat tedious recital of the historical facts of the famous negro revolt against slavery in San Domingo at the end of the eighteenth century. Mr. James would appear to lack experience of the the-atre. He has sincerity and industry, but he does not know how to make his story live on the stage. The incidents are dully marshalled, and one or two of the eight scenes are as clumsy as the grotesque army of negro warriors which answered the whistle in the first act. Thanks to Mr. Robeson's vital and tre-mendously sincere acting, the leading character came to life and held one's attention.

He seemed to infuse the story with some of his own passion, and he was particularly moving in the grand moment when, in the presence of God, Toussaint realises his great mission. Mr. Peter Godfrey's production was imaginative, although some of the lighting was too tricky.

G[EORGE] W. B[ISHOP], *SUNDAY TIMES*, 22 MARCH 1936

Saint-Like Negro

Whether there will be a West End run for "Toussaint Louverture" by C. L. R. James, I cannot say. It was given a try-out performance by the Stage Society a week ago.

This is another biographical drama. The hero is the noble negro who first gave the slaves of Haiti their freedom and died through the treachery of their French masters.

Paul Robeson rose magnificently to his chances in the leading part. But as a whole the production stressed the melodramatic side of the story instead of aiming at making it as convincing as possible.

"THE PROMPTER," [*MANCHESTER*] *EMPIRE NEWS*, 22 MARCH 1936

Criticisms in Cameo: The Stage

At the Westminster, where the Group Theatre people have been offering the very last word in English drama their season of six months' hard work was bravely concluded with some performances of the very first word in that theatrical literature.

At any rate, Medwall's "FULGENS AND LUCRECE" is one of the earliest English plays, and by no means the least amusing.

Prior to that, the Stage Society had used the same house in order to present Mr. Paul Robeson in "TOUSSAINT LOUVERTURE," the negro rebel and ruler of St. Domingo, an Emperor Jones who was dirtily treated by the Emperor Bonaparte; trapped himself, he left his legacy of a free Haiti to the plantation-folk of his own kith and colour.

Mr. C. L. R. James, a West Indian who can write as vividly and learnedly about cricket as he does about the captains and the kings, gave us an interesting play, despite the fact that some of his episodes needed tightening and cutting.

Toussaint was a real tragedy hero, and Mr. Robeson bestowed tremendous power on the picture of this tribal hero in victory and frustration. Toussaint's negro generals liked dressing-up, and the coloured actors seemed to like dressing-up as generals dressing-up. I liked them too.

IVOR BROWN, *THE SKETCH*, 25 MARCH 1936

Toussaint Louverture; The Story of the Only Successful Slave Revolt in History

It was a privilege to see the Stage Society's presentation of Mr. James' play in the Westminster Theatre on Sunday and Monday last, produced by Mr. Peter Godfrey, with Paul Robeson in the title role.

The story of Toussaint is one of the most dramatic in history; the story of a negro slave, who became leader of a revolution, Governor of a colony of over half a million people, a General of the French Army, and the victim of white treachery, martyr of the cause of negro liberty.

. . . The play opens with plantation slaves pledging themselves to "Liberty or death" and Toussaint awakening to the "call" of leadership. In eight years they freed the slaves, trained and equipped an army, and reorganised the whole life of the island; and we have a glimpse of the attempts to win Toussaint over by the English, Spanish, and American interests, but he remained loyal to France.

France was the one country which he was sure would never be able to restore slavery, and so he maintained the French tradition, and San Domingo remained a loyal colony of France. By this time, however, the French Revolution was over, and Napoleon established as First Consul of France; and the next scene depicts his reception of Colonel Vincent, the French officer to whom Toussaint had entrusted the constitution he had drawn up for the colony.

Napoleon would have none of it, arrested Vincent for his support of Toussaint, and sent out an expeditionary force with instructions to win peacefully the confidence of the negro leaders, arrest Toussaint, and establish the old order of slavery. But Toussaint had builded [*sic*] too well, and although he was arrested by a trick, sent to France to rot in a French prison, he kept his faith. "Re-establish slavery in San Domingo? Never; never!"

His work was done, and the last scene shows the Negroes and mulattoes joining forces, and, fired by the death of their hero, tearing out the white from the tricolour, to drive out the French, and establish an independent "Haiti."

Paul Robeson, with his wonderful voice and his acting ability, made Toussaint live again, revealing, as the play progressed, the genius of statesmanship, the sincerity and wisdom, and the command of the love and loyalty of the people which was Toussaint's.

The part was, of course, ideal for him, and the play as a whole is a fine piece of negro propaganda, without any of the evidences of the "inferiority complex" which characterises much negro thought today, "different" and intensely interesting.

It shows certain weaknesses of style, due to the author's inexperience in play-writing for production, and perhaps also to the wealth of material from which he had to choose in these episodes in the life of a great man.

One felt, as one watched and listened, that the words of Rev. "Dick" Shepherd were not merely a personal tribute to Robeson, when he said, "How can one listen to Paul Robeson, and still think in terms of white superiority?"

E[DNA] R[OBINSON], *NELSON LEADER*, 27 MARCH 1936

The West Indian Drama

Debunking Napoleon at the moment is a popular sport in literature and the drama. I sometimes feel that it is a little overdone. In their indignation at his insatiable appetite for conquest and his desire to find remunerative positions for his family most authors seem to overlook the fact that it was Napoleon who put the French Republic on the map, and that from a mere rabble of undisciplined and half starved men he created his unconquerable army of defence.

Mr. Sherriff and Miss Jean de Casalis show us Napoleon in his last days at St. Helena. His admitted pettiness, the sudden rushes of anger which must have convulsed him at the realisation that his power had gone, are skilfully sketched in but, to my mind, there is little to show in their delineation that the prisoner on that lonely isle had once been a colossus.

Napoleon is also the villain of Mr. C. N. R. [*sic*] James's play "Toussaint L'Ouverture" recently produced by the Stage Society. The author has presented the story of the rising in Hayti when the French were swept from the island most effectively. The negro who developed into a military genius and broke the power of slavery in the island was magnificently played by Paul Robeson. For once at least this great artist had a part worthy of his genius.

His dignity, eloquence, the quick play of his wit, presented an unforgettable picture.

We are given a glimpse of Napoleon as First Consul when Toussaint L'Ouverture's campaign has reached a successful issue. The black general has never cut adrift from France; he wishes the island to remain a part of her possessions and for that reason refused England's offer of help if he would establish himself as king.

Napoleon, however, has no use for black genius and regards it as impertinent that mere Negroes should have attempted to abolish slavery. He dispatches his brother-in-law to quell what he regards as a rising with instructions to send Ouverture captive to Europe, to bribe his generals to leave him and when the insurgents have been repressed to re-establish slavery.

The betrayal of Ouverture has an uncomfortable likeness to European diplomacy of a more recent date. The General signs terms of peace, and extracts the pledged word of the French Commander in Chief that slavery shall never be re-established. He dismisses his men and is promptly taken prisoner and dispatched to a Swiss prison where he dies. The play ends with the triumph of Dessalines, Ouverture's aide-de-camp, who drives the French out of the island.

The moral of the whole business is that Ouverture had armed the black populace and had instructed them never to give up their means of defence. For this reason they could not be subdued. The play needs shortening and tightening up and there were moments when I felt that Mr. Peter Godfrey's production was a touch fantastic. Mr. Charles Maunsell was admirable as the Republican envoy to Ouverture and Mr. Norman Shelley played a die-hard planter to perfection. With these two exceptions, however, the black artists outplayed the white from start to finish.

I wish this drama could be performed at a West End Theatre. It is calculated to provoke argument and thought, two of the most considerable assets of the theatre, which today are but rarely found.

J. K. PROTHERO [ADA ELIZABETH CHESTERTON],
G.K. [CHESTERTON]'S WEEKLY, 2 APRIL 1936

"Toussaint L'Ouverture": Success of
C. L. R. James' Play in London

Judging from the reception given Mr. C. L. R. James' play "Toussaint L'Ouverture" in London by the leading newspapers, it has been a success and the "Port of Spain Gazette" is informed that Mr. James has received a cable from a Broadway producer asking him to arrange a production in New York.

PORT OF SPAIN GAZETTE, 19 APRIL 1936

Paul Robeson in "Toussaint L'Overture"

Mr. C. L. R. James, a young West Indian journalist, has written a play, "Toussaint L'Overture," which was produced for two performances on Sunday and Monday, by the Stage Society, at the Westminster Theatre. The title role was played by Mr. Paul Robeson, well known to London playgoers as a singer and as an interpreter of negro parts, particularly in Eugene O'Neill's plays.

The play concerns the life of the negro liberator of Haiti or San Domingo in the West Indies. The action being at the time of the Napoleonic wars, and shows how, from being merely a coachman, Toussaint rose to become the leader of all the Negroes of the island; and in doing so, defied the forces of all the colonial powers: England, France and America.

It reveals the appalling conditions prevailing in a slave colony and the more than selfish attitude of the planters towards their human property, as well as the greatness of the negro people in a time of stress.

Toussaint and Dessalines, portrayed by Mr. R. Adams, turn these abject rebels against a system into a formidable army of blacks who defeat even an army of Napoleonic France. There is only one answer to this — the personality of one man. Such a man was Toussaint. Mr. Robeson gives us the greatness of the leader who, realising the littleness of his followers and their ignorance, deals with them as children, and with his enemies, the whites, as an incarnation of subtlety.

The theme itself is excellent propaganda for the negro side of the colour question but as treated by Mr. James it is more than this; it is a remarkable piece of literature, which fact has been appreciated by *Life and Letters Today*, who are publishing it serially.

The acting of the minor characters suffered from an excess of zeal which came, perhaps, from their intensity of feeling in their parts. An exquisite cameo of deliverance came from Mr. Wilfrid Walter as Colonel Vincent, Toussaint's white envoy. Mr. Robeson appeared at times to be afraid to allow himself to live in the part and it was only in the death scene that he really gave the impression of great acting.

As a whole this may be said to be a play which, although dealing with a highly controversial theme, the colour question, deserves public presentation in London as a vivid piece of dramatic writing.

L. F. H., *THE LITERARY REVIEW*, APRIL 1936

Toussaint L'Ouverture, Westminster Theatre (Stage Society)

I have always wanted to see Paul Robeson in a play worthy of his powers. At long last my wish has been fulfilled.

This play is built round events in Haiti at the time of the French Revolution. Led by Toussaint Louverture the slaves make a bid for freedom at the same time as the peasants are fighting for it in France. Their revolt is successful, slavery is abolished, and in the name of the French Republic Toussaint establishes freedom and prosperity among the Negro people of Haiti.

But this does not satisfy the white planters; to them Negroes are fit only to be slaves on plantations. On their behalf Napoleon sends a force to Haiti, tricks the Negroes into submission, throws Toussaint shamefully into prison, where he dies, and finally attempts to re-establish slavery. At this the Negroes rise once more; Haiti is declared a republic, and to this day she remains an independent Negro state.

This is the story enfolded in a swiftly moving drama; a play which grips the audience from beginning to end, and takes it completely out of itself into the atmosphere of the Napoleonic era. Yet this is a first play; its author, Mr. C. L. R. James, is a Negro journalist who has spent most of his life in Trinidad.

Robeson plays the part of Toussaint, and he does not fail to show what a great Negro actor can do, given the scope. And he receives able support from a group of coloured amateurs and white professionals.

The performance at the Westminster was private, under the auspices of the Stage Society. The name of Peter Godfrey, as producer, is itself a mark of the excellence of the play; but whether it will ever have the long run it deserves is a more doubtful matter. The play tells the truth about Negroes, and there are few white audiences which want to know the truth about Negroes.

Some months ago Mr. Robeson promised to launch a theatre in London for presenting Negro art. Such a theatre is long overdue, and when it does materialise *Toussaint L'Ouverture* will have first claims upon it. Meanwhile let us hope that the play will be produced again shortly so that the public may get the chance to see what is really a first-class play.

G. M., *THE KEYS; THE OFFICIAL ORGAN OF THE LEAGUE OF COLOURED PEOPLES*, 3, NO. 4 (APRIL–JUNE 1936)

APPENDIX

| | | | |

C. L. R. James at the congregation for his honourary Doctorate of Letters, University of Hull, 28 July 1983. Courtesy of the University of Hull.

"The Intelligence of the Negro" by C. L. R. James

In the last issue of *The Beacon* appeared a paper by Dr. Sidney C. Harland entitled "Race Admixture." In it he stated that the negro race was inferior in intelligence to the white.

Perhaps before going any further it should be just as well to take a glance at certain aspects of the history of the subject. Gobineau at once springs to mind. It was in the year 1853 that Gobineau published the first volume of his famous work, *On the Inequality of Human Races.* In his book Gobineau proved among other things that the white race was the first of races in its capacity both to absorb and to create culture. In that part of his book at least, Europe agreed with him: Europeans were very sure of themselves in the third quarter of the last century. Doubtless Gobineau as a student of race and culture was very interested in the accounts brought back by Commodore Perry of that backward people, the Japanese, whom the Commodore first in 1853 and again in 1854 visited and brought once more into contact with Western civilisation. The Japanese at this time were still a mediaeval people who, living out of touch with Europe, had apparently remained stationary for three hundred years — a living proof of Gobineau's theory. Gobineau unfortunately died sometime in the seventies, but some of those very Marines who in 1854 marched through the streets of this backward country must have been alive in 1905 to see Japan, having mastered with amazing quickness and completeness the culture and organisation of Europe, administer such a beating to one of the most powerful of Western nations that her power has ever since been one of the cardinal factors in any consideration of world affairs. No nation in history has ever done what Japan did in those fifty short years. So much for the capacity to absorb.

And as for creation, I take it that Dr. Harland knows the place which Japanese art, for instance, holds in the history of culture. Hokusai, who is only one of a group, ranks with Titian, Michael Angelo, and Rembrandt among the greatest artists of all time. The achievements of Japan more than anything else caused a sharp revision of this theory of the inequality of races.

In this connection I cannot do better than quote Mr. Wells:

> Even today there are many people who fail to grasp the essential facts of this situation. They do not realize that in Asia the average brain is not one whit inferior in quality to the average European brain; history shows Asiatics to be as bold, as vigorous, as generous, as self-sacrificing and as capable of strong collective action as Europeans . . .

In the short space of less than three-quarters of a century there has been a complete revolution in scientific and historical thoughts as to the relative quality of Eastern and Western minds.

Now, in historical matters, least of all in a matter of this kind, one cannot take logical inferences as final. Nevertheless it is unwise to neglect them. They are useful if only for the purpose of indicating a valuable line of investigation.

Let us now take the case of the negro. The ninth edition of the *Encyclopaedia Britannica*, published in 1884, was very definite in its statement of the absolute mental inferiority of the negro to other races. More than that, it not only was certain of the fact, it knew the cause. Let me quote:

> . . . the cranial sutures, which close much earlier in the negro than in the other races. To this premature ossification of the skull, preventing all further development of the brain, many pathologists have attributed the inherent mental inferiority of the blacks, an inferiority which is even more marked than their physical differences.

"An inferiority which is even more marked than their physical differences." Nothing could be plainer. And this is how the article ends:

> No full-blood negro has ever been distinguished as a man of science, a poet, or an artist, and the fundamental equality claimed for him by ignorant philanthropists is belied by the whole history of the race throughout the historic period.

Let us step forward twenty-seven years and see what the eleventh edition of the *Britannica*, 1911, has to say on the same subject:

Mentally the negro is inferior to the white. The remark of F. Manetta, made after a long study of the negro in America, may be taken as generally true of the whole race. "The negro children were sharp, intelligent and full of vivacity, but on approaching the adult period a gradual change set in. The intellect seemed to become clouded . . . the growth of the brain is . . . arrested by the premature closing of the cranial sutures and lateral pressure of the frontal bone." This explanation is reasonable and even probable as a contributory cause; but evidence is lacking on the subject.

And later:

But though the mental inferiority of the negro to the white or yellow races is a fact, it has often been exaggerated . . .

The difference in tone is clear. No longer is the inferiority "more marked than the physical differences." Further, the writer admits that the suggested cause of the inferiority, though probable, lacks proof. He deprecates exaggeration.

That was in 1911. The fourteenth edition was published in 1929. In the article "Negro" under the heading "Mental Qualities," we read:

In reviewing the comparative studies of the differences between the Negro and the modern European, Carr Saunders concludes that "there seems to be no marked difference in innate intellectual power. The differences are rather differences in disposition and temperament . . . The apparent arrest of development may not be so much an inevitable result of the kind of mental faculties which are inherited as the coming into play of a peculiar tradition."

Could any progression be clearer?

Carr Saunders's book was written before 1922, the *Britannica* article very probably late in 1927 or early in 1928. During the last few years I have met at every turn evidence of the changed attitude towards the intelligence of the negro. In fact to be unaware of it is inexcusable ignorance. The phrase is not my own. Writing in the *Spectator* of May 16, 1931, on "Skin Colour," Professor L. W. Lyde begins thus:

The two main forces behind our persistent colour prejudice are fear and vanity, but the strength of both is largely dependent on habit and on ignorance.

And lest that would not be clear enough he is even more emphatic at the end of his article where, after referring to different kinds of fear that white people have for the negro, he says:

> This fear, though inarticulate, probably has been and still is more harmful than even the vanity of any belief in racial superiority; but the ignorance—on which both are based has been excusable till quite recently.

"The vanity of any belief in racial superiority." We have travelled a long way from "an inferiority which is even more marked than their physical differences."

I am not writing here to convince Dr. Harland of the error of his views. He may very well be inclined to stick to his own opinion. Some men are very hard to convince. Some, as Pope well knew, cannot be convinced at all. But what I do say is this. No competent reader of Dr. Harland's paper will deny that despite the general survey which he attempted, his main concern was with the negro. Of the negro he claimed special knowledge. It was with the negro that his statistics chiefly dealt. And yet the Doctor put forward his antiquated opinions with a confidence and self-sufficiency which betoken his total, his teetotal abstention from recent views on the subject. And I do not think that he can shelter himself behind Professor Lyde's statement that the evidence on which his ignorance is based has not been available until recently. It has been available long enough for me to know, the moment I saw Professor Harland's article, in what decade his mind was moving.

But perhaps it is too much to expect a scientist to take or be in any way influenced by the historical view. Let us suppose then that Dr. Harland, having lived in the West Indies a long time, had used his eyes and observed the relative intelligences of the people around him. Surely quite casual observation would be enough to tell him that in no field of human enterprise where the competition is open can the negro's intelligence be considered inferior. In the open professions, law and medicine, in the sphere of higher education, in the Civil Service, in politics, in journalism, the negro's record, especially when one considers his immense initial disadvantages, shows intelligence second to that of no other race. And not only in the West Indies where the European is naturally at a disadvantage. Trinidad has but a third of a million people. Her educational facilities are of necessity inferior to those of more highly developed and wealthier centres of civilization. Yet since the War, from Trinidad alone we have seen negro students defeating all comers at English law examinations, we have seen them winning gold medals at competitions of the Royal Academy of Music. They win scholarships and distinguish themselves at hospitals of the standard of St. Bartholomew's. Today there is a young negro surgeon in Trinidad whose extraordinary ability is fully recognised, if not here, by his colleagues in London. Whoever has any doubts on this question cannot do better than consult masters at the Queen's Royal or St. Mary's Colleges who have an experience extending back many years. I do not make excessive claims for West Indian negroes. I know only too well the shortcomings of my own people. But in one thing they are not inferior. And that thing is intelligence. Let Dr. Harland leave his books for a while and sit up and take notice. Wherever the negro is given a chance, he establishes himself. And this from a people barely three generations away from the physical and moral degradation of slavery.

That Dr. Harland knows little of the history of his subject is, though deplorable, not irremediable. A little application can set that right. That the evidence around him should have taught him otherwise but failed to do so is also understandable. Aesop's astronomer, engaged in scanning the stars, fell into an ordinary well. But it is when the Doctor is on what I may call his own ground, when I look at the reasons that he advances for his view, that I find it hard to forgive him. Says the learned Doctor:

> Ferguson, in testing the intelligence of 486 white and 421 coloured children, found that pure negroes scored 69.2 per cent as high as the whites, that the three-quarter negro scored 73.2 per cent as high as the whites, that the mulattoes scored 81.2 per cent as high as the whites and the quadroons obtained 91.8 percent of the white score.

He continues:

> Most of the other investigations which have been made confirm the results obtained above. Our conclusion is therefore . . .

Now a colleague writing a short notice of Dr. Harland, for a newspaper, say, would hardly write as a statement of the Doctor's achievements: "He has written on Race Admixture and has done other scientific work." He would be much more likely to say that the Doctor was head of a Cotton Research Station, had travelled widely in botanical pursuits, etc. etc., the etceteras being all the Doctor's lesser achievements, right down to the paper on Race Admixture. Where space or time is limited or where there is no necessity to say too much a man states his main point or points and goes on.

And I take it therefore that when Dr. Harland quotes Ferguson he states what he considers his most important argument. I need not comment on the looseness of his succeeding sentence. "Most of the other investigations which have been made confirm the results obtained above."

That is obviously untrue (it would mean that the modern evidence I have indicated is based not on investigation but on fancy). More than that, its general flabbiness shows that Dr. Harland only pushed it in to bolster up his case. Ferguson alone was good enough for him. The kind of proof he offers is a measure of the kind of proof he accepts. He gives us no hint of what these tests were like. He does not tell us of the almost overwhelming difficulties that are inseparable from all such tests, above all, in the United States. He is unaware or does not think it necessary to state (either of which is equally heinous) that even in families apparently of the same social grading, a comparison is not fair because the negro child in America, constantly discriminated against, always made to feel inferiority ("No dogs nor negroes in this park") inevitably suffers in spirit; that the grand-parents of millions of negroes in America today were slaves, and anyone with a little imagination can think of what the mental atmosphere of many of the homes must be; that the worse quarters of any town or district are reserved for the negro; that sanitary conditions and all the departments of public health are usually far less cared for than in the corresponding white section; that unemployment is the negro's portion not only in abnormal but also in normal times: he usually is employed only after the supply of white men has given out; and England today knows the effect on any home of the continued unemployment of the head of the house. When Ferguson made his tests the Doctor does not say (from internal evidence I should say before 1900). Things are improving steadily in America, but even today there is so much disparity between the relative environments of white and black that there is a wide-spread scepticism about most of these tests.

Dr. Harland has space for a long and pretty useless statement of types of ability by Galton. But to prove the inferiority of the negro all that is necessary is this: "Ferguson tested, etc. Most of the other investigations confirm his results. [I cannot get over the raw dishonesty of that sentence.] Therefore the negro is inferior." And then very naively the Doctor gives himself away. He attempts to comfort the negro for any loss of pride he may sustain at this hurtful conclusion. Without the slightest cause (except the sentimental one I have pointed out) he adds, "There is little doubt also that the aborigines of Australia are innately inferior to the negro." No proof, no "investigation," no "Ferguson," nothing; just the bare statement, showing to all the world that despite his parade of scientific knowledge and scientific method Dr. Harland's approach to this subject is the same as that of the average uneducated European, an approach in essence emotional and not rational.

It can serve no useful purpose to go into his exposition of Galton's divisions of grades of intelligence. These things are useful but extremely dangerous when handled in the amateurish way Dr. Harland handles them. He says that "the proportion of Negroes with intelligence about equal to the foreman of an English jury is about 1 in 413." Maybe. Maybe not. I have no time to argue about a statement such as that. But all through this part of his paper I can see that Dr. Harland has fallen into the elementary error of using symbols of a wide variability as constants. And it comes as no surprise to me that when he pays heavily for this silliness by a monstrous blunder. Who is responsible for it I do not know. All the evidence points to Dr. Harland. But, if it is Galton, then the less Galton he.

Toussaint L'Ouverture was a coachman in Hayti until he was well over forty. About 1790, when about fifty years of age, he joined the Haytian army as a physician and rose rapidly to high command. But Toussaint had one passionate aim—the liberation of the blacks from slavery. He joined the Spaniards of San Domingo and swept the French before him. When the French, however, ratified the freedom of the slaves, Toussaint, faithful always to the cause he had at heart, joined the French again and "in a campaign scarcely equalled for its vigour in all military history," he broke the power of his former allies. The English under Maitland he defeated in pitched battles until they were glad enough to fly to Jamaica. A rebellion of the French soldiers against their general was crushed by Toussaint, and the French, the proudest military nation in Europe, appointed the ex-coachman Commander-in-Chief. Toussaint set to work, and from the dregs of humanity into which the slaves had been turned by centuries of unparalleled cruelty, he formed an army. By 1800 he was master of the whole country. "No one before him had succeeded in uniting both the Spanish and French settlements and the all but impassable mountain ranges under a single ruler. Never in the history of the world has as barren a human field yielded in a little time so marvellous a flowering of greatness." (All my quotations are from white historians.) Toussaint devoted himself to government. Let the letter written to Napoleon by Colonel Vincent, who was at one time Toussaint's private secretary, speak. "Sire," wrote the Colonel, "leave the country alone; it is the happiest spot in your dominions. God raised this man to govern; races melt under his hand . . ." Toussaint (this was in 1800, mind you) introduced Free Trade, he introduced full religious toleration. He wiped out all old disputes and called on Frenchmen of Hayti, and Spaniards of San Domingo, to come home. "The negro only sought that liberty which God gave him," he said. But Napoleon's ambition would not let the island rest. He sent his brother-in-law and one of his finest armies to peaceful and prosperous Hayti. Toussaint, Henri Christophe, and Dessalines waged a guerrilla warfare with masterly skill. The French, unable to pin them down, proposed a treaty, promising freedom to the blacks. That was all Toussaint was fighting for and he signed. A few weeks after the French invited him for dinner. The moment he entered the room the officers drew their swords and told him he was a prisoner. They could have paid him no greater compliment than this treachery. Such in bare outline is the story of Toussaint, whose latest biographer (1931) entitles his book *The Black Napoleon*, and whose personal quality, apart from his achievements, was such that he could dictate to three secretaries at once. His whole marvellous career barely covers ten years.

Now, Dr. Harland, having given his exposition of Galton's scheme of classification proceeds to classify Toussaint. He puts him in Class F, the lowest of the superior classes, 1/4,300. In other words among every 4,300 men the Doctor expects to find a Toussaint L'Ouverture. He will pick a Toussaint from every tree. According to this theory Port-of-Spain has fifteen such men, San Fernando two, there is one between Tunapuna and Tacarigua. Or if Dr. Harland prefers it that way there are about 80 in Trinidad today. I need carry this absurdity no further. But what respect can anyone have for a man who in the midst of what he would have us believe is a scientific dissertation produces such arrant nonsense!

But there is more to come. In the very same paragraph he produces another gem, of almost but not quite the same water as the Toussaint clarification. "From another point of view we seldom hear of a white traveller meeting with a black chief whom intellectually he feels to be the better man."

This for proof of the inferiority of the negro race! A European, with a European education, with a European background, meets a negro Chief in Africa, talks to him (about Genetics, and the Reform of the House of Lords I expect) and goes away without feeling any sense of inferiority. "Our conclusion is therefore . . ." Isn't this pathetic? I wonder if I turned that argument round what Dr. Harland would say. But perhaps Dr. Harland believes that the average negro meets white men with a sense of innate intellectual inferiority. Let me assure the Doctor, let me earnestly and religiously assure him that it is not so. I may seem to have strayed. I do not think I have. It seems to me that some such idea is moving at the back of Dr. Harland's mind, a "Prejudice" which he is trying to "rationalize." I cannot believe that it is purely bankruptcy of intellect and information which explains his proffering this ghastly ineptitude as a proof of negro inferiority.

I do not think it worthwhile even to discuss his endorsement of Ferguson's statistics which would have us believe that the fairer the skin of the man of mixed blood, the more intelligent he is. Where a man is so mixed as Dr. Harland is even before he mixes the races, we can guess at the nature of the racial admixture which he will wish to administer. He forgets the essential fact. The fairer skin always gets the better chance. So that it will always appear to the superficial observer that the fairer-skinned crosses have more ability than the dark.

And so all through his paper I can point to his lack of proper acquaintance with his subject, his inability to see more than the surface of any statement, and that only from his own carefully-chosen angle. Take for instance where he says "the negro race has rarely produced such men as Toussaint L'Ouverture." Would the Doctor (if we can imagine the transference) have accepted as proof of the innate mental inferiority of his ancestors, the following statement from one of the earlier Roman governors of Britain, "You Britons are not only barbarians but innately inferior because you have rarely, in fact you have never produced any such men as Julius Caesar, Virgil, Scipio Africanus, and Cicero." Yet that is exactly what the Doctor is saying. Any educated man, in fact any man with a little commonsense, exercises some sense of historical proportion in these matters. Let the Doctor take warning from the quotation I made from the 1884 *Britannica*, that the negro was obviously inferior because no full-blood negro had risen to eminence as scientist, writer, or artist. How stupid that argument sounds today! I do not know if Dr. Harland has ever heard of James Weldon Johnson. I doubt if he has. Mr. Johnson has just retired from his post as secretary of the National Association for the Advancement of Coloured People, and a public dinner was given in his honour in New York on May 14th. At the dinner (I quote from *The Nation's* editorial columns), "there were hundreds of guests both white and coloured," there were speeches by "various associates and admirers of Mr. Johnson through his long life as song-writer, poet, diplomat, public man." Finally, concludes *The Nation*: "There are few men in the country of whatever colour who could have called forth such whole-hearted tributes from persons so enlightened; there are few who could have responded to these tributes with such distinction."

How many white people, particularly Colonials, hear of a man like Johnson? How many men today know what was the real quality of Booker T. Washington? To most he was a clever, even a distinguished negro, and nothing more. Time will right all these things. When names like Hoover, Coolidge, Mellon, Stimson, and Walker, which fill the American news today, are as dead as dust, there will yet be a place in history for Booker T. Washington, James Weldon Johnson, Moton of Tuskegee, Burghardt du Bois, and others of their kind who, in the face of every imaginable difficulty, have fought and are still fighting the case of negro emancipation.

I think I have written enough. I would have far preferred to write on Toussaint L'Ouverture for instance. But I have thought it necessary to reply to Dr. Harland's view of the negro for two reasons.

The first is that there may be negroes who might read his article and, misled by his reputation, feel some internal disquiet. Dr. Harland, I think it fair to say, means well. He obviously likes to think of himself as a man with no prejudices, a truly scientific man, compelled after deep study and thought to come to the conclusion that the negro is about 5 (or is it 10?) percent inferior to the white man in intellect. But Science is the only department of human life where the heart must not lead the mind. It is not necessary for Dr. Harland to mean well. It is far more requisite that he should think well. But far from thinking well, it seems to me that the Doctor has not thought at all.

Which brings me to my second reason for writing. This, strangely enough, has nothing to do with the race question at all. I am not "touchous" on the race question. If at times I feel some bitterness at the disabilities and disadvantages to which my being a negro has subjected me it is soon washed away by remembering that the few things in my life of which I am proud, I owe, apart from my family, chiefly to white men, almost all Englishmen and Americans, men, some of them of international reputation, who have shown me kindness, appreciation, and in more than one case, spontaneous and genuine friendship. Looking back at my life I see that on the whole white people have befriended me far more than negroes have done, so that I am unlikely to see red on the race question, however much I am provoked to it by people who will not realise that the more they discriminate the less discriminating they show themselves. No, as I think over the Doctor's article I find that my chief reaction to it is not racial but educational. Apart from the fact that I have made some money by it off and on for some years, I am very much interested in education, particularly in the claims that it makes for the training of the mind as distinguished from the mere imparting of information. Today the old classical culture is gone. Only a few weeks ago Yale decided to drop Latin and Greek from the list of subjects required for an undergraduate degree. What will take their place as the foundation of a liberal education? Something must—and it seems as if that something will be science. Huxley had hoped that England would be a scientific nation, not so much a nation with scientific knowledge, but scientific in temper, scientific in outlook. But the strange case of Dr. Harland makes me doubtful. Here is a man admittedly eminent in his profession, yet who, the moment he steps outside it, betrays the typical vices of the unscientific: disregard of essential facts, large conclusions drawn from small premises, random statements of a patent absurdity; in fact, taking it for all in all, the very negation of the scientific temper, the very antithesis of the scientific attitude.

If the high priests of the temple cannot apply the doctrine, what hope is there for the multitude without!

THE BEACON, 5 AUGUST 1931

"A Century of Freedom" by C. L. R. James

The great-great-grandson of a freed slave tells how, since emancipation, the West Indian Negro has been able to attain to high positions of trust and responsibility in Trinidad and the West Indies.

The emancipation from slavery is the greatest event in the history of the West Indies. For the average West Indian Negro it is his Magna Carta, Bill of

Rights, Independence Day, and French Revolution, all in one. If anyone attempts to encroach on their rights the country people will reply that, maybe, it could have been done in slavery-time but not today.

The West Indian Islands and British Guiana vary very much in size and population. The total population is something less than two million; four-fifths of the inhabitants are Negroes, of about 20 percent have a varying degree of white blood. Any general survey of the last hundred years, therefore, would need to be hedged about with so many qualifications that it would be best for me to start with a concrete picture, the history of my own family.

My great-great-grandfather was a slave in the southern port of Trinidad. He was a carpenter and his master allowed him to go from place to place, sometimes thirty or forty miles away, to work for other people. He thus made money for his master and a little for himself. Working in one estate, he fell in love with a female slave, my great-great-grandmother. He worked hard, bought her from her master, married her, and stayed on working on the estate, more or less permanently separated from his master. It does not seem that he worried very much about being a slave, and in his particular circumstances there was no reason why he should have done. Two children were born on the estate but they were slaves. Then he brought his wife away from the estate into the village and after a time was able to buy his two children from the owner. One of these was my great-grandmother. In 1833 he became absolutely free. He bought a piece of land and life was fairly easy for him.

Then you have one class and rather a small class of the Negroes at the time of emancipation, the house-slaves, for whom slavery was not physically a very oppressive state. There were, too, a few free people of colour, pure Negroes and mixed, some of whom had attained to wealth and education. But by far the larger majority—for instance, in Jamaica about a quarter of a million—were agricultural labourers, and though this is a controversial point, yet from what my grandmother's aunt, old cousin Nancy, used to say—and I remember her quite well—the slaves in the fields used to have a dreadful time.

My grandmother was born in 1846. She is in her eighty-seventh year and is still able to go to church and follow the service in her prayer-book, as she has done all her life. I mention this because too many people believe that the West Indians even today are a primitive people slowly emerging into civilisation. But, chiefly through the devoted work of the nonconformist churches, there was a little education, and my grandmother learnt to read and write. About ten years ago she had to witness some document dealing with the transfer of land. The solicitor suggested that she should make a cross and he would sign. My father tells me that in all his life he had never known the old lady so angry, and though rather shaky in the fingers she insisted on signing.

In 1870 Sir Patrick Keenan had visited Trinidad to report on the system of education, and by 1886, when my father was about ten years old, there was a new system, which, though not compulsory and far from adequate, yet was a great advance. But my grandfather had been struck down with paralysis and things had gone very badly with the family, and my grandmother was working as a cook to a clergyman. In other words, except for the land and the house, they were in much the same position as the majority of those who had started with nothing in 1834.

My father's elder brother was a wheelwright, but my father wanted to be a teacher, which meant a long and unremunerated apprenticeship. Strangely enough, his chief support in this determination was his grandmother, the ex-slave. He continued his schooling, learnt to play on the school harmonium, and in 1900 he became a trained certificated teacher at the Government Training College. He taught me very carefully and I won a free exhibition to the Government secondary school. He himself taught my sister music for seven years and then gave her two years with a German professor in the island. He gave my brother a secondary school education and my brother is now in the Civil Service. I taught first for many years as an acting master at the Queen's Royal College (to which I had won the free scholarship), and then I used to lecture at the Government Training College in the institution where my father had lived for two years and gained his certificate; and where his grandmother, who had been born a slave, used to visit him on Saturdays, bringing him a little money and special things to eat from home.

There you have roughly the history of thousands of middle-class families in the West Indies. In Trinidad and all through the West Indies today, elementary education is almost entirely in the hands of the Negro people. My father has acted for long periods as inspector of schools, and two of the present inspectors of schools in Trinidad are ex-schoolmasters whose origin is much the same as my father's. The splendid police force, up to the highest ranks of the non-commissioned officers, are 99 percent coloured. Nearly the whole mechanical and clerical staff of the railways, electrical, and other engineering enterprises are coloured men. The civil services are over 90 percent coloured, the medical and legal professions over 75 percent; the majority of the stipendiary magistrates are coloured men. In Jamaica the coloured people are particularly powerful, for in addition to filling the majority of the black-coated occupations they are now filling some of the highest posts in the Government as well. Take the coloured members of the West Indies side, playing cricket at present in England. Of the eleven of them there are two teachers, two sanitary inspectors, three or four doing clerical work of some kind connected with business, one a cashier, another a solicitor. Negroes have produced a Chief Justice of Barbados, Sir Conrad Reeves; and an Attorney-General of Trinidad, Mr. Vincent Brown. The present Attorney-General of British Guiana, Mr. Hector Josephs, is a Negro, and if we haven't had more posts, it is not because we were not qualified to fill them.

Now we must look for a moment at the general economic position of the people. When slavery was abolished in 1833, or to be strictly correct, in 1834, many of the more energetic struck out for themselves and squatted in the remote parts of the various islands. However, the planters who for the most part were in control of the Government were naturally hostile to this; they would not build roads to these districts, and many of these Negroes suffered from their isolation and neglect. However, the peasant proprietary movement thus begun has on the whole held good, particularly in Jamaica, and today five families out of every six in Jamaica own land. Large and flourishing co-operative societies have been established and the Jamaican Negro is the most independent in the West Indies. In Trinidad also there is a large peasant proprietary and quite a number of lower middle-class Trinidadians own and work land themselves, though, owing to the memories of slavery and also to the heat of the sun, no one does agricultural labour unless he cannot do otherwise. The situation is much the same in Grenada. In Barbados, however, it was rather different. All Barbados was owned and cultivated. There was no room there and the Negro had to take what wages he got. The result is that in no important island in the West Indies are the Negroes on the whole, comparatively speaking, so poor, and the population is pretty sharply divided into white landowners and Negro proletariat. But the Barbadian under this severe training has developed into a very hard-working, thrifty, and clever Negro; and the Barbadians may be said to be the Scots of the West Indies. The difficult situation at home has sent them abroad and wherever they have gone they have done well. That is how my maternal grandfather came to Trinidad. The son of an ex-slave, he could get nothing to do in Barbados. He came to Trinidad and, joining the mechanical department of the railway, rose to be fireman and then engine-driver, for years the only coloured engine-driver in the service. But those days are over; more and more local men are filling local posts, and in another generation a white engine-driver will be as unique as my grandfather was. His wife died early and he sent my mother to live with some nonconformist old maids. My mother was very well brought up indeed and passed on what she had been taught to us. The result is that Victorianism to me is not a thing to be amused at in books, but a very vivid and sometimes painful memory.

Now you may want to know what sort of life Negroes in the West Indies live. Well, there is work, cricket, football, tennis, books, dancing, debating societies, music, vegetating at home; much the same as you have here. Motoring is very popular. Barbados, twenty-one miles long and fourteen broad, is divided into fourteen parishes, and a Barbadian editor has told me that in a single one of those parishes, St. Michaels, there are over a thousand motorcars. As the more motor-cars there are the more civilisation, you can see that Barbados is quite civilised. There is no doubt that among too many of the labouring classes, housing and living conditions are far from what they should be. There is much ignorance and, with it, its twin brother, superstition.

But I have been told by those who have experience of judging that, taken as a whole, the West Indian working-man, even in the remoter country districts, need not be afraid of comparison with those of the countries of Europe, and is superior to many. Take education: in Kingston, the capital of Jamaica, there is compulsory education. In Trinidad we have not got compulsory education, but it has been on the statute book since 1921. Barbados has other claims to civilisation besides its motor-cars. In that island, with a population of nearly 200,000, the percentage of literacy is over 80, while in Trinidad among the Negro population it is nearly 75 percent.

With the social question, one can bracket the colour question. There is race prejudice in the West Indies, but no race antagonism. I have heard of few clubs or associations of any kind in the West Indies which did not have some very rich and powerful coloured men as members. Usually you will find that while Mr. White and Mr. Rich Coloured are members of the aristocratic men's club, Mr. and Mrs. White are members of another club to which

Mr. and Mrs. Rich Coloured are not admitted. But quite often Mrs. White and Mrs. Rich Coloured meet on social welfare boards and on committees arranging functions for the poor, and some of these meetings are held in one another's homes and they meet and are very cordial and friendly in a semi-official way. Now and then a rather distinguished coloured man is taken up by the white people, or at least by a majority of them, and accepted as one of themselves. That is equivalent to being given a peerage in England, for there is no doubt that the white people in the West Indies still exercise an enormous prestige.

There is little intermarriage in the ordinary sense of the word. That is to say that you will rarely find a dark West Indian black man, however rich or however distinguished, marrying a West Indian white woman, but the three-quarter white will try to marry white; the mulatto, that is the half-breed, will very often marry a three-quarter white, the dark brown Negro more often than not marries the mulatto. What the middle-class Negro rarely does is to marry darker than himself, for the various shades of the coloured people have quite as much prejudice against one another as the whites have against them. On the other hand, the large majority are quite black and marry among themselves.

The full effects of emancipation can only be judged by a review of the political as well as the social activities of the coloured people, and so I propose to say something of the political situation in the West Indies today. In 1833 most of the islands had representative government and if not altogether in theory, in fact had pretty complete control of internal affairs. When the slaves became free, however, it was clear that sooner or later they would begin to move towards political power, and while still unfit for full political rights would hopelessly out-vote the few white people. Then the labour troubles following on emancipation, coupled with England's free trade policy, contributed to economic decline, which in turn led to political disorder. The consequence was that after forty years the British Government was able to persuade nearly all the islands to give up their representative government and to submit to a form of Crown Colony government by which the Crown gained full powers in the legislature, coupled with full financial responsibility. Most of the islands accepted, except Barbados, for, owing to the fact that the Barbados Negro had no choice but to stay where he was and accept such wages as he was offered, the Barbados planters had the situation well in hand and successfully resisted the attempts of the British Government to gain control. They and the Bahamas still have their representative government, and the House of Assembly in Barbados goes back nearly 300 years. In most of the other islands, however, although there are elected members of the governing council, yet the will of the Governor is still the Sovereign will. It is towards control of internal affairs that the democratic movement is directed.

Most, though not all, of the white people in the West Indies, say that the coloured people are not yet ready for full control, and that self-government will result in internal chaos. They say that capital from abroad will cease to come into the islands and there will probably be a flight of some of the capital at present invested. They say also that the islands have made great progress under the present system, which may well be allowed to continue, or at least extended very slowly instead of attempting a risky experiment such as full democratic control. These views are also held by quite a number of coloured middle-class people, who view with suspicion the increasing organisation of the working classes.

The democratic party denies all this. We — and you will understand that I personally associate myself with the democratic movement — believe that such questions as education, labour legislation, the proper adjustment of taxation and distribution of expenditure, are matters which can only be satisfactorily settled by a democratic constitution. But there is more in the movement than that. People who are governed from abroad often feel that they are considered in some way inferior, backward, or immature, and that many of us resent. Education and all intellectual and political life take their colour and direction from those who have power. The masses cannot respect their own people and respect themselves when the highest positions are so regularly filled from abroad, and many of the better educated Negroes feel the time has come through a free political life to begin building up some sense of background, some consciousness of responsibility which will fortify and stimulate us in our development. There is no treason in this. The West Indian Negro in the West Indies is the most loyal subject in the British Empire, and any move towards giving the island to any other country would immediately cause revolution. But perhaps you will allow me to say that the coloured West Indian of decent up-bringing and good education on holiday or studying for the professions in England is often treated in such a way that he loses much of the goodwill which he brought with him. Englishmen who respect the Empire would do well not to forget that it is the West Indians studying in England who will be moulding West Indian political opinion in the future.

As for myself, I have lived in the West Indies all my life. I came here just over a year ago and I have not had the slightest difficulty in entering into the phases of the life I see around me. I should do wrong not to say that, particularly from the intelligentsia (a horrible word, but I know no other), I have received a warm welcome and much kindness. But, were it not for a few institutions like the Student Movement House, and the League of Coloured Peoples, the average West Indian student would have a dreadful time. I say this and state our political aims because a centenary is a time when one should look not only backwards but forwards.

A few weeks ago I wanted a typist and after some difficulty I found one. I started to dictate to her about the West Indies and after a few lines, she asked me what island I was from. I said Trinidad, and she told me that her people had lived there and held slaves before emancipation. When we had finished we walked down the steps together, she in front and I behind, for I had stayed to turn on the light. As we neared the end of the steps she said, "Strange, isn't it, that your people used to work for mine and now I work for you?" At the bottom of the steps she waited for me and standing on the level we shook hands.

THE LISTENER, 31 MAY 1933

"Slavery Today: A Shocking Exposure" by C. L. R. James

One hundred years ago this month, the famous Act of Parliament was passed which abolished all slavery within British possessions. Then Parliament dealt with 700,000 slaves. Today, throughout the world, there are 5,000,000. And there are still slaves within the British Empire.

I am the great-grandson of a freed slave. Although I am still a young man I knew personally a great-aunt of mine who had been a slave in her early days, and I have often heard her speak of what slavery meant in those days before the Abolition.

In the West Indies, where I come from, the Act of Abolition, passed through Parliament one hundred years ago this month, is the great background to our lives. We discuss it sometimes as if it were only yesterday.

Our history begins with it. It is the year One of our calendar. Before that we have no history.

Therefore, you will see that I have some direct *personal* interest in this article which the Editor of *Tit-Bits* has asked me to write.

A few weeks ago I broadcast from the B.B.C. stations on the progress and advancement made by the men of my race since the Act of Liberation. But my theme now is very different. I want to deal now, not with the freed and their future, but with the shackled who have no future.

In 1833, the Act of Abolition involved no more than 700,000 slaves. *Today, a century after, there are more than 5,000,000 slaves, distributed throughout fifteen different areas of the world.*

When that Act, which all Englishmen are today justly and proudly celebrating, went upon the Statute Book, it was hoped that by example, by persuasion and, sometimes, by force, the rest of the world would follow, and all men would be soon free. We know now that we were wrong in that belief, in that hope.

While you are reading this there are thousands of men and women, chained and shackled together, being whipped and driven along forests and jungle paths of the Central African hinterland, driven into slavery hundreds and hundreds of miles away from their burnt and plundered villages.

FIRE AND CARNAGE

In great cities of Arabia, over which are flying Imperial Airways passenger machines which left Croydon a few days ago, there are slave markets by the score, where human merchandise is bought and sold. At the very gates of the Great Mosque in the Holy City of Mecca itself there is a huge market where the slaves, men and women, are penned, chained to benches until they are sold to some passer-by.

All of them are Negroes, and there is ample evidence that many have been taken from villages in parts of Africa *which are under British protection.*

In Abyssinia, a stronghold of the Christian Church, there are upward of two million slaves. Almost every Abyssinian owns one or two, the chiefs or Rases owning sometimes more than a thousand. In that enlightened country slaves are sometimes used as currency, being exchanged for land, arms, and ammunition.

The Arabs in Africa are the great slave traders, Abyssinia and Southern

Arabia their greatest market. They are the most expert, the most ruthless, and the most persistent as raiders, ranging sometimes a thousand miles from their bases collecting their pitiful human cargoes.

No white man has ever seen a slave raid, but we have descriptions of them from refugee slaves. Here is one as told recently to a District Officer by a slave who escaped into the British Sudan from a caravan bound for the markets of Abyssinia: —

The raiders must have surrounded our village at night while we were sleeping. Our huts were in a clearing, and the Arabs, about 500 of them, had advanced to the edge of the forest all round us during the night. We were 200 — men, women, and children.

Just before the dawn they flung blazing fibre on to the thatch of the huts nearest them, and the wind began to blow the flames towards the other huts. There was a terrible confusion as we all rushed out on the alarm and then tried to save our possessions.

Meanwhile, the Arabs lay concealed, watching to see how many we were. Suddenly, above the crackling of the flames and the shrieks of the women, I heard the crackling of gunfire and the next minute they were on us. We could see them coming in the glare of the flames but we were helpless. Those of us who had weapons in their hands were shot down, others were knocked down by blows from chain flails and rifle butts. They plunged in amongst us, flinging some old men and women back into the blazing huts and shooting and killing others, including women with babies and small children.

In only a few minutes it was all over. They had weeded out the young men and women amongst us, together with some girls and boys who were old enough to walk. There were forty of us left all told. In the daylight, which came soon, we were all herded out of the clearing, leaving behind us our still burning homes and the bodies of our families and the rest of our tribe.

Two days' march through the forest we passed the remains of another village, and a little way beyond it we came to another band of Arabs with about four hundred prisoners. We were put among these, and the next day the whole of us set out, chained and roped together, on a long march.

On the journey many of us died. Usually we had only a handful of maize flour for each day's journey. Those who through sickness, hunger, wounds or misery fell out were roughly handled and beaten onwards. When they fell at last, too weak to go on, they were stabbed or shot where they lay.

This happened to six of my tribe, two of them women whose children had been killed in the village on the night of the raid.

On the night of the eighteenth day of the march I escaped. During the day I had worked my arm out of the raw hide loop which bound me to the men on either side, and in the middle of the night I crawled out and through the ring of guards into the high grass. They tracked me afterwards but I got away.

That is the tale, shorn of much detail, and sparing much of the horror of the full narrative, of one man who had been through a slave raid and lived to tell his story in freedom.

The most terrible aspect of it, however, to anyone with thought and feeling, lies in the fact that it is a common story. It is happening continually the year round. The slave trade is the one trade which has never felt a slump.

All civilized countries must bear their share of the blame for the continuance of this hideous evil. Our record, as befits the country which first proclaimed the freedom of every man within its sway, is less bad than the others which I shall name.

But let us be frank. One hundred years after that famous Act of Abolition there *are still thousands of slaves within the British Empire.* Most people believe that Act of 1833 ended all slavery beneath the British flag. It did not.

Only a few years ago Mr. Amery freed 215,000 slaves in Sierra Leone. Sir Harcourt Butler freed nearly 8,000 in Burma. In the last ten years nearly 200,000 have been liberated in Tanganyika. That is more than ninety years after the work of Wilberforce and Buxton.

And there are still more.

THE BLACKEST RECORD

In British Hong Kong, for instance, there is a system called *mui-tsai* whereby little girls are sold into Chinese households for domestic labour by their parents or guardians. There are several thousands of children owned in this way by Chinese residents of Hong Kong and registered as *mui-tsais*.

Missionaries and other investigators have compiled a huge catalogue of the horrors inflicted on girl children in China under this system. Floggings, gagging, torture with hot irons are only a few of the often unmentionable cruelties which have been commonly used on these children.

When protests were made by various Governments to the Chinese Government, the slave dealers of Shanghai merely said: "Look at Hong Kong, a British possession. They have the *mui-tsai* system there."

As long ago as 1922, Mr. Winston Churchill, then Colonial Secretary, ordered in a famous despatch, "This thing must stop." But it did not stop. Only in 1929 was the final legislation passed. And leaders and observers of the Anti-Slavery movement say that it still flourishes.

Vested interests are the prime cause of the persistence of slavery in China, Arabia, and Abyssinia. Strike at the slave-raider and the slave-trader, and the slave-owner will soon cease to exist. It was those interests which the Maharajah of Nepal had to fight a few years ago when he liberated 60,000 slaves in his kingdom. It had always been a good business and he had to persuade them that it was a bad business — or was shortly going to be so.

It is vested interests which keep the trade going against all opposition in the Portuguese dominions (the Portuguese have the worst slavery record of any civilized country), and in Abyssinia. The present King Ras Tafari is doing his best to stamp it out in his country, but he has a terrific task in front of him.

The Christian Church there gives slavery its authority, and the King has also most of the conservative elements of the country against him. One thing he has succeeded in doing, and that is to make a law providing that all children born of slaves are free.

That action stamps out the dreadful slave-breeding system which still holds in many countries which recognise slavery. Under it a woman slave who gave birth to a child received a reward for doing so. The child merely added to the slave owner's capital of flesh and blood.

It is vested interests, finally, which are behind that other subtle form of slavery — forced labour. Most European countries are stained with the same dye in regard to their countenancing of forced labour in their dominions. Portuguese East Africa is easily the worst.

But the fine flower of it is seen in Liberia. The government of this republic, controlled by a mere handful of American Negroes, has practically enslaved the whole of the 2,000,000 native inhabitants.

A League of Nations Commission which investigated conditions there published a report recently which shocked the whole of the civilised world.

British ex-officers who went out to direct labour on the rubber plantations for an American firm came home in disgust. They were given "labour" which had been marched into the plantations under the guard of armed Liberian soldiers. Some of the men were brought in chain-gangs from villages hundreds of miles away. They had been torn ruthlessly from their families and compelled to "sign on" for a number of years, labouring and living under the most terrible conditions for supposed rates of pay which, in fact, never reached them.

UNDER THE LASH

The League Commission confirmed many of the statements made by these British officers. One native witness told them: "The whip is our only pay." As a result of the Report, the President of Liberia resigned, together with many of his Cabinet. The new administration has promised to make reforms, but so far they have chiefly remained promises.

This, then, is what we have to face a century after the Emancipation. Five million fellow human beings still in bondage and sentenced to a lifetime of servitude and suffering. Over half the earth, while I am writing this, while you are reading it, the thud of the slave-drivers' flail on bare human flesh, the clanking of chains, the cries and supplications of slavery's victims resound to high heaven.

It is your responsibility and mine. What are we going to do about it?

Britain led the way one hundred years ago, and by an interesting coincidence it was British efforts a few months ago which have led to the setting-up of a Permanent Commission of the League of Nations to deal with slavery.

Our Government asked for permission to treat all slave ships as pirates, which would have had the effect of virtually ending slavery in Arabia. Permission was refused, but our demands led to the appointment of the Commission. In that there is a weapon close at hand which can end the evil.

But first we must set our own house in order. We owe that at least to the memory of Wilberforce and the other pioneers whose work we are celebrating today.

Then pressure must be brought to bear on the League to see that all nations who tolerate slavery are indicted, with no concealment and respect to none.

Public opinion, ten times more powerful now than it was in 1833, will do the rest. It worked a miracle then, it can do so again.

TIT-BITS, 5 AUGUST 1933

"I Want Negro Culture" by Paul Robeson

All the world knows by now that I have faith in the future of the negro. I believe that negro culture merits an honourable place amongst the cultures of the world. I believe that as soon as negroes appreciate their own culture, and confine their interest in the European to learning his science and mechanics, they will be on the road to becoming one of the dominant races in the world.

But the trouble is that the negro has lost faith in himself. Slavery and the white man's machines have been too much for his confidence. He has repudiated the best in himself, tried to find salvation by imitating Europeans. In the nature of this imitation he has made a most serious mistake.

Realising, quite rightly, that a nation is ultimately judged not by its might but by its culture, he has set out to try and absorb Western arts. What he has not understood is that culture cannot be put on from the outside. A certain artificial grace may be achieved by such means, but only at the cost of strangling the natural creative impulses. That is too big a price to pay, and the race which pays it can never be an influential people.

That is the tragedy of the negro at the moment. It could cease to be his tragedy tomorrow if something gave him back his self-respect. Nothing would do that so quickly as to find himself being accorded respect by Europeans.

At present white men are apt to take him at his own estimation. It is true that certain people of discrimination have freed themselves from prejudice and pronounced with respect and even enthusiasm upon negro music and negro art. But these are still too few to affect world opinion. The mass of people does not know them. Least of all does the negro know them. He continues to accept the valuation of the ignorant mass.

The one way to change his views is to demonstrate his worth practically and win world recognition for it. That was my problem. How best demonstrate to the world the quality and possibilities of negro culture? Well—being an actor—my thoughts flew to the theatre.

If one could make a start by establishing before the whole world a permanent negro theatre giving performances whose quality the critics recognised, the seeds of negro self-respect might be planted and the great swing back to African traditions begun.

Now, whenever I make that statement, I find that people misunderstand me. They imagine that I am advocating a return to grass huts and the jungle. Nothing is further from my mind. I want to see my people win a place among the great nations as educated equals, not as some quaint survival of more primitive times.

I want to see them master the European's machines and learn his control over nature. I want to see them use these to win the wealth and power which bring that liberty and leisure in which a great culture can flower. When they have that liberty and leisure they will not need to strain after the white man's culture — they have their own complete traditions developed to a stage perhaps comparable with that of England before the Reformation and Renaissance.

Out of these traditions will grow with spontaneity and power an art perhaps comparable with that of Elizabethan England — but unique art, negro art, yet as far removed from the negro art we know as modern British poetry is from that of Chaucer.

I do not think this is an impossible dream. Once remove the initial barrier — the negro's lack of faith in himself and his traditions — and anything might be achieved.

Russia is staggering the world by the results of harnessing her immense vitality to technical and industrial development but she is only doing this that she may win that liberty and leisure for her people in which she believes a great culture can flower.

I think that in this there is a lesson for the negroes. They are right in aiming at culture, but instead of trying to borrow someone else's they must develop their own. Mechanical technique can be borrowed because it is an external thing — but culture is the essence and expression of a man's own soul.

Therefore, let us learn the world's technique, but stick to our own arts. Once we have won freedom from the domination of nature, art — living and individual — will come singing and flowing spontaneously of itself.

I regard my theatre as the first step on this road. Through it we aim to win world recognition for negro productions and so help the negro back to self-respect. I intend shortly to launch this theatre in the West End.

We do not intend to confine ourselves to negro plays. That would be defeating our object. We want to produce some of those classics written by Europeans but which deal with man, the human being, irrespective of his colour, caste, or creed. We want also to produce negro plays by Europeans, negro plays by negroes, and a few plays calling for a mixed cast.

We want to do revue, and we shall aim at producing some purely African plays — plays which may hold in them the seed of a new dramatic form, since they consist of a perfect welding of drama, music, and ballet such as has never been achieved on the Western stage.

To the African, dancing, singing, and acting are not separate and divorced from life as they are among Western people. They are a spontaneous expression of different sides of his personality, and rank as naturally in his life as eating, drinking, and sleeping.

This gives his stage performance a naturalness and ease comparable with that of the Russian, and, when disciplined, gives his playing a power extremely moving to those used to the artificiality of the West.

The nearest thing London has so far seen to what we aim at achieving was provided by the "Ohel" Hebrew players last year.

For a start we shall recruit our players from those negroes already in London, but later we hope to draw them from all over the world. We may even bring a whole company from the heart of Africa. Naturally, it will take time to build up a disciplined core of first-class actors, but I am confident that we can do it, and in so doing make a decisive step towards winning the negro a new place in the world.

NEWS CHRONICLE, 30 MAY 1935

"'Civilising' the 'Blacks': Why Britain Needs to Maintain Her African Possessions" by C. L. R. James

Never was a book more timely than George Padmore's *How Britain Rules Africa*. The chapter on South Africa is particularly relevant. By false documents, by making chiefs drunk, by setting tribes against each other, by missionaries preaching religion, by every sort of dishonesty, and when that failed, by ruthless conquest, all of which is described in this book, Dutch and British brought the natives under their control, steadily fighting each other meanwhile. The British defeated the Boers, and both British and Dutch settled down to joint exploitation.

The native proletariat on the mines live in huge concentration camps, guarded night and day. They sleep like cattle on the concrete floor. After a meal of cold mealie porridge they are in the mines at 3 A.M. They may have to work in water to the waist for days. The white miners have tall rubber boots, stand in dry places, and order about and kick the blacks who do the work. If the black does not do his quota, the whole day's pay is forfeit.

At 4.30 work stops, and the native gets a warm meal consisting of the same mealie with beans—once a week, three-quarters of a pound of meat. His wage is £36 a year, and "skilled labour" gets on the average £376 a year. But by law no native may become skilled.

The British worker may say, "I am sorry for these poor beggars, but I can't take the troubles of the whole world on my shoulders." He would be wrong. In the last twenty-five years the mineral wealth of South Africa alone has produced for British and allied capital £1,578,541,929. The annual income of the gold-mining industry is over £65 millions per year. Some of Britain's share, but very little, goes in the form of super-tax towards the social services. Some goes seeking investment elsewhere and laying the basis for Imperialist war.

But its most important function is to swell the ranks of the parasitic petty-bourgeoisie at Brighton and Southport, to give good wages to certain workers who create a firm support for Citrine, Attlee, Bevin, Morrison, Lansbury and Co., and thus, in the last analysis, keep the great millions of British workers in firm subjection. And that is why Mussolini will risk his regime for Abyssinia.

The book relentlessly exposes the "civilisation" lie. In South Africa 1,800,000 whites have stolen 80 percent of the best land, 7,000,000 Bantu have 8 percent. After that you only have to tax him, and to pay the tax he must come to work at whatever wages you want to pay. Out of the funds raised by native taxation the South African Government spends £650,000 on the education of 500,000 native children, but out of general revenue, contributed to by white and black, £10 million on 400,000 Europeans. There are today in South Africa, after 300 years of European domination, but five native doctors.

LIES AND HYPOCRISY

Except in parts of West Africa and Uganda, where the Europeans cannot settle, the tale is the same. In Rhodesia and Kenya the natives are paid fourpence and fivepence a day, and then taxed to help educate European children. The imperialists strive to keep him ignorant. They educate him through missionary schools which confuse him with talk about suffering and obedience and the life to come. In Kenya the natives tried to organise their own schools. The Government closed them down. In Tanganyika they forbid English in the schools, lest the native might learn things not good for him.

Tyranny and oppression in the Colonies, and lies and hypocrisy at home, in order that the British worker may be acquiescent and peaceably assist in forging his own chains. In West Africa the native has his land, but in 1930 Imperialists paid £29 16s. per ton for cocoa at Lagos and sold for £35 12s. at Liverpool. So capitalism, by its control of prices at home and abroad, keeps its profits up though people buy less.

The book is not easy reading; it could have been better arranged; it badly needs an index. But as a picture of Africa today, economic and political, it is a masterpiece of reliable information, knowledge, and understanding, and easily the best book of its type that has yet appeared.

WORKERS' CO-OPERATION

It is on the future of Africa that the author, himself a man of African descent, is grievously disappointing. He heads one section "Will Britain Betray Her Trust?" as if he were some missionary or Labour politician. In the true tradition of Lenin, he insists on the rights of the African people to choose their own development. But, astonishingly, he welcomes the appeal of "enlightened far-sighted sections of the ruling classes of Europe with colonial interests in Africa" to co-operate with Africans. That is madness. How does the lion co-operate with the lamb?

Africans must win their own freedom. Nobody will win it for them. They need co-operation, but that co-operation must be with the revolutionary movement in Europe and Asia. There is no other way out. Each movement will neglect the other at its peril, and there is not much time left. The great cracks in the imperialist structure are widening day by day.

Africa Answers Back, by Prince Nyabongo, himself an African educated at Yale and Oxford, describes the native life of an East African tribe. The book, authoritative and written with disarming simplicity, is a powerful satire on the imperialist claim that it "civilises" Africa. It was an enormous success in America, and will be here also.

NEW LEADER, 29 MAY 1936

Letter from George Padmore to Dr. Alain Locke

Dear Esteemed Friend,

I was very disappointed not seeing you this summer. Nevertheless I was glad to have been in indirect contact with you. Shortly after your departure from Paris for the U.S.S.R. I arrived in France and remained there for several weeks doing a book "Africa in World Politics" which I have submitted to a publisher. I just received a copy of the German edition of my book on Africa. They made a splendid job of it, and strange it might sound, it is doing well in Germany. It is all the more ironical when it is recalled that the Nazis expelled me from there after Hitler came to power. The Germans are making a drive for colonies and no doubt feel that a book indicting their opponents — the British imperialists, by a Black would help to prove that they are not the only villains. It is all a game of Real politics.

I have discovered a young writer — novelist and dramatist for you — C. L. R. James. I could recommend him to no better mentor. James is an old school friend of mine. He was for some time a junior worker at Queen's Royal College in Trinidad, where our younger friend, Eric Williams, also did his secondary work. I presume you know of Mr. W. D. Innes, a former Senior master at that college. James came to London in 1932 to exploit a larger world to conquer. He has done well; but opportunities here for people of colour are not as great as in the States. James, like myself, is interested in Left politics. He is doing a book on Soviet Foreign Policy. His play on Toussaint was written especially for Robeson; to give him something dignified to say from the stage. It was put on by the British Stage Society, the most exclusive of its kind, but despite a good press, was not a financial success. For the British public is not too keen for such stuff on Black Revolutionaries when they have so many black colonies of their own to keep such ideas from. I wonder if you could get the following done for James.

1. Submit the play to some journal for publication in whole or part. I have sent you "Life and Letters" perhaps that published therein could be sold to some American journal.
2. Get some theatre group (Howard) or other coloured society to stage it;
3. Review James' novel (see British reviews). The book came out in Nov: His first novel.

4. Suggest how James can get a little money which he, like myself, is badly in need of. Perhaps it could be sold to a magazine for reproduction. I shall await your kind suggestions. By the way, Nyabongo has taken his B.Litt at Oxford this term. He joins in sending seasons greetings.

Yours truly,
George Padmore.

19 DECEMBER 1936; FROM THE ALAIN LOCKE PAPERS, MOORLAND-SPINGARN RESEARCH CENTER, HOWARD UNIVERSITY, WASHINGTON, D.C., REFERENCE NO. LOCKE 164–76 F16.

["The Maverick Club"] by C. L. R. James

How many people today ever heard of the Maverick Club? It came into existence in Trinidad after World War I. People said that Negroes could not organise anything. The Maverick Club consisted solidly of Negroes. There were the late C. T. W. E. Worrell, Jack Procope, the Davis girls (Meta, Beryl, and Kathleen) the Jameses (Ellen, Ruby, and Mabel), J. T. C. Prescott, the late E. B. Grosvenor and his three daughters, the late Cecil Adams, and many others. I was at one time Secretary. We met every Saturday night in a hall attached to All Saints Church. Later we progressed to a new house in Woodbrook.

We gave some fabulous concerts. The Grosvenor girls, Amy Gibbons, Elise Braithwaite were good musicians and fine amateur singers and S. Arthur Walke was our musical director. The best thing we ever did was a musical comedy (I forget the name) and I remember clearly Lois Procope, Jack's wife, practising the piano version of the orchestral accompaniment which she had to play. A bandsman from the Police Band came down to help, and at rehearsals conducted her as if she were an orchestra, while Walke put the singers through their paces.

Why recall all this? Because it is part of the history of nationalism in Trinidad. I ought to know. I was just from Queen's Royal College and I was familiar with Wordsworth, Keats, Dickens and Thackeray, Flaubert, and Victor Hugo. I had some knowledge of English politics. But in the Maverick Club, Worrell, Procope, and others were reading W. E. B. Du Bois, they read an American Negro magazine called *The Crisis*. They were familiar with the Negro Question in the United States. About all this I knew nothing. They were not militant, but the intellectual atmosphere and the very existence of the club was a symbol of things to come.

The club faded away and many of the women joined the Coterie of Social Workers. But the Coterie was never any club. From the first minute Audrey Jeffers knew what she was about. I remember well the impact she made when she unfolded her plans and started to work. They would make an impact today so you can imagine what they meant then.

I am pretty certain that I was Secretary of the first fair the Coterie gave at the Princes' Building, and the word soon passed. "When the day is approaching, leave Audrey alone." Years after the English wife and children of a West Indian were destitute in London, I took Audrey to see them. I shall never forget her reaction. At the mere sight of the children, the formidable organizer nearly broke down and I believe if I were not there she would have cried. Then she took over. Wherever I have been, in England and the United States, during talk about the West Indies and West Indians, the name of Audrey Jeffers will come up and there is a silence. I know the reason. You may like or not like, you may want to criticize, but the general attitude is "Audrey Jeffers. She is in a class by herself. You get one in a million like her."

All this is history. In England people write books of reminiscences, publish diaries, biographies. So the history of the country is built up. I know what to do here and how to do it, but how to get all this, as well as the regular routine of political and social life into 12 pages, that is what I don't know. The only thing is to manage somehow until the daily comes. The public needs it, but, friends, we need it more than you.

"WITHOUT MALICE," *THE NATION*, 28 FEBRUARY 1959

"A Unique Personality" by C. L. R. James

This is a review by James of the collection "Paul Robeson Speaks: Writings, Speeches, Interviews 1918–1974," edited by Philip S. Foner.

This is an extraordinary book. First the subject: a recent description of Robeson calls him, "The most marvellous human being I have ever known or seen." The writer had reason to believe that he knew Robeson quite well. This book proves that he didn't.

It consists of eight pages of contents, twenty pages of introduction by Philip Foner, a chronology of twenty pages, four hundred and fifty pages of

Robeson's career decade by decade and nearly one hundred pages of notes by the learned, rigorous, and sympathetic editor. Not to be ignored is an excellent index of thirty-two pages.

Robeson's story is well known. The most successful concert artist of his times, by 1948 he had associated himself indelibly with the policies of the USSR. The US government, by taking away his passport, confined him to the United States, and in the States Robeson was denied appearance at all concert halls and public forums.

In England, where he spent twelve successful years, Robeson used to talk constantly of the music and civilisation of the west and the folk music of blacks and orientals. We who listened did not understand. Here the truth cannot be missed:

> In the east this quality has never been damaged—to that is traceable the virility of most eastern peoples. In the west it remains healthy and active only amongst those sections of the community which have never fully subscribed to western values—that is, the exploited sections, plus some rebels from the bourgeoisie. For the rest, mathematical thinking has made them so intellectualised, so detached and self-conscious that it had tended to kill this creative and emotional side.

Robeson learned to speak twenty-four languages in order to sing the folk songs in the original words. He claimed to have learned to speak Russian in six months, whereas he had the usual difficulties with English and French. But this unity he found in the folk music of the various countries is why he always sang the spiritual and work songs of American blacks and other countries.

His politics seemed to be concentrated on the emancipation of US blacks. But Robeson travelled all over the world, including, late in life, a visit to Australia and New Zealand where he claimed his folk singing was welcomed as much as anywhere else.

With Stephen Spender, John Strachey, and André Malraux, he was one of the intellectuals of the thirties who turned their backs on capitalism. All of them, however, except Robeson, returned. Perhaps the following explains why he didn't:

> Once I was driving in Jamaica. My road passed a school and as we came abreast at the building a great crowd of school children came running out

to wave at me. I stopped, got out of my car to talk with them and sing to them. Those kids were wonderful. I have stopped at similar farms in our own deep south and I have talked to Negro children everywhere in our country. Here for the first time I could talk to children who did not have to look over their shoulders to see if a white man was watching them talk to me.

I was the person who wrote the appreciation with which this review began. Paul had played the leading part in a play of mine, and we had spent four weeks rehearsing. But, while I recognised what a remarkable man he was, I had no idea of the study of languages, of music, the incessant political activity, and the simple human feeling which integrated themselves into this astonishing and perhaps unique twentieth-century personality.

NEW SOCIETY, 8 FEBRUARY 1979

"Paul Robeson" by C. L. R. James

Paul Robeson is in his own way a very famous figure. Even up to today people remember him. First of all he was a public performer: he was a singer, he was an actor, and in addition he was known as a man who stood for equality between the races, in general for all progressive classes.

I have not to add too much to that, but I want to explain its full significance. I do not believe that any human being in the twentieth century, which is what I know, achieved the world-wide fame and recognition that Paul Robeson did. It was not only his singing, his public performance, his tremendous personality. At the time he came forward, in the late twenties and in the thirties, moving to the war and after the war, a great change was taking place in the world at large. People were beginning at last to recognise that black people were people like anyone else.

Previous to that they had looked upon us as some sort of subordinate type. But if in the thirties, particularly after the crisis in 1929 and the recognition that a new state had come into the world, Soviet Russia, people began to have a different attitude. And the attitude was not only in politics and in word, the attitude was not only in people who were acting and singing—the attitude was expressed very sharply and concretely in the personality of Paul Robeson.

People of all kinds, particularly those advocating equality, were able to point to him and say: "Look, here is a black man. See the kind of person he is. You can't look upon him and think he is inferior." And that is why Robeson represented so much. His performances and the force of his personality represented and symbolised the great change that was taking place in the new conceptions that were flooding human consciousness in the thirties.

RACE TODAY, 16, NO. 4, MAY/JUNE 1985

C. L. R. JAMES (1901–89) was a Trinidadian intellectual, writer, and political activist whose work included a pioneering West Indian novel, *Minty Alley*; one of the very first histories of the Communist (Third) International, *World Revolution*; the classic account of the Haitian Revolution, *The Black Jacobins*; a theoretical treatise on Hegel, Marx, and Lenin, *Notes on Dialectics*; a landmark study of Herman Melville, *Mariners, Renegades, and Castaways*; and a seminal cultural study of cricket, *Beyond a Boundary*.

CHRISTIAN HØGSBJERG has completed doctoral research on C. L. R. James for the Department of History at the University of York. He is the author of *C. L. R. James in Imperial Britain* and is currently coediting a volume of new critical essays regarding C. L. R. James's *The Black Jacobins* (both forthcoming from Duke University Press).

Library of Congress Cataloging-in-Publication Data
James, C. L. R. (Cyril Lionel Robert), 1901–1989.
Toussaint Louverture : the story of the only successful slave
revolt in history ; a play in three acts / C. L. R. James ; edited
and introduced by Christian Høgsbjerg ; with a foreword by
Laurent Dubois.
p. cm. — (The C. L. R. James Archives)
Includes bibliographical references.
ISBN 978-0-8223-5303-4 (cloth : alk. paper)
ISBN 978-0-8223-5314-0 (pbk. : alk. paper)
1. James, C. L. R. (Cyril Lionel Robert), 1901–1989 — Criticism
and interpretation. 2. Toussaint Louverture, 1743–1803 — Drama.
3. Haiti — History — Revolution, 1791–1804 — Drama. 4. Revolutionaries — Haiti — Drama. 5. Slavery — Haiti — History — Drama.
I. Høgsbjerg, Christian. II. Dubois, Laurent, 1971- III. Title.
IV. Series: C. L. R. James Archives (Series)
PR9272.9.J35T68 2013
812'.52 — dc23   2012033858